CHILD LABOUR IN INDIA

Legal Regulation

CHILD LABOUR IN INDIA

Legal Regulation

DR. LINGARAJ M. KONINKAR
Professor of Law and Principal,
S.S.L. Law College and Director Child Line 1098 Nodal Centre,
Gulbarga-585102 (Karnataka)

Foreword by

JUSTICE SHIVARAJ V. PATIL
Former Judge
Supreme Court of India

REGAL PUBLICATIONS
New Delhi-110027

CHILD LABOUR IN INDIA: Legal Regulation

ISBN 978-81-8484-304-0

Typeset by
S.S. COMPOSERS
3190, Mohindra Park, Shakur Basti, Delhi-110034.

Printed in India at
MAYUR ENTERPRISES
WZ Plot No. 3, Gujjar Market, Tihar Village, New Delhi-110018.

Published by
REGAL PUBLICATIONS
F-159, Rajouri Garden, New Delhi-110027.
Phone: +91-11-45546396
E-mail: regalbookspub@yahoo.com

:THIS BOOK IS DEDICATED TO MY BELOVED PARENTS
LATE SHRI MALSHETTEPPA KONIN AND
LATE SMT. MAHADEVI KONIN'

Contents

Justice Shivaraj V. Patil

Former Judge
Supreme Court of India

Foreword

I am happy to learn that the book entitled "An Empirical Study of Socio-Legal Problems of Child Labour with Special Reference to Gulbarga City in Karnataka" submitted by Mr. Lirigaraj M. Koninakar to the Karnataka University, Dharwad, for the award of the degree of Doctor of Philosophy in Law, has successfully earned Doctorate for him. This Thesis is being published in the form of a book. I am deeply delighted to deliver Foreword to this book.

Mr. Lingaraj M. Koninakar is presently serving as the Principal of S.S.L. Law College of H.K.E. Society, Gulbarga. I myself was the student of the 1st Batch of his college and later served in the same college as Honorary Principal for about three years. This work of him reflects his hard work, dedication, commitment painstaking in the field and quality research. I congratulate him for this.

Gabrial Mistral, the Noble Laureate said: "We are guilty of many errors and faults, but our worst crime is abandoning the children neglecting the foundation of life. Many of the things we need can wait. The child cannot, right now is the time his bones are being formed, his blood is being made and his senses are being developed. To him we cannot answer 'tomorrow'. His name is 'today'."

One of the greatest achievements of progressive democracies in the last century is to have recognized the rightful place of the child in the societal fabric. Both in the international forum as well as domestic policies, positive action for the child's welfare is evidenced by way of various United Nation's Conventions, State legislations and Judicial interpretations. The efforts towards preserving environment and bringing about sustainable development are aimed at giving our children what is naturally theirs. Child centric human rights jurisprudence has come to be a new dimension to the larger role of law in social engineering.

Children are the supreme asset of any nation, they being the greatest gift to the humanity. Children are the potential and useful human resources for the progress of the country. They are to be looked after and groomed well, not merely on the basis of the constitutional or statutory provisions, but also with great human touch and concern. We have both obligations and duty towards them.

The Supreme Court of India in *Rosy Jacob* vs. *Jacob, A.* Chakrammakkal observed that "children are not mere chattels, nor are they mere play things, for their parents. The Supreme Court in the judgment in *Bandhua Mukti Morcha* vs. *UoI and others* case observed that "....Neglecting the children means loss to the society as a whole. If children are deprived of their childhood—socially, economically, physically and mentally—the nation gets deprived of the potential human resources for social progress, economic empowerment and peace and order, the social stability and good citizenry. The founding fathers of the Constitution, therefore, have bestowed the importance of the role of the child in its best for development."

The General Assembly of the United Nations Resolution, brought into force on 2/9/1990 recognizes that "every child has the right to be protected from economic exploitation and from performing any work that is likely to be hazardous or to interfere with the child's health of physical, mental, spiritual, moral and social development".

Children are subjected to different kinds of abuse. Protection of children from verious forms of abuse and exploitation across the world is both urgent and immediate need, right now without loss of any time, as those children who are/will be subjected to abuse and exploitation suffer each day.

In most of the countries of the globe, with a difference in degree, be it developed, developing and underdeveloped, child labour is a complex and controversial issue, besides being serious violation of human rights. The existence of child labour even now is a curse and challenge to human society. It is a scar and stigma on the very human civilization itself. This is an evil which seriously affects economic strength and human development.

This work of the author on such a vital, complex, difficult, controversial and important subject, is useful and valuable addition to the literature in the field. It may be useful and helpful to all the stakeholders and public of concern in dealing with the issue of the child labour. Though the field work is related to the city of Gulbarga as sample, gives practical insight to the ground realities which may enable to understand and appreciate the issue of child labour and consequences thereof. Mr. Koninakar having made in-depth study has given reference to various books, statements, articles, Conventions and Constitution of India wherever relevant and necessary. This is in a way, a value addition to the book, increasing its utility and focus.

The author has made a study primarily with the objective to examine the problem of child labour and to evaluate the measures adopted by the State with a view to determine their suitability and effectiveness besides:

1. To analyze the various forms of abuse of the children,
2. To study the concept of the child and child labour and the factors leading to child labour,
3. To study the evolution of the child labour practice in different countries including India,
4. To study the various 'international instruments' dealing with the child labour,
5. To make comparative analysis of the positions of child labour in United States of America, England, Russia, China, South Africa and other countries,
6. To study the legal regulation of child labour in India and judicial response,
7. To make an empirical study of the status of the child labour in Gulbarga and the role of NGOs in the rehabilitation of the child labour, and
8. To present the general findings of the study and to offer suggestions for effectively tackling the problem of child labour in India.

Investigation into the problem pertaining to eradication of child labour in India and in particular in Gulbarga city is designed and covered in Ten chapters.

Chapter 1 is introductory. It deals with the general elucidation of the problem, hypothesis, objectives of the study, methodology, importance of the study and scheme of the study.

Chapter 2 analyses concept of child. It says definition of the age of child under various legislations be brought in conformity with U.N. Convention on the Rights of the Child, 1989. It emphasized on the importance of childhood and growth of children. The study, as can be seen in this chapter, focused on constitutional provisions, legal framework, various national policies, plans and programs meant to protect and promote the best interest of children.

Chapter 3 deals with various forms of abuse of children stating that the problem of child abuse is a clear case of serious violation of human rights, socio-economic conditions prevailing in the society are mainly responsible for children during abusive situations.

In Chapter 4, the author analyses child labour and factors leading to it. He examines as to how child labour force is engaged and exploited. He points out that the poverty and lack of education are two primary reasons for social evil of child labour. The need to adopt comprehensive and integrated approach to tackle and combat child labour, the origin and development of problem of child labour in different periods is tried to be traced in Chapter 5. This chapter also deals with the prevalence of child labour even after independence and refers to constitutional provisions in respect of children in particular to Articles 24, 39(e) and (f) and various Five Year Plans made by the Government of India.

Chapter 6 highlights on international instruments, Conventions and Laws having bearing and impact on child labour. The UN Convention on the Rights of the Child, 1989 has proclaimed the child to be the more privileged ward of humanity. It stated that the "mankind owes to the child, the best it has to give". Article 32 of this Convention having a direct bearing on elimination of child labour says that every child has the right to be protected from economic exploitation and from performing any work that is likely to be hazardous or to interfere with the child's health of physical, mental, spiritual, moral and social development.

In Chapter 7, a comparative analysis of the problem of child labour and issues connected thereto is made with reference to situations prevailing in some countries like USA, UK, China, etc. and as with there.

Chapter 8 speaks of statutory provisions, legal framework and judicial response to the child labour. The contribution of judiciary and in particular of the Supreme Court in the direction of eliminating child labour is mentioned.

In Chapter 9, empirical study on child labour status in Gulbarga city and role played by the NGOs in rehabilitation is covered. Investigation was made in Gulbarga city to understand the actual reasons for the prevalence of child labour at the grass-root level. Data for the study is collected from four fields—Automobile/Workshop/Garages; Hotels; Brick-kiln industry, and construction works to get the true picture of the problem. A sample consisting of 41 child labours, 41 employers, 6 NGOs and 6 law enforcing officers was drawn. Out of 41 child labourers 10 child labourers are working in garages, 13 children are working in hotels/restaurants, 13 are working in brick-kiln and 5 children are working in construction works.

From the analysis of the data, the findings are recorded in the concluding Chapter 10 as under.

The study has led the investigator to conclude that large number of children are working as child labourers due to number of factors like socio-economic and socio-legal problems. And poverty being the root cause for the prevalence of child labour. It is found that the child labourers predominantly belong to under privileged backward communities.

The study has further revealed that though there are child labour laws, they are not properly enforced due to apathy on the part of administrative authorities. The attitude of parents, who push their children to become child labour has been found to be one of the major causes for the evil practice.

Based on the findings, the author has made a few good suggestions which are worth considering and implementing. They are:

(1) Improving the content of laws through amendment.
   (i) The Child Labour (Prohibition and Regulation) Act, 1986 should be suitably amended to bring it on par with Articles 24 of the Constitution which provides prohibition and not regulation.
   (ii) The age of the child be increased from 14 years to 18 years in conformity with the Convention on the Rights of the Child, 1989.
   (iii) Proviso annexed to Sec. 3 of Child Labour Act is misused by the family members/occupiers. Therefore, it is required to be amended to prevent misuse.

(2) Adequate training shall be provided to the enforcement agencies to bring about a change in their attitude.

(3) A systematic and idealistic scheme to rehabilitate the rescued children should be devised.

(4) Government should assign greater role for providing necessary facilities.

(5) The Childrens Right to Free and Compulsory Education Acts, 2009 should be implemented in letter and spirit.

(6) Mid-day meal scheme and other incentives should be liberally provided to motivate the children to attend schools.

(7) Anti-poverty programmes and providing alternative employment opportunities to the parents must be launched by the Government.

(8) There is a need to make a provision for rehabilitation of rescued child in the Child Labour (Prohibition and Regulation) Act, 1986 by amendment.

Mr. Koninakar has written several articles, attended/organized number of workshops/conferences and courses. This experience gained by him is also put in the book

In my view, the work undertaken by the author is well done. When it is published in the form of book, it will be informative and educative besides being very useful to all the concerned. I hope the book will be well received to serve the benevolent purpose of eradicating child labour in the country, if not completely but certainly in minimizing it. I wish Mr. Lingaraj M. Koninakar all the best to contribute more.

JUSTICE SHIVARAJ V. PATIL

Preface

The welfare of the entire community, its growth and development depends on the health, strength and well being of its children. The prosperity and development of any country certainly depend upon "Human development" or the wellbeing of its people in general and children in particular, than the development of their military or economic strength or the splendor of their capital cities and public buildings. "Children are the greatest gift to the humanity and they are the representation of the beautiful creation of God". Children are indeed, the future great scientists, rulers, administrators, philosophers, legislators, teachers, judges, engineers, technologists, industrialists, politicians on whom the nation rests. The children are innocent, weakest and defenseless and most vulnerable segment of the society. The protection of children from all forms of abuse and exploitation across the world is the need of hour. Unfortunately, the children are subjected to various forms of abuse. The problem of child labour is one amongst serious abuses of the children. Child Labour is a universal problem and is prevailing in every country across the world whether it is developed, developing and under developing country, but there is difference only in degree. It is a complex and controversial issue and is one of the major human right issues and highly emotive one and a socio-economic phenomenon. India has the largest number of child labourers in the age of 6-14 in the world. As per the 2001-Census there are 1.26 crore working children in the country in the age group of 5-14. According to 12th Five Year Plan, there are 27 crores children in the age group of 6-18 years and 40% children are in difficult circumstance i.e. Child labourers. In order to address this issue, there are various international instruments like Universal Declaration of Human Rights 1948, United Nations Convention on the Rights of the Child 1989 and other international bodies which prohibit the practice of child labour and recognize the rights of the child to be protected from economic exploitation and performing any work that is likely to be hazardous: or interfere with his education; or be harmful to the child's health or physical, mental, spiritual, moral, or social development. Constitution of India under Article 23 prohibits traffic in human being and beggar and other similar forms of Forced labour. Under Article 24, it has laid down that "No child under the age of 14 years shall be employed to work in any factory or mine or engaged in any other hazardous employment". In order to implement international instruments and Constitutional obligations towards eradication of Child Labour, plethora of legislations were brought. Child Labour (Prohibition and Regulation) Act 1986 is an outcome of various recommendations made by a series of commissions like National Commission on Labour 1969; The Gurupad Swamy Committee on Labour 1976 and Sanat Mehata Committee 1984. The preamble to the Child Labour (Prohibition and Regulation) Act 1986 prohibits the employment of children in certain employments and prohibits the employment of any person who has not completed his 14 Years of age. Government of India has amended Child Labour (Prohibition and Regulation) Act in 2006 banning the employment of children as domestic servants and in the hospitality industry. In pursuance of amendment to the Constitution in 2002, Parliament has enacted, Children's Right to Free and Compulsory Education Act, 2009 which makes access to education a fundamental right between the age of 6 and 14 years.

The present book is based on the thesis submitted to Karnataka University, Dharwad for the award of Ph.D. Degree in Law.

The present book "CHILD LABOUR IN INDIA—LEGAL REGULATION" is quite comprehensive, educative and informative. The Problem of child labour, its development and the nature has been examined thoroughly and painstakingly from a historical perspective. Various international declarations, conventions, convenants, and constitutional mandates and various Indian statutes and rules, regulations, polices, programmes, and various judgements of the courts have been appropriately and correctly taken into consideration while dealing with the subject. The book highlights the role of various organizations namely Universal Declaration of Human Rights, United Nations Convention on the Rights of the Child, International Labour Organization, UNESCO, UNICEF, which are working in the field of protection of child rights.

To understand the ground realities of the probem in a socio-legal framework, best efforts has been made by conducting empirical study relating to unorganized sectors. A sincere attempt has been made in this book to highlight the problems faced by children, the laws to safeguard their interests and judgements given by various courts. Inspite of may best efforts, I could not comprehend the depths of topics and therefore, I solicit suggestions for the improvement of this book from the readers.

With the divine blessings of Lord Mahadasohi Sharanabasaveshwara of Gulbarga, this book is being written.

The author wishes to acknowledge with deepest sense of gratitude to Prof. and Guide Dr. C. Rajashekhar, Professor of Law and Dean Faculty of Law, Karnataka University, Dharwad who is the guiding force and encouraged me to write this book.

Justice Dr. Shivaraj V. Patil, Former Judge of Supreme Court of India has kindly blessed this work by writing a Foreword. His insights about children in general and problem & practice of child labour in particular and solutions have made value addition to the work. I immensely thank the learned Judge for sparing his valuable time in writing an encouraging Foreword.

I express my sincere thanks to Shri. Shashil G. Namoshi, MLC and President and to Vice-President and all the Governing Council Members of H.K.E. Society, Gulbarga for the support and encouragement in completing this work.

I gratefully acknowledge the guidance and encouragement extended by my learned teachers Prof. T. Veerbhushan, Senior Advocate and Prof. P.G. Pandhararpurkar, Principal (Retd) and to all the faculty members and staff of H.K.E. Society's S.S.L. Law College Gulbarga.

My sincere thanks are also due to Prof. M.S. Devarmani and Sri. D.Siddappa President OM Yoga kendra Gulbarga.

I express my deep sense of gratitude and acknowledge the blessings of my parents Late Shri Malshetteeppa Konin and Late Smt. Mahadevi Konin who are the guiding source of inspiration and positive force in writing this book.

I wish to express regards to my eldest sister Smt. Sharadadevi Subhash Maisalgikar for her unconditional love and support in all my endeavour. I am very much grateful to my daughter Ms. Mahadevi Konin who helped and assisted throughout in completing this work I also sincerely thank my wife Mrs. Parvati Konin and my son Mr. Mahesh for their invaluable assistance in completing this work.

Lastly I express my gratitude, thanks and appreciation to Regal Publications, New Delhi for publishing this book.

DR. LINGARAJ M. KONINKAR

Abbreviations

AIR - All India Reporter
BC - Before Christ
BLS - Bureau of Labour Statistics
BPL - Below Poverty Line
CAB - CHILDLINE Advisory Board
CBR - Community Based Rehabilitation.
CEHAT - Centre for Enquiry into Health and Allied Themes
CIF - Child India Foundation
CLPRA - Child Labour (Prohibition and Regulation) Act, 1986
CPS - Current Population Survey
CRC - Convention on the Rights of the Child
CREPA - Centre for Rural Education and Development Action
Cri.L.J. - Criminal Law Journal
CRY - Child Relief and You
CULR - Cochin University Law Review
CWC - Child Welfare Committee
DRC - District Rehabilitation Centre
ECOSOC - United Nations Economic and Social Council
Edn - Edition
FLASA - Fair Labour on Standard Act
GNP - Gross National Product
GM - General Merit
GOI - Government of India
GSD - General Station Diary
HIV - Human Immuno Virus
HMGA - Hindu Minority and Guardianship Act
IBID - Ibidem
ICCPR - International Covenant on Civil and Political Rights.
ICDS - Integrated Child Development Services
ICESCR - International Covenant on Economic Social and Cultural Rights
ICPS - Integrated Child Protection Scheme
ILO - International Labour Organisation

IMR - Infant Mortality Rate
INDUS - Indo US Co-operation for Elimination of Child Labour
IPC - Indian Penal Code
IPEC - International Programme for the Elimination of the Child Labour
IRDP - Integrated Rural Development Programme
JILI - Journal of Indian Law Institute
Kar. - Karnataka
MDGs - Millennium Development Goals
MVF - M. Venkatarangaiya Foundation
NCLP - National Child Labour Projects, National Child Labour Policy
NCMP - National Common Minimum Programme
NCPCR - National Commission for the Protection of Child Rights
NCRB - National Crime Record Bureau
NCRC - National Children's Rights Committee
NGO - Non-Governmental Organisation
NHRC - National Human Right Commission
NICDR - National Information Centre for Disabled and Rehabilitation
NICP - National Institute for Child Protection
NILP - National Child Labour Policy
NIPCCD - National Institute for Public Co-operation and Child Development
NISD - National Institute of Social Defense
NRCCL - National Research Centre on Child Labour
NREP - National Rural Employment Programme
OBC - Other Backward Communities
RRTC - Regional Research Training Centre
SAARC - South Asian Association for Regional Co-operation
SC - Supreme Court
SCC - Supreme Court Cases
SCIU - Save the Children International Union
SCs - Scheduled Castes
SHGs - Self-Help Groups
SSA - Sarva Sikshana Abhiyan
SSL - Seth Shankarlal Lahoti Law College
STD - Sexually Transmitted Diseases
STs - Scheduled Tribes
SVT - Strengthen Vocational Training
UDHR - Universal Declaration of the Human Rights
UNESGO - United Nations Education, Scientific and Cultural Organisation

UNICEF - United Nation's Children Emergency Fund
UPE - Universal Primary Education
USA - United States of America
v. - Verses
VRC - Vocational Rehabilitation Centre
w.e.f. - With effect from
WHO - World Health Organization

List of Cases

A. Sriram Babu v. *Chief Secretary, Govt. of Karnataka,* ILR (1997) Kar. 2269.

Bandela Aillaiah v. *State,* (1995) Cri. L.J. 1083.

Bandhua Mukti Morcha v. *Union of India and others* 1984 2, SCR.

Bandhua Mukti Morcha v. *Union of India,* (1984) 3 SCC 161.

Centre for Enquiry into Health and Allied Themes (CEHAT) and others v. *Union of India,* AIR 2001, S.C.

Francis Coralie Mullin v. *Union Territory of Delhi* (1981) 1 SCC 608.

Gaurav Jain v. *Union of India* (1997) 8 SCC 114: AIR 1997 SC 3021.

Hayatkhan v. *Deputy Labour Commissioner, Regional Office, Belgaum and others,* 2008-1-LLJ.

J.P. Unnikrishnan and others v. *State of A.P. and others,* AIR 1993, SC 2178, SC 2178 (1993) 1 SCC 645.

K.C. Chandra Segaram v. *State of Tamil Nadu and others,* AIR 1993, SC 404.

Labourers Salal Hydro Project v. *State of Jammu & Kashmir* (1983) 2 SCC 181, AIR 1984 SC 177.

M.C. Mehta v. *State of Tamil Nadu,* AIR 1997, SC 699.

M/s P.M. Patel and sons v. *Union of India* AIR, 1987 SC 447.

Menaka Gandhi v. *Union of India,* AIR 1978 SC 597, 1978 (1 SCC 248)

Mohini Jain v. *State of Karnataka,* AIR 1992, SC 1858.

Neeraj Choudhary v. *State of M.P.,* AIR 1984 SC 1099, 1984 3 SCC 243.

P.A. Inamdar v. *State of Maharashtra,* AIR 2005 SC 3226.

P. Shivashwamy v. *State of AP,* AIR 1988 Lab IC 1680.

Peoples' Union for Democratic Rights v. *Union of India—Asiad Workers case,* AIR 1982, SC 1473.

Rajangam, Secretary Dist. Beedi Workers' Union v. *State of Tamil Nadu and others,* AIR 1993 SC 404, 1993 Lab. IC 4.

Reftakes Brett and co. v. *others,* Civil Appeal No. 4336 of 1991.

Rosy Jacob v. *Jacob. A. Chakramakkal* (1973) 1 Sec 840.

Satyavan Kottarakkara v. *State,* AIR 1997 Ker., 133.

Sheela Barse v. *Secretary, Children Aid Society*, AIR 1989 SC 656, 659.
Sheela Barse v. *Union of India*, AIR 1986 SC 1873.
St. Therasa's Tender Loving Care Home v. *State of A.P.*, AIR 2005, SC, 4375.
T.M.A. Pai Foundation v. *Union of India*, AIR 1996, SC 2652.
University of Delhi v. *Ramanath*, AIR 1963, SC 1873.
Vishal Jeet v. *Union of India*, AIR 1990, SC 1412.
Walker T. Ltd. v. *Martindale*, (1916) 85 FL KB, 1543.

1

Introduction

> *'We are guilty of many errors and many faults, but our worst crime is abandoning the children, neglecting the foundation of life. Many of the things we need can wait. The child cannot wait. Right now is the time his bones are being formed, his blood is being made, and his senses are being developed. To him we cannot answer 'Tomorrow' his name is 'Today'".*
>
> ***—Gabriela Mistal***
> ***Noble Prize Winning Poet from Chile***

The right to childhood is a sacred entitlement of mankind. Children are not just tomorrow's citizens but today's as well. Children are universally recognized as the most important asset of any nation. The future of the nation depends directly on how they are brought up and cared for. Children are like today's seeds for tomorrow's societies. Children are the very soul of any nation. Therefore, every society must, devote full attention to ensure that children are properly cared for and brought up in a proper atmosphere where they would receive adequate training, education and guidance in order that they may be able to have their rightful place in society when they grow up. It is aptly relevant to quote Justice Subba Rao, former Chief Justice of India, on Social Justice to Children, who remarked, "Social Justice must begin with children, unless tender plant is properly nourished, it has little chance of growing into strong and useful tree. So the first priority in the scale of social justice should be given to the welfare of children".[1]

But unfortunately millions of children are forced to work as child labourers due to various reasons and child labour continues to prevail, based on exploitation, abuse and deprivation.

Child labour is a universal problem, and is prevailing across the world whether it is developed, developing and underdeveloped country. Child labour is a complex and controversial issue. The existence and perpetuation of child labour is a challenge to the human society. It is really a curse and stigma upon the society; disgrace for the world of the mankind, a malady which may destroy the economic backbone of the country. The practice of the child labour would be an impediment in the way of human development in almost all the third world countries including India. The issue of the child labour is one of the major human rights issues and is highly emotive one. The problem of child labour in underdeveloped and developing countries is quite high and abnormal. It is a global phenomenon which exists in almost all the countries of the world, but there is difference only in degree. It has been in existence, more or less in all periods of time though varies in its nature and dimension, depending on the existing socio-economic structure of the society.[2]

Children need to grow in an environment that enables them to lead a life of freedom and dignity where opportunities of education and training are provided to grow into a worthy citizen. Every child has the right to receive the best that the society can offer. But unfortunately a large proportion of children are deprived of their basic rights and are found working in various sectors of economy.[3]

One of the great world leaders, Nelson Mandela had said: "All countries today need to apply affirmative action to ensure that the women and the disabled are equal to all of us". He also focused on the position of the children. Every nation, developed or developing, links its future with the status of a child. Childhood holds the potential and also sets the limit to the future development for the society. Children are the most sensitive gifts to humanity. The children signify external optimism in the human being and always provide the potential for human development. Kofi, A. Annan, in 1999 in his statement has stated that "To look into some aspects of the future, we do need projections by super computers. Much of the next millennium can be seen in how we care for our children today. Tomorrow's world may be influenced by science and technology but more than anything, it is already taking shape in the bodies and minds of our children.[4]

Children are innocent, vulnerable and dependent. Children cannot and should not be treated as chattels or saleable commodities or playthings. They are in flesh and blood with life as much as we elders are and they are also capable of becoming as great, as good and as useful as we are and even more.[5]

(a) Magnitude of the Problem

According to the 12th Five Year Plan, recommendations there are

43 crores children in the age group of 0 to18 years and 16 crore children are in the age group of 0 to 6 years, of this 8.5 crore children are male children and 7.88 crore are female children. There are 27 crore children are in the age group of 6 to 18 years and 40% children are in difficult circumstances, i.e. Child Labourers, etc. According to the 2011 Census overall sex ratio has improved between 933 to 940 females to 1000 males. National Sample Survey Organization (NSSO) in 2004-05 reported that there were 90.75 lakh working children but its survery report in 2009-10 discloses that 49.84 lakh are working children in India.

(b) Inspection, Prosecution and Conviction

It is significant to mention that there were 13,60,117 inspections were carried out under the Child Labour Law since its inception in 1986, barely 49,092 prosecutions were launched and nearly 4,774 employers convicted in court of law. A meager sum of Rs. 200 to 400 was imposed as penalty in most of the cases and in some cases the penalty imposed was as low as Rs. 20 to 25. This shows there was lack of effective implementation of law.

According to Gurupadswamy Report of 1979, chronic poverty is the most important factor for prevalence and perpetuation of child labour. Nearly half of Indian population subsists below the poverty line. In this context the child since its very appearance in the world is endowed with an economic mission. Socio-economic factors and compulsion weigh so heavily on poor parents that they do not mind colluding with the child's employer in violating the laws and placing the child under risks of inhuman employment situation. Poverty of child labour always begets each other. International Labour Organisation is of the opinion that poverty is not only reason for the exploitation of children. Inadequate schooling also must be taken into account. Lack of political will and adequate machinery to monitor children further compounds the issue of the abolition of child labour.

According to the World Bank Report, 2007,[6] the child labour and child economic activity is defined as all paid work and certain forms of unpaid work (e.g., Unpaid work in one's own household enterprises).

Child Labour is keeping children out of school and contributing to the growth of illiteracy, especially among girls.[7] Child labourer is basically, a child who is deprived of the right to education and childhood.[8]

In order to protect and secure human rights of the children, there are various international instruments regulating child labour. Universal Declaration of Human Rights, 1948 had proclaimed that childhood was entitled to special care and protection. The U.N. Convention on the Rights of the Child, 1989 proclaims in Article 6, that every child has the inherent right to life and that the State parties shall ensure to the maximum extent possible the survival. Article 32 of the Convention on the Rights of the Child mandates that the State parties, "to recognise the right of the child to be protected from economic exploitation and from performing any work that is likely to be hazardous or to interfere with the child education, or to be harmful to the child's health or physical, mental, spiritual, moral and social development". The Government of India has ratified United Nations Convention on the Rights of the Child in December, 1992 and undertakes to initiate measures to progressively implement the provisions of Article 32.

The Convention on the Rights of the Child is really a '*Magna Carta*' and it is a most important human rights document focusing and concentrating on children. The Convention on the Rights of the Child is the most complete statement of child rights ever made. It is indeed an innovative document in overall human rights theory and practice.

In India, there are various constitutional provisions in Part III and Part IV providing for fundamental rights and directive principles of State Policy, which are relevant for the elimination of child labour. Article 24 of the Constitution which prohibits the employment of children in factories, provides "no child below the age of 14 years shall be employed to work in any factory or mine or engaged in any other hazardous employment". In the year 2002, the Indian Constitution, through its 86th Amendment Act, has made "Right to Education a Fundamental Right". Article 21-A of the Constitution provides that "the State shall provide free and compulsory education to all children of age of 6 to 14 years in such manner as the State may, by law, determine". Article 45, a directive principle, imposes an obligation on the state to endeavour to provide early childhood care and education for all children until they complete the age of six years. In pursuance of this the Parliament has enacted the Child Labour (Prohibition and Regulation) Act, 1986 which prohibits the employment of children in certain employment and to regulate the conditions of work of children in certain other employments. It prohibits the employment of any person who has not completed his fourteenth year's of age,[9] in occupation and processes set forth in Part A and Part B of the Schedule of the Act. The National Policy on Child Labour, 1987 focuses mainly on three welfare aspects of the child. Firstly, on the enforcement of child labour; secondly, on the families of the child labourers to avail the benefits of welfare and development programmes meant for this purpose; and thirdly, to take-up projects in areas of child labour concentration.[10]

Recently, Government of India has amended the Child Labour (Prohibition and Regulation) Act, 1986 on 01.08.2006 banning the employment of children below the age of 14 years as domestic servants and also in the hospitality industry with effect from 10th October 2006 and violation of ban shall be an offence with imprisonment which may extend to 3 months to one year or with fine from Rs. 10,000 to Rs. 20,000 or with both.

Government of India in 2002 amended the Constitution by 86th Amendment Act, 2002. In pursuance of this, in August 2009, Parliament has enacted, Children's Right to Free and Compulsory Education Act, 2009 which makes access to education a fundamental right from 1st April, 2010 and places the obligation of enrolment of every child in school on the Government. The Commission for Protection of Child Rights Act, 2005[11] was enacted by the Parliament which provides for the constitution of a National Commission and State Commission for Protection of Child Rights and Children's Courts for providing speedy trial of offences against children or of violation of child rights and for matters connected therewith or incidental thereto.

Inspite of having various international instruments, constitutional provisions both as fundamental rights and directive principles of state policies, plethora of legislations, Government policies and programms, practice of child labour is perpetuating even after attaining independence for 66 years. The problem has become a harsh reality and cause of severe violation of human rights of children.

Today children are employed in all sectors. In cities and towns they are engaged in almost every occupation like hotels, restaurants, automobile workshops, brick kiln, Construction work, domestic and household services, trade and commerce, tailoring shops, printing press, farms and fields, agricultural works, besides in traditional occupations. Reviewing the existing literature, it was found that at the National level, a very few research works have been done on the problem of child labour in brick kiln and Automobile workshops, whereas not a single work from the socio-legal approach was noticed on the same in the State of Karnataka and that is the driving force and intution behind the attempt to conduct the present empirical study. Accordingly a case study of the Hotels and Restaurants, Construction work, Brick kiln and Automobile workshops in Gulbarga City was undertaken. Gulbarga city is continued as most backward region due to socio-economic reasons prevailing in the area since after state re-organisation.

The problem of child labour is a socio-economic, socio-legal, complex, controversial, human rights and multi-dimensional problem across the world:

(a) Multiple causes are responsible for perpetuating problem of child labour;

(b) Various practical difficulties involved in the design and implementation of laws;

(c) There is a problem of differences in perception about what constitutes a child or child work or child labour and child labour and exploitive child labour;
(d) Problem with regard to prohibition and regulation of child labour;
(e) There is a problem of difficulty in understanding, the term child labour in hazardous and non-hazardous sectors;
(f) There is a problem of difficulty in understanding organized and unorganized sectors;
(g) Early involvement of children in continuing family tradition work also causes child labour problem;
(h) Defective education system, drawbacks in laws, low economic growth, breaking of joint families, urbanization, migration, corporal punishments in the schools are the factors responsible in perpetuating the child labour problem;
(i) Poor implementation of child labour provisions; and Gender inequalities; and
(j) Lack of political, administrative, political and social will which are also the factors responsible in perpetuating the child labour problem.

Thus, there is a need to make an objective assessment at grassroot level to understand the ground reality in a socio-legal frame- work and to ascertain whether international instruments, constitutional and legislative porovisions, Government policies and programmes are adequate to protect children from physical and economical exploitation in order to eliminate the problem of child labour.

1. To study the child and child labour and factors leading to child labour.
2. To analyse their socio-economic background.
3. To know practical difficulties of enforcement agencies.
4. To analyse rehabilitation programmes for the rescued children.
5. To look into the working conditions of the children at work.
6. To conduct èmpirical investigation at the grassroot level to understand ground reality.

Based on the above objective assessment empirical investigation has been undertaken at Gulbarga city to understand the actual reasons for the prevalence of the child labour. Data for the study is collected from four fields—automobile shops and garages; hotels; brick-kiln industry; and construction works to get the true picture of the problem. A sample consisting of 41 child labourers, 41 employers and 6 NGOs was drawn. Out of 41 child labourers 10 child labourers are working in garages, 13 children are working in hotels/restaurants, 13 are working in brick-kiln and 5 children are working in construction works. Data was collected through administering the questionnaires and schedules to the respondents. Thorough analysis and interpretation of data was undertaken and for this purpose data was tabulated and graphs were prepared for the presentation of the findings. From the analysis of the data, the findings are made and the same are presented.

The study has led the investigator to conclude that large number of children are working as child labourers due to various socio-economic factors. Poverty is the root cause for the prevalence of child labour, as it is found that the child labourers most predominantly belong to under privileged backward communities.

The study has further revealed that though there are child labour laws, they are not properly enforced due to apathy on the part of administrative authorities. The attitude of parents, who push their children to become child labourers, has been found to be one of the major causes for the evil practice.

It is true that law alone cannot eliminate the problem of child labour. The involvement of voluntary and Non-Government Organisations, local bodies like panchayats will go a long way in protecting the interest of children and thereby elimination of child labour can be ensured. The study has established that the NGOs can play a vital role in dealing with the problem.

Now the Union Cabinet approved a proposal for amending a Child Labour (Prohibition and Regulation) Act, 1986 to ban employment of children aged upto 14 in any form of industry. It will be an cognizable offence to employ such children not only in factories or industries, but also in homes or on farms, if their labour is meant to serve any commercial interest. Thus, employing a child under 14 for any work will be a cognizable offence punishable with imprisonment upto two years or a fine upto Rs. 50,000 or both, and increase from the current one year jail or Rs. 20,000 punishment. Repeat offenders can be imprisoned for upto three years. Untill now, Child Labour (Prohibition and Regulation) Act, 1986 permitted the children under age 14 to work in non-hazardous industries including some agricultural work in contravention of the Right to Free and Compulsory Education Act. It says that all children between 6 and 14 must be in school.

Children between the age of 14 and 18 have been termed in the amendment as adolescents and can only be employed in non-hazardous industries. Earlier any one over the age of 14 could be employed for hazardous work. The newly proposed legislation could be entitled as "Child and Adolescents Labour Prohibition Act. Amended legisltation should focus and ensure that Government must recognize that the best way of eliminating child labour is to eliminate poverty. It is aptly relevant to say that, if we lose the war against poverty, we cannot win the battle against child labour.

The three major challenges that the government is confronted with are ascertaining enforceability, assessing the real magnitude of the problem and devising appropriate rehabilitative measures. The pre-requisites for all lie in political will substantiated with appropriate budgetary allocations and building effective partnerships with a sense of utmost urgency.

Let us hope and trust that Ministry of Labour, Govt. of India may introduce amendment bill in parliament soon and the amended legislation will ensure true justice to the children.

Notes and References

1. K. Subba Rao, *Social Justice and Law*, Delhi: National Publications House, 1974, p. 5.
2. Umesh C. Sahu, "Child Labour in Surat Textile Industry Social Change", Vol. 20, No. 3, September, 1990, p. 29.
3. Helen R. Sekhar, *Towards Combating Child Labour*. 2nd edn., Noida: V.V. Giri National Labour Institute, 2005, p. 2.
4. Kofi A. Annan, Secretary General of the United Nations, 1999.
5. Presidential address by Hon'ble Mr. Justice Shivaraj V. Patil at the 10th Justice Sunanda Bhandara Memorial Lecture on 8-11-2004.
6. Jeen Fares and Dushyanth Raju (2007): "Child Labour Across the Developing World Patterns and Co-relations", *The World Bank Report*, Policy Research Working Paper-4119, pp. 1-36.
7. Neera Burra, *Born to Work Child Labour in India*, Delhi: Oxford University Press, 1995.
8. Nanjuda, D.C., *Child Labour and Human Rights—A Perspective*, Delhi: Kalpaz Publications, 2008, p. 52.
9. CLPRA, 1986, Section 3, *"No Child shall be employed or permitted to work in any other occupations set forth in Part A of the Schedule or in any workshop, any of the process set forth in Part B of the Schedule is carried on"*.
10. Sudesh Kumar Sharma, "Child Labour: Problems and Prospects", *Cochin University Law Review*, 1999, p. 263.
11. Received the Assent of the President on 20 Jan. 2006 and Published in the Official Gazette of India, Extra Part II, S-1 (Central Act, No. 4 of 2006) came into force w.e.f. 15-02-2007 vide No. 229 E, dated 15-02-2007.

2

Concept of Child: An Analysis

> *"No one is born a good citizen; no nation is born a democracy. Rather, both are processes that continue to evolve over a lifetime. Young people must be included from birth. A society that cuts-off from its youth severs its lifeline".*
>
> —*Kofi Annan*

1. INTRODUCTION

The significance and importance of the child lies in the fact that the child is the universe. If there was no child, there would be no humanity and there cannot be a universe without humanity. Children are the greatest gift to the humanity and they are the representation for the beautiful creation of God. They must be nurtured with care and affection within the family and the society, and they constitute the nation's human resources.

Children are like a seed, a seed in which a grand tree is hidden so in children abundant strength, intellectual sense, potential power is hidden. A child of today develops to be a responsible and productive member of tomorrow's society unless an environment which is conducive to his social and physical health is assured to him. Justice K. Ramaswamy, observed, "Children of the world are innocent, vulnerable and dependant. They are all curious, active and full of hope. Their life should be full of joy and peace, playing, learning and growing. Their future should be shaped in harmony and co-operation. Their childhood should mature, as they broaden their perspectives and gain new experience. Abandoning the children, excluding good foundation of life for them, is a crime against humanity.[1] Noble Prize Winner and great Poetess, Gabriela Mistral of Chile chastised the leaders of the society: "We are guilty of many errors and many faults, but our worst crime is abandoning the children, neglecting the foundation of life. Many of the things we need can wait, the child cannot wait. Right now is the time his bones are being formed, his blood is being made and his senses are being developed. To him we cannot answer 'Tomorrow'. His name is today".[2] Maria Montessori has made a marvelous observation that, "Humanity shows itself in all its intellectual splendor during this tender age as the sun shows itself at the dawn, and the flower in the first unfolding of the petals; and we must respect religiously, reverently, these first indications of individuality. If any educational act is to be efficacious, it will be only that which tends to help towards the complete unfolding of this life".[3]

"Child is an 'organic cell' of the society". Great Poet John Milton very aptly and admirably said, "Child shows the man as morning shows the day". The physical and mental health of the nation is determined largely by the manner in which it is shaped in the early stages. "The child is a soul with a being, a nature and capacities of its own, who must be helped to find them, to grow into their maturity, into fullness of physical and vital energy and the utmost breadth, depth and height of its emotional, intellectual and spiritual being; otherwise there cannot be a healthy growth of the nation".[4] Supreme Court said, "Today's children will be leaders of tomorrow who will hold country's banner high and maintain the prestige of the nation. If a child goes wrong for want of proper attention, training and guidance, it will indeed be a deficiency of the society and of the Government of the day. Every society must therefore, devote full attention to ensure that children are properly cared for and brought up in a proper atmosphere where they would receive adequate training, education and guidance in order that they may be able to have their rightful place in the society when they grow up".[5] Children are the future custodians and torch bearers of the society; they are the messengers of our knowledge, cultural heritage, ideologies and philosophies. Children are really future components in the form of Great teachers, scientists, judges, rulers, doctors, planners, engineers, politicians on whom the entire society founded (rests). Thus, children are important asset not only for their country but also for the whole mankind. So children are supremely important 'National Asset' which was endorsed and approved in the leading case *Sheela Barse* v. *Union of India*.[6] Children have the Right to joyful childhood. Every child has the Right to grow up in a safe and nurturing environment with protection and guidance from their guardians/parents. Our Constitution mandates the State, under Article 39, to ensure that "Children are not abused and that childhood and youth are protected against exploitation and against moral and material abandonment".[7]

2. THE LEGAL DEFINITION OF A CHILD

All social backgrounds and culture of the society equally contribute the view that the younger children are more vulnerable and exploitable, both physically and psychologically. Age limits are a form and reflection of society's judgments of the evolution of children's capacities and responsibilities. Almost everywhere age limits formally regulate children's activities: When to join and leave the school; when they can marry; when they can vote; when they can be treated as adults by the criminal justice system; when they can join the armed forces and when they can work but age limits differ from activity to activity and from country to country.[8] While making use of standard demographic data, social scientists include females, in the age group of 15-19 years under the category of the girl child. Most of the government programs on children are targeted for the age group below 14 years.[9] The legal concept of child varies depending upon the purpose: Whether it is for imposing legal disabilities, (in the political rights sphere), for spelling out duties and obligations (e.g. In the Juvenile Justice System), for affording protection (e.g. from exploitative or hazardous employment), or for establishing eligibility to receive benefits or special services. (e.g. health, education and maintenance benefits).[10] The primary definition of child is the immediate progeny of human parents. The ordinary meaning of "Child" or Children refers to parentage and embraces only the first generation of the offspring. The Primary meaning of the word "Child" is an infant and that the text allowable use in meaning is one of tender years, young persons and a youth.[11] *Black's Law Dictionary* defines the term "Child" as Progeny: Offspring of parentage. Commonly it implies one who had not attained the age of fourteen years, though the meaning now varies in different "statutes". The Shorter Oxford Dictionary defines 'person' in two ways: 'an individual human being or a man, woman or child'. The Webster's New World Dictionary defines a child as *inter alia* 'an unborn offspring'. The American Bar Association's Standards Relations to Rights to Minors proposes that, "all persons who have attained the age of eighteen years should be regarded as adults for all legal purposes".[12]

The word 'Child' has been used in various legislations as a term denoting relationship, as a term indicating capacity and as a term of special protection. Relationship of child is with the parents, relatives, community and nation. Capacity is a term of status, competency find variations in view of age, maturity, understanding causing temporary disabilities etc...these makes viewing children as a 'burden' which invokes rights to maintenance and support. Further, it leads to temporary disabilities to the children which demands special treatment and special discrimination. Children are most vulnerable and exploitable which requires protection of their rights. Thus, recognising children as resources for the country's development necessitating their nurturing and advancement.[13] As per accepted definition 'child' means someone who needs adult protection for physical, psychological and intellectual development until able to become independently integrated into the adult world.[14]

2.1. Age of the Child

The Constitution of India under Art. 24 defines 'child' as any one below the age of 14 years and who shall not be employed to work in any factory or mine or engaged in any other hazardous employment. Article 21-A of the Constitution states that, the State shall provide free and compulsory education to all children of the age of six to fourteen years in such manner as the state may, by law determine.[15] Article 45 of the Constitution states that, the state shall endeavour to provide early childhood care and education for all children until they complete the age of six years.[16] Article 51-A clause (K) of Constitution lays down a duty that the parents or guardians should provide opportunities for education to his child/ward between the age of six to fourteen years.[17] According to Art. 1 of the United Nations Convention on the Rights of the Child 1989, A child means every human being below the age of 18 years unless, under the law applicable to the child, majority is attained earlier" [18] The Article thus grants the discretion to individual countries to determine by law whether childhood should cease at 12, 14, 16 or whatever age they find appropriate. In India, the age at which a person ceases to be a child varies in different laws. The Census of India, 2001 treats persons below the age of 14 years as children.[19] The Indian Penal Code defines that it is not an offence by a child under 7 years of age and further not an offence which is done by a child above seven years of age and under twelve, who has not attained sufficient maturity of understanding to judge the nature and consequence of his conduct, on that occasion.[20] The Juvenile Justice Act, 1986 defines Juvenile as a boy who has not attained the age of 16 years, and a girl who has not attained the age of 18 years.[21] The Juvenile Justice (Care and Protection of Children) Act, 2000, defines Juvenile or child as a person who has not completed eighteenth year of age.[22] The Child Marriage Restraint Act, 1929 defines 'Child' as a person who, if a male, has not completed twenty-one years of age, and if a female, has not completed eighteen years of age and 'minor' means a person of either sex who is under eighteen years of age.[23] Similarly, under The Prohibition of Child Marriage Act, 2006, "Child" means a person who, if a male, has not completed 21 years of age, and if a female, has not completed 18 years of age.[24] Under Child Labour (Prohibition and Regulation) Act, 1986 'Child' means a person who has not completed his 14th year of age.[25] Factories Act, 1948 defines 'child' as a person who has not completed his fifteenth year of age and no child who has not completed his fourteenth year shall be required or allowed to work in any factory.[26] Further, The Factories Act, 1948 distinguishes between 'child', 'adolescent' and 'adult'. 'Child' is a person who has not completed the age of 15 years; an 'adolescent' is a person who has completed the age of 15 years, but is below the age of 18 years, and an 'adult' is a person who has completed the age of 18 years. The Act defines a young person as one who is either a child or an adolescent. A child below the age of 14 is not allowed to work in a factory. A child above the age of 15 and below the age of 18 cannot be employed to work for more than four and half hours and cannot be employed during the night.[27] Mines (Amendment) Act, 1952 defines Child means no person below eighteen years of age shall be allowed to work in any mine or any part thereof.[28]

The Indian Majority Act, 1875 defines the normal age of majority in India is 18 years, but if a guardian is appointed before that age by a court or property is taken under superintendence by a court of wards, the age of majority is 21 years.[29] The Hindu Minority and Guardianship Act (HMGA), 1956, defines a 'minor' as a person who has not completed the age of eighteen years.[30] The age of majority for the purposes of appointment of guardians of person and property of minors according to the Mohammedan law is also completion of eighteen years.[31] Christians[32] and Parsis[33] also reach majority at eighteen. Under Apprentices Act, 1961 a person shall not be qualified to be engaged as an apprentice...unless he completes fourteen years of age.[34] In Plantation's Labour Act, 1951, 'Child' means a person who has not completed his fifteenth year.[35] The Merchant Shipping Act, 1958 defines Child as a person who has not completed 14 years of age.[36] The Karnataka Shops and Commercial Establishments Act, 1961 prohibits employment of children who has not completed 14 years of age.[37] The Dangerous Machines (Regulation) Act, 1983 prohibits employment of children who have not completed 14 years of age.[38] Under Orphanages and Charitable Homes (Supervision and Control) Act, 1960 'child' means a boy or girl who has not completed the age of 18 years.[39] The Children Act, 1960 defines child as a boy who has not attained age of 18 years.[40] The Employment of Children Act, 1938 prohibited Employment of child who has not completed his 14 years in any workshop are process.[41] The Motor Vehicle Act, 1939 defines child as a person under the age of 14 years.[42] Sec. 361 of Indian Penal Code provide different definitions, a boy less than 16 is defined as a child and a girl less than 18 is considered as child.[43] According to Immoral Trafficking Act, 1956, age for children is 18 or less.[44]

Under Indian Contract Act, 1872 child is a person below the age of 18 years who has no capacity to enter into contract. In Beedi and Cigar Workers (Conditions of Employment) Act, 1966 'Child' means a person who has not completed 18 years.[45] Minimum Wages Act, 1948 defines a child as a person who has not completed his 15 years of his age.[46] Under Motor Transport Workers Act, 1961 defines child as a person who has not completed his 15th year.[47] The Maternity Benefit Act, 1961 defines child includes a still born child.[48] The Protection of Women from Domestic Violence Act, 2005 defines 'child' as any person below the age of 18 years and includes any adopted, step or foster child.[49] The National Plan of Action for Children, 2005 defines the 'child' as person upto the age of 18 years and its clear declaration that 'all rights apply to all age-groups, including before birth.[50]

The Right of Children to Free and Compulsory Education Act, 2009 defines 'child' as a male or female child of the age of six to fourteen years.[51]

The Constitution regards a person as child until 14 years. India has now recognized that the period of childhood and the protection it should imply extend to the age of 18 years. The National Plan of Action for Children, 2005 officially acknowledges this higher age ceiling.[52]

To bring uniformity, the Child Labour (Prohibition and Regulation) Act, 1986 amended certain other related enactments already in force. After clause (b) in Sec. 2 of the Minimum Wages Act, 1948 a new clause (bb) has been inserted by Sec. 23 of the present Act, which defines "child" as a person who has not completed his fourteenth year of age and Child Labour Act by Sec. 23 has further amended the Minimum Wages Act (Act 11 of 1948) as follows:

For clause (a), the following clauses have been substituted, namely,

(a) "adolescent" means a person who has completed his fourteenth year of age but has not completed his eighteenth year;

(aa) "adult" means a person who has completed his eighteenth year of age.

The Plantations Labour Act (Act of 69 of 1951) has also been amended by Sec. 24 of Child Labour Act, 1986 to bring the age of the child in conformity with the definition under the said Act. Under the amended Sec. 2 clauses (a) and (c) child means a person who has not completed his fourteenth year of age for the word fifteenth, the word fourteenth has been substituted. Similarly, Sec. 109 of the Merchant Shipping Act, 1958 has been amended by Sec. 25 of Child Labour Act,

1986 and under the amended Act "child" means a person who is under the age of fourteen years. In a like manner Sec. 2(a) and (b) of Motor Transport Workers Act, 1961 has been amended by Sec. 26 of Child Labour Act, 1986 and now child means a person who is under the age of fourteen years.

2.2. The "Age of the Child": An Analysis

From the above analysis it is observed that there is no criteria or scientific parameters in defining the age of the child and is not uniformly defined in various laws. The age of the child has been differently defined in different laws. Different Indian Laws have varying versions on when a child turns adult. Some laws say the age of attaining adulthood is fourteen, while in other it ranges between sixteen and eighteen.[53] The Child Labour (Prohibition and Regulation) Act, 1986 has an altogether different definition. Only those below a fourteen are considered as children. Children between 14 and 18 are still are now allowed to work in hazardous industries.[54] The age 14 was fixed may be on the ground of biological aspect. The Child Labour Act does not specify the minimum age of employment of children in the occupation and process other than the prohibited ones. Since this legislation was enacted way back in the year 1986, age of the child under this legislation continued and remains a debatable concept.

Sec. 361 of IPC is confusing as it gives different definitions with regard to age of boy child and girl child. There is no gender parity in IPC for children. Most law enforcers wonder how to deal with girls between 16 and 18 years, caught in prostitution rackets or rescued from trafficking. There is a confusion and difference between the IPC and Immoral Traffic Act. There is an inherent contradiction in the IPC, while sex with a girl who is 16 or younger is considered rape, in the case of married woman the offence can be registered only if she is less than 15. This is contradictory to the provisions of the Prohibition of Child Marriage Act, 2006 which says that the legal age of marriage is 18. Further the age of marriage for boy is 21 years and for girl is 18[55] years which is differently defined under the present legislation, The Prohibition of Child Marriage Act, 2006. As such the age of the marriage for both boys and girls should be made 18 years, as there is no scientific reason why this should be different[56] and there is no justification for defining the age of the child differently. At the age of 18 girl child do not complete her education and hence this provision deprives the girl child of opportunities to growth and development.[57] Further the legalization of the Prevention of The Immoral Trafficking Act is also under debate, Sec. 7(aa) states, that "child" means a person who has not completed the age of sixteen years. There are no different provisions for women and girl children. So, while the age for voting and marriage is put at 18, this Act defines the age of the girl child at 16! Maximum punishment for procuring a girl child under the age of 16 is 5 years. But under the Prevention of Immoral Trafficking Act, it can go till 7 years and continue till life. Detaining a child under this Act, is a crime. Similarly, if a child is found in a brothel, it is assumed that it is for commercial exploitation.[58] The Indian Penal Code defines the punishment for procuring a minor girl, for illicit intercourse, importing of a foreign girl from other country. Sec. 366-A which states – "procurement of minor girl – girl below the age of 18 years with the intent of illicit intercourse with another person- punishable with imprisonment of 10 years and fine". Sec. 366-B states—"importation of girl from foreign country—outside India—under the age of 21 years with intent of illicit intercourse with another person—punishable with 10 years imprisonment and fine". The age of a foreign girl is put at 21 years old. The offence is same, but an Indian girl is treated differently. Also, the courts have refused to change the definition of Rape.[59]

In the Child Marriage Restraint Act, 1929 there is difference between the age of the boy and that of the girl. The minimum age of marriage for girls is 18 but the age of sexual consent under the rape laws is 16 and it is 15 if she is married.[60] Thus Child Marriage Restraint Act, 1929 itself is a very weak and dilatory. Child Marriages are valid even though there is prescribed minimum age of marriage. The procedure to prevent child marriages are very cumbersome and time consuming. Illiteracy and orthodoxy of the people have proved to be other stumbling blocks.[61]

There is a disparity of age of the child in child labour laws and Juvenile Justice laws. In the existing Child Labour (Prohibition and Regulation) Act, 1986 those below 14 years of age are considered as child labourers but the Juvenile Justice Act considers 18 as the age bar, may be on the ground of the legal aspect. Further the Right to Education Act, 2009 narrows the definition down to persons between six to fourteen years. Though the Act expresses interest in taking necessary steps in providing free pre-school education for children above 3 years of age, leaving out this critical segment of the child population from the definition is worry some not only does the Act fail to cover all children, does not provide definite timeless for many provisions.[62]

The definition of children given under Child Labour (Prohibition and Regulation) Act, 1986 is in contradiction with United Nations Convention on Rights of the Child, 1989 and Juvenile Justice (Care and Protection of Children) Act, 2000. Other legislations concerning child labour include: The Factories Act, 1948; The Mines Act, 1952; The Plantation Labour Act, 1951; The Merchant Shipping Act, 1958, The

Motor Transport Workers Act, 1961; The Beedi and Cigar Workers (Conditions of Employment) Act, 1966; The Bonded Labour System (Abolition) Act, 1976. All these Acts prohibit employment of children under 14 years only, which is not in accordance with the United Nations Convention on the Rights of the Child and the Juvenile Justice legislation in India. Therefore, an amendment to these Acts is required for ensuring that children are protected from economic exploitation and their rights are not violated. [63]

Thus clarity is missing on the basic understanding of 'who is a child'.[64] The different connotations, versions defining 'child' invites gaps in legal procedures, provides scope to the vested interests and guilty to escape from prosecution and punishment. This further consequently causes injustice to the children. The UN Convention on the Rights of the Child mandates, the age of the child should be 18 years and 'best interest of the child' be adhered in all situations, and the Convention was ratified by Government of India and is signatory. So the definition of the term, 'child' be brought in conformity with Convention on the Rights of the Child viz. "below 18 years of age" by establishing one standard "age of majority".[65]

3. DEFINITION OF CHILDHOOD

Child is called the father of man, but it is more proper to call it as father of whole mankind. Child's innocence and smile assures us of great future. Childhood is the most precious stage of a person's life. Therefore, the guardians of the children including the Government must fulfil the Constitutional obligation of ensuring right to life for them. "Childhood is the foundation of hopes for better future".[66] Childhood was considered to be the golden age in individuals' life history rather than adulthood. Every child has to enjoy the childhood, as it is the basic and natural right of a child for building the personality of a person, childhood is very remarkable bearing. This demands proper environment and atmosphere and the child is suppose to have the love, care, protection, education and nurturing too. Parents owed responsibility to provide opportunity to the child to grow and develop in a environment which is healthy, safe and from danger/violence free.

Undoubtedly childhood is the golden period of physical, mental and moral growth. M. Edwards[67] rightly observes: "Children are the future: childhood is a once-and-for-all biological window of opportunity for investment in human beings. Losses incurred can never be made good and a failure to support children as children will have permanent effects on society's capacity to develop".

Justice V.R. Krishna Iyer says that: "A generation which fails to recognize that the baby is its first charge is lost in barbarity. The hall-mark of culture and advance of civilization consists in the fulfilment of the obligation to the young generation by opening up all opportunities for every child to unfold in its personality and rise to its full stature-physical, moral, mental and spiritual". He further adds that it is the birth right of every child to get justice from the world as a whole.[68]

The Right to childhood is a sacred entitlement of mankind. Children are not just tomorrow's citizens but today's as well. Childhood is more than just the time before a person is considered an adult. It means more than just the time between birth and the attainment of adulthood. Childhood refers to the state and condition of a Child's life: To the quality of those years. Childhood implies a separate and safe space, demarcated from adulthood, in which children can grow, play and develop.[69]

The Directive Principles of State Policy under Constitution are basic cardinal Principles of justice as they stand for guarantee to safeguard the interest of women and children. The tender age of children are not be abused and not forced by economic necessity to inter avocations unsuited to their age or strength.[70]

In *Sheela Barse* v. *Union of India*,[71] the Supreme Court called upon the state governments to bring into force and to implement vigorously the provisions of the Children' Acts enacted in various states to implement the directive contained in Article 39(f) of the Constitution that, "the state shall direct its policy towards securing that Children are to be given opportunities and facilities to develop in a healthy manner and conditions of freedom and dignity and that childhood and youth are protected against exploitation and against moral and material abandonment by the state.

Though it is a matter for the state government to decide as to when a particular statute should be brought into force, the court felt it appropriate that every state should bring the Act into force without any delay and administered in accordance with provisions contained therein.[72]

State has to provide early childhood care and education for all children until they complete the age of 6 years.[73] Way back in the year 1948, The United Nations General Assembly had adopted the Universal Declaration of Human Rights which contains specific references about children and their rights. "Motherhood and Childhood are entitled to special care and assistance", and adds that "all children whether born in or out of wedlock shall enjoy the same special protection".[74]

Judiciary has laid down various guidelines on the concept of childhood. In *Bandhua Mukti Morcha's case*[75] Justice P.N. Bhagwati has held that: "This right to live with human dignity enshrined in Article 21 derives its life breath from the Directive Principles of State Policy and particularly clauses (e) and (f) of Article 39 and Article 41 and 42 and at least, therefore, it must include protection of the health and strength of workers, men and women, and of the tender age of children against abuse, opportunities and facilities for children to develop in a healthy manner and in conditions of freedom and dignity, educational facilities, just and humane conditions of work and maternity relief. These are the minimum requirements which must exist in order to enable a person to live with human dignity..." The observations made by the Supreme Court in another judgment in *Bandhua Mukti Morcha* v. *Union of India,*[76] are relevant in the context, which read: "The child of today cannot develop to be a responsible and productive member of tomorrow's society unless an environment conducive to his social and physical health is assured to him. Every nation, developed or developing, links its future with the status of the child... Neglecting the children means loss to the society as a whole. If children are deprived of their childhood—socially, economically, physically and mentally—the nation gets deprived of the potential human resources for social progress, economic empowerment and peace and order, the social stability and good citizenry. The founding fathers of the Constitution, therefore, have emphasized the importance of the role of the child and the need of its best development". The Supreme Court of India in *Rosy Jacob* v. *Jacab A. Chakramakkal,*[77] observed that: "The children are not mere chattels: nor are they mere play things for their parents. Absolute right of parents over the destinies and the lives of their children has, in the modern changed social conditions, yielded to the considerations of their welfare as human beings so that they may grow up in a normal balanced manner to be useful members of the society...".

3.1. Childhood—Growth of Children

Children are innocent, trusting and full of hope, this childhood should be happy and loving their lives should mature gradually, as they gain new experiences. But for many children, the reality of childhood is altogether different. Right through history, children have been abused and exploited. They suffer from hunger and homelessness; work in harmful conditions, high infant mortality, deficient health care and limited opportunities for basic education. A child need not live such a life. Childhood can and must be preserved. Children have the right to survive, develop, be protected and participate in decisions that impact their lives. Children should be carrying books, not bricks. They should be playing with footballs not stitching them. They should be sitting inside the classrooms, and not sweeping them.[78]

Our two great epics *Ramayan* and *Mahabharata* also appraised the Indian view of childhood regarding intense parental longing for children, and their upbringing is characterized by affectionate indulgence.[79] The ancient rulers King Ashoka, (268-31 B.C.), Chandragupta Vikramaditya (A.D. 375-415) stressed on loyalty and obedience by children to their elders. This was also considered not only a moral but also socially approved and valued behaviour.[80]

Children rarely figured as individuals in their own rights, with activities, reactions and feelings separate from those of their all powerful parents.[81] Rama's love for Lava and Kusha, Prabharkaravardhan's love for his son, Harsha and Kanwa's love for his daughter Shakuntala are well known examples.[82] The songs of Surdasa on Krishna's childhood and that of Tulasidasa on Rama's childhood, which are rich resources for childhood.[83]

The 19th century saw the birth of the child-saving movement, the growth of the orphanage, the development of child protection legislations, schooling and the construction of separate institutions, including the Juvenile courts, for delinquent children, in different parts of the western world. One of the reasons for this kind of development was that in the wake of industrial revolution there was severe exploitation of many working-class children who were widely employed in textiles, mining, agriculture, domestic service, docks and navigation. Moreover, the so-called 'advances' of industrialization and urbanization had serious consequences.[84] All the leaders and reformers invested their time, knowledge and resources towards better health, education and growth of the weaker children.[85]

The ideals of childhood are one of love, care and protection, in a family environment with ample scope to survive growth, develop and participate. Childhood as a time when children are allowed to grow and develop to their full potential; healthy children in school and at play, growing strong and confident with the love and encouragement of their family and an extended community of caring adults gradually taking on the responsibility of adulthood, free from fear, safe from violence, protected from abuse and exploitation. Firstly, childhood is an empty word and broken promise. Secondly, childhood is the foundation of the world's hope for better future.[86] There is a gap between the reality and ideal childhood. Childhood implies a separate and safe space, demarcated from adulthood, in which children can grow play and develop. A new definition of childhood based on human rights is reflected in the Convention on the Rights of the Child, adopted by the UN's General Assembly in 1989. The Convention is the First International Human Rights treaty to bring together the Universal set of standards concerning children in a unique instrument and the first to understand child rights as a legally binding imperative.[87] The Convention on the Rights of the Child defines childhood is separate space demarcated from adulthood.

Historically, the needs and obligations of children were not well differentiated from those of adults. Like adults, able-bodied children traditionally engaged in arduous labour and were often combatants in battle. But the Convention, citing the "special care and assistance" that children require, recognizes that what is appropriate for an adult may not be suitable for a child. This is why, for instance, it sets a minimum age for recruitment into the armed forces and participation in armed conflict. Its recognition of childhood as a 'separate space' means that even when children face the same challenges as adults, they may require different solutions.[88] Supreme Court Judge Ruma Paul said while addressing[89] a gathering of lawyers, Jurists and Judges that, ensuring justice to children is the responsibility of every citizen, every institution and every limb of the Government.

In *M.C. Mehta* v. *State of Tamilnadu and others*,[90] Supreme Court had opened the paragraph of the Judgment with a beautiful poem by Mamie Gene Cole, it proceeds with the importance of the statement, "Child is the father of the man". It proceeds to emphasize how a child be groomed, and receive education and nutrition, so as to enable the petals of childhood to blossom to the flowers of youth and manhood.

4. CONSTITUTIONAL PROVISIONS AND LEGAL FRAMEWORK

In order to protect best interest of children and their childhood the Constitution of India, the fundamental law of India, came into effect on 26th January 1950, which provides, measures to protect for the rights of the citizens. These rights include right to equality (Article 14), right to freedom including freedom of speech and expression Article 19(1)(a), personal liberty, right to due process of law including right to life (Article 21), right against exploitation (Article 23), religious, cultural, educational rights (Article 29); and right to Constitutional remedies (Article 32). In addition to the above basic rights the Constitution provides certain fundamental rights especially for children. As this class is vulnerable for various kinds of exploitation, due to their physical and mental immaturity, they need special protection. Article 15 of the Constitution prohibits discrimination of citizens on the grounds only of religion, race, caste, sex, place of birth, or any of them. But clause 3 adds: 'Nothing in this Article shall prevent the state from making any special provision for women and children.' Therefore, laws can be made giving special protection to children. These rights are included in Part III and Part IV of the Constitution. The fundamental rights in Part III are enforceable in courts whereas the Directive Principles of State Policy in Part IV are guidelines and principles that are fundamental to the governance of the country. It is the duty of the state to apply these principles in making laws. If the fundamental rights are violated, a writ petition can be filed in the Supreme Court or the High Court Arts. 32 and 226. Under the Constitution, it is the duty of the state to secure that children of tender age are not abused and forced by economic necessity to enter vocations unsuited to their age and strength Art. 39(f). Rights provided under Part IV (Directive Principles) of the Constitution can be read into the fundamental rights provided in Part III and thus become enforceable in courts. Because of judicial interpretation, many of the directive principles have now become enforceable through legal actions brought before the courts (for example, the right to education). There are certain aspects relating to children that are dealt with in the state and concurrent lists of the Constitution of India. It is estimated that there are more than 250 Central and state statutes under which the child is covered in India. Some of the important, special legislations that deal with children are as follows:[91]

(a) The Child Marriage Restraint Act, 1929: This Act, as amended in 1979, restrains the solemnization of child marriages by laying down the minimum age of marriage for both boys and girls. This law is applicable to all communities irrespective of their religion;
(b) The Prohibition of Child Marriage Act, 2005: This Act prohibits the marriage of a boy if he is below 21 years and the girl if she is below 18 years. Thus the Act stipulates the age bar;
(c) The Child Labour (Prohibition and Regulation) Act, 1986: This Act prohibits the engagement of children in certain employment and regulates the conditions of work of children in certain other employments;
(d) The Juvenile Justice (Care and Protection of Children) Act, 2000: This Act deals with the law relating to juveniles in conflict with law and children in need of care and protection, by providing for proper care, protection and treatment by catering to their development needs and by adopting a child-friendly approach in the adjudication and disposition of matters in the best interest of children and for their ultimate rehabilitation through various institutions established under the Act;
(e) The Pre-Natal Diagnostic Technique (Regulation and Prevention of Misuse) Act, 1994: This provides for the regulation of the use of prenatal diagnostic techniques for the purpose of detecting genetic or metabolic disorders or

chromosomal abnormalities or certain congenital malformations or sex-linked disorders, and for the prevention of the misuse of such techniques for the purpose of prenatal sex determination leading to female feticide;

(f) The Children (Pledging of Labour) Act, 1933: This prohibits pledging the labour of children;

(g) Probation of Offenders Act, 1958: This law lays down the restrictions on imprisonment of offenders under twenty-one years of age;

(h) Young Persons Harmful Publications Act, 1956: This Act prevents the dissemination of certain publications that are harmful to young persons;

(i) Apprentices Act, 1961: This lays down qualifications for persons above fourteen years of age to undergo apprenticeship training in any designated trade;

(j) The Infant Milk Substitutes, Feeding Bottles and Infant Foods (Regulation of Production, Supply and Distribution) Act, 1992: This Act regulates the production, supply and distribution of infant milk substitutes, feeding bottles and infant feeds with a view to the protection and promotion of breastfeeding and ensuring the proper use of infant feeds and other incidental matters;

(k) The Guardian and Wards Act, 1890: This Act deals with the qualifications, appointment and removal of guardians of children by the courts and is applicable to all children irrespective of their religion; and

(l) The Hindu Minority and Guardianship Act, 1956: This provides for the appointment of guardians of minors among Hindus.

Further there are other provisions relating to employment of children in The Factories Act, 1948; The Minimum Wages Act, 1948; The Plantations Labour Act, 1951; The Mines Act, 1952; The Merchant Shipping Act, 1958; The Motor Transport Workers' Act, 1961; The Payment of Bonus Act, 1965; The Beedi and Cigar Workers' (Conditions of Employment) Act, 1966; The Bonded Labour System (Abolition) Act, 1976; The Trade Unions Act, 1926; and the various State Shops and Establishment Acts. The Contract Act, 1872; The Indian Partnership Act, 1932; and The Indian Trust Act, 1882; contain provisions relating to civil and commercial rights and liabilities of minors.

5. GOVERNMENT POLICIES AND ACTION PLANS

The Government of India has introduced various National Policies, Plans and Programmes relating to children. The Policies focus on planning and implementation. Some major policy and plan documents are as follows:

(1) National Policy for Children, 1974.
(2) National Children's Fund, 1979.
(3) National Policy on Education, 1986.
(4) National Policy on Child Labour, 1987.
(5) National Plan for SAARC Decade for the Girl Child, 1991-2000.
(6) National Plan of Action for Children, 1992.
(7) National Nutrition Policy, 1993.
(8) National Population Policy, 2000.
(9) National Health Policy, 2001.
(10) National Charter for Children, 2003.
(11) National Plan of Action for Children, 2005.
(12) The Commission for Protection of Child Rights Act, 2005.
  (a) National Commission for Protection of Child Rights;
  (b) State Commission for Protection of Child Rights; and
  (c) Children's Courts.

5.1. National Policy for Children, 1974

In 1975, following The National Policy Resolution for Children 1974, A National Children Board was constituted with the Prime Minister as its President. The main objective of creating this Board was to bring about greater awareness and promote the welfare of children and to plan, review and co-ordinate programmes and services directed at children including working children.

In pursuance of the Constitutional provisions embodied in Article 39 clauses (e) and (f), Government of India evolved and adopted the National Policy for Children.[92] The policy for the welfare of children starts with a goal-oriented preamble:

> "The nation's children are supremely important asset. Their nurture and solicitude are our responsibility. Children's programs should find a prominent part in our national plans for the development of human resources, so that our children grow upto become robust citizens, physically fit, mentally alert and morally healthy, endowed with the skills and motivations needed by society. Equal opportunities for development to all children

during the period of growth should be our aim, for this would serve our larger purpose of reducing inequality and ensuring social justice".

As per the preamble and declaration of the Government, it is crystal clear that child is a national asset. Further as observed by the Supreme Court in *Sheela Barse* v. *Union of India,*[93] that, if a child is a national asset, it is the duty of the State to look after the child with a view to ensuring full development of its personality. The National Policy, sets out the measures which Government of India proposes to adopt towards attainment of the objectives set out in the prefatory introduction and they include measures designed to protect children against neglect, cruelty and exploitation and to strengthen family ties "so that full potentialities of growth of children are realized within the normal family neighbourhood and community environment". The National Policy also lays down priority in programme formation and it gives fairly high priority to maintenance, education and training of orphans and destitute children. There is also provision made in the National Policy for Constitution of a National Children's Board to provide a focus for planning and review and proper co-ordination of the multiplicity of services striving to meet the needs of children and to ensure at different levels continuous planning, review and co-ordination of all the essential services. The National Policy also stresses the vital role, which the voluntary organizations have to play in the field of education, health, recreation and social welfare services for children, and declare that it shall be the endeavour of State to encourage and strengthen such voluntary organizations.

The above policy is now outdated as it does not conform to the standards laid down in the United Nations Convention on the Rights of the Child which India has ratified and in conformity of which it is obliged to make laws.[94]

5.2. The National Children's Fund, 1979

The Fund was created during the International Year of the Child in 1979 under the Charitable Endowment Fund Act, 1890. The Fund provides financial assistance to voluntary agencies for implementing programmes for the welfare of children including rehabilitation of destitute children. The Fund should be enhanced and energized. It should have flexibility in supporting new and innovative ventures, to benefit children and the ability to respond promptly to emergencies.[95]

5.3. National Policy on Education, 1986 (Modified in 1992)

The National Policy on Education, 1986 was the second policy on education since Independence. It was regarded as a landmark. It redefined educational priorities and made a fresh attempt to cope with the three stands that have influenced educational policy in India, viz., issues relating to quantity, quality and equity. The policy gave the highest importance to Universal Primary Education (UPE).[96] Under the Seventh Five Year Plan (1985-90) Govt. of India has adopted a new National Policy on Education. Taking holistic view, the National Policy on Education visualized education as a dynamic cumulative, life long process providing diversity of learning opportunities to all segments of society. It's main purpose was to fulfil the objective of "*Education for All*" by providing early childhood care and education, universalizing elementary education through formal and non-formal methods, reducing wastage and involving the local community in the management of early education. As a result, new schemes were implemented like the 'District Primary Education Programme' in 1986 and the 'Operation Black Board' in 1987. The Scheme of Non-formal education was revised. The National Policy on Education tried to provide scope for equal access to education for all, irrespective of class, caste, creed or gender. Further The National Policy on Education envisaged, a common educational structure like 10+2+3 and common core curriculum throughout the country. It also sought to remove disparities by catering to the needs of Schedule Castes, Schedule Tribes, the handicapped and other minority groups.[97] The Policy sets a target whereby all children who attained the age of 11 years by 1990 will have received five years of schooling or its equivalent in a non-formal system of education. With this goal in view, 4,90,000 non-formal education centers are proposed to be opened nationally to supplement the formal education system.[98] The National Policy on Education in India was modified in 1992. Thereafter, Parliament approved a programme of action which sought to launch National Elementary Education Mission-Education for All-in 1993 and the District Primary Education Programme launched in 1994. Currently the emphasis is on universal primary education.[99] To spread education, top priority should be given to universalisation of elementary education for children between 6 to 14 years. The focus is upon the Non-formal education to help the children who are unable or unwilling to attend full time school. These facilities should be provided by Non Governmental Organizations.

5.4. National Policy on Child Labour, 1987

The Government of India announced the National Policy on Child Labour in August, 1987. The Policy focuses mainly on three welfare aspects of the child. Firstly, on the enforcement of child labour; Secondly, on the families of the child labourers to avail the benefits of welfare and development programmes meant for this purpose; and Thirdly, to take up projects in areas of child labour concentration.[100] The basic goals of the National Child Labour Policy were to rehabilitate the children withdrawn from employment and reduce the incidence of child labour in areas of high concentration of child labour; (a) By improving health condition for child labour; (b) By providing nutrition through schemes like Integrated Child Development Scheme; and (c) By intensifying the anti-poverty programmes, such as Integrated Rural Development Programme (IRDP), National Rural Employment Programme (NREP), etc.

Child labour is a subset of the total child population and policy on child labour is also a fragment of National Labour. The National Policy on Child Labour is therefore, a combination of how the nation views children *vis-à-vis* other segments of the population and how it views working children *vis-à-vis* the rest of the working population.

The National Child Labour Policy was adopted in 1987 to deal with a situation where children are compelled to work, on a regular or a continuous basis to earn a living for themselves and their family, and where conditions of work result in their being disadvantaged and exploited. The Policy is intended to have Legislative Action Plan:

(1) Setting up of Child Labour Technical Advisory Committee to advise the Central Government on addition of occupations and processes to the schedule contained in the Child Labour (Prohibition and Regulation) Act, 1986 and other child related legislation.
(2) Envisages the strict enforcement of the provisions of the Child Labour (Prohibition and Regulation) Act, 1986 and other child-related legislation.

Further, The Policy is focusing on General Development Programmes for benefiting Child Labour: To successfully rehabilitate child labour withdrawn from employment and to reduce the incidence of child labour progressively, the focus is on the environment of the child. By utilizing the ongoing development programmes of other Ministries and Departments for the benefit of the child and his family, child labour can be discouraged.

(1) By providing better and readily accessible education, through formal or non-formal systems of education;
(2) By improving health conditions for child labour; and
(3) By providing nutrition through programmes such as Integrated Rural Development Programme, National Rural Employment Programme, etc.

The Policy is focused on areas known to have high concentration of child labour and to adopt a project approach for identification, withdrawal and rehabilitation of working children.[101]

The National Child Labour Policy was formulated with the basic objective of suitably rehabilitating the children withdrawn from employment and reducing the child labour in areas where there is a known concentration of child labour. The policy consists of three main ingredients: the legal action plan, focusing of Central Government programmes, and project based plan of action.

5.5. National Plan for SAARC Decade of the Girl Child, 1991-2000

In 1992, the Government of India prepared a separate National Plan for the Girl Child for the period 1991-2000. This plan identified three major goals:[102]

(1) Survival and protection of the girl child and safe motherhood;
(2) Overall development of the girl child; and
(3) Special protection for vulnerable girl children in need of care and protection.

5.6. National Plan of Action for Children, 1992[103]

India is a signatory to the World Declaration 1990 on the Survival, Protection and Development of Children and the Plan of Action for implementing it. The National Plan of Action is a follow-up of the promises made by the global fraternity at the World Summit for Children. The major goals of the Plan of Action for 1990-2000 were:

(1) Reduction of infant mortality rate to less than ten;
(2) Reduction of maternal mortality rate by half;
(3) Reduction in severe and moderate malnutrition among under-5 children by half;
(4) Universal access to safe drinking water and improved access to sanitary means of excreta disposal;
(5) Universal enrolment, retention, minimum level of learning, reduction of disparities, and universalization of effective access of schooling;
(6) Achievement of adult literacy rate of 80 percent in the age group of 15-35, with emphasis on female literacy;
(7) Improved protection of children in especially difficult circumstances;
(8) Assistance to children affected by one or more disabilities,

having no access to proper rehabilitative services and especially upliftment of the status of those most marginalized;

(9) Removal of gender bias and improvement in the status of the girl child;

(10) Conservation and protection of the environment for the well-being of children; and

(11) Promotion of advocacy and people's participation for the child.

5.7. National Nutrition Policy, 1993

This was adopted by the government in 1993 identified a series of actions for different departments in the area of food-production and distribution, health and family welfare, education, rural and urban development, women and child development, etc.

The National Nutrition Policy reflects the understanding that malnutrition is not simply a matter of 'not enough food', but is most frequently caused by a combination of factors, including lack of time and attention to child care, inadequate feeding of the child especially in the first year of life, poor health, unhygienic conditions as well as the lack of purchasing power of poor families. A National Plan of Action on Nutrition was formulated in 1995.[104]

5.8. National Population Policy, 2000

It aims at improvement in the status of the Indian child. The National Population Policy, 2000 of the Government of India aims at gender-balanced stabilization but also underscores the need for addressing issues such as child survival, maternal health and contraception, while increasing the provision and outreach of education, extending basic amenities such as sanitation, safe drinking water, and housing, besides empowering women and enhancing their employment opportunities.[105]

The National Population Policy, 2000 recognizes the link between high infant mortality and excessive population growth. The policy statement commits the nation to a reduction of the infant mortality rate to under 30 per 1000 by the year 2010. This necessitates a rapid reduction in neonatal deaths which form a major component of infant mortality. The Policy also aims to achieve 80 percent deliveries in institutions and 100 percent deliveries by trained personnel by the year 2010.[106]

5.9. National Health Policy, 2002

This accords primacy to preventive and first line curative care at primary health level and emphasizes convergence, and strategies to change care behaviours in families and communities.[107] National Health Policy, 1983, in a spirit of optimistic empathy for the health needs of the people, particularly the poor and underprivileged, had hoped to provide 'Health for All by 2000', through the universal provision of comprehensive primary health care services. National Health Policy, 2002 has attempted to set out a new policy framework for the accelerated achievement of public health goals in the socio-economic circumstances currently prevailing in the country. National Health Policy, 2002 has been formulated taking into consideration the ground realities in regard to the availability of resources. In the period when centralized planning was accepted as a key instrument of development in the country, the attainment of an equitable regional distribution was considered one of its major objectives. Despite this conscious focus in the development process, the attainment of health indices has been very uneven across the rural-urban divide. National Health Policy, 2002 also envisages giving priority to school health programmes which aim at preventative health education, providing regular health checkups, and promotion of health-seeking behaviour among children. The school health programmes can gainfully adopt specially designed modules in order to disseminate information relating to 'health' and 'family life'. This is expected to be the most cost-effective intervention as it improves the level of awareness, not only of the extended family, but the future generation as well. It is widely accepted that school and college students are the most impressionable targets for imparting information relating to the basic principles of preventive health care. The policy will attempt to target this groupto improve the general level of awareness in regard to 'health-promoting' behaviour. Social, cultural and economic factors continue to inhibit women from gaining adequate access even to the existing public health facilities. This handicap has an adverse impact on the health, general well-being, and development of the entire family, particularly children. This policy recognizes the catalytic role of empowered women in improving the overall health standards of the community including children.[108]

5.10. National Charter for Children, 2003

The National Charter for Children emphasizes commitment to children's right to survival, development, and protection. It also stipulates the duties of the state and community towards children and emphasizes the duties of children towards family, society, and the nation.[109]

In order to ensure protection of rights of children, one of the recent initiatives that the Government of India has taken for Children is the adoption of National Charter for Children 2003 to reiterate its commitment to the cause of children in order to see that no child remains hungry, illiterate or sick.

The object of the Charter is to secure for every child its inherent right to be a child and enjoy a healthy and happy childhood, to address the root causes that negate the healthy growth and development of children, and to awaken the conscience of the community in the wider societal context to protect children from all forms of abuse, while strengthening the family, society and the Nation.

The State and Community shall undertake to provide to the children for protecting their best interest. Some of the important components of Charter are as under:

(1) To ensure and protect the survival, life and liberty of all children; (2) Promoting high standards of health and nutrition; (3) To provide all children from families below the poverty line with adequate supplementary nutrition and ensure to provide safe drinking water and environmental sanitation and hygiene; (4) Assuring basic Minimum Needs and Security; (5) To recognize play and leisure to all children; (6) To provide early childhood care for survival, growth and development; (7) To recognize that all children shall have access to free and compulsory education; (8) To provide protection to children from economic exploitation and all forms of abuse especially to move towards a total ban of all forms of child labour; (9) To recognize that all children have a right to be protected against neglect, maltreatment, injury, trafficking, sexual and physical abuse of all kinds, corporal punishment, torture, exploitation and degrading treatment; (10) To take measures against use of children in conduct of illegal activities; (11) To ensure to provide protection to the girl child; (12) To take steps in empowering adolescent by providing necessary education and skills to equip them to become economically productive citizens; (13) To take steps to treat equally without discrimination on the grounds of race, colour, caste, sex, etc.; (14) To provide opportunity for freedom of expression for the all-round development of the personality and creativity of the children; (15) Ensure to provide freedom to seek and receive information; (16) To provide opportunity of freedom of association and peaceful assembly to all children; (17) To provide support in strengthening the family of the child; (18) To recognize the responsibilities of both parents of their children; (19) Recognize to provide protection with disabilities; (20) To provide Care, Protection, Welfare of Children of Marginalized and Disadvantaged Communities; (21) To recognize that children from disadvantaged communities and weaker/vulnerable sections of the society; and (22) To ensure to provide child-friendly procedures in the Juvenile Justice system for children in conflict with law and for children in need of special care and protection.

5.11. The National Common Minimum Programme (NCMP), 2004

The Government has formulated this program towards the cause of children. The National Common Minimum Programme specifically highlights the government's commitment to protect the rights of the children, strive for the elimination of child labour, ensure facilities for schooling and extend special care to the girl child. The National Common Minimum Programme also commits to universalize the Integrated Child Development Services Scheme, to provide a functional Anganwadi in every settlement and ensure full coverage for all children. In order to strengthen primary education, The National Common Minimum Programme highlights the role of NGOs and promises to provide full support to all NGO efforts.[110] The main components of The National Common Minimum Programme are: (a) Commitment to the well-being of the common man; (b) Preservation, protection and promotion of social harmony; (c) Enhancement of welfare and well-being of farmers, farm labour and workers, particularly in the unorganized sector; (d) A pledge to provide a corruption-free, transparent and accountable government at all times; (e) Administration that is responsive and responsible at all times. It provides a basic affirmation of the Government's resolve to "protect the rights of children". The test of National Common Minimum Programme is in how it gets translated into practical programming and investment in children; the National Plan of Action for Children, 2005 spells out goals, objectives and strategies to achieve this.[111]

5.12. National Plan of Action for Children, 2005

The National Plan of Action for Children, 2005 was introduced in the Parliament to provide a road map for steps to be taken for improvements in the lives of Indian Children.[112] It was implemented throughout the country through national measures and through State Plans of Action for Children. This Plan re-affirms the Nation's commitment to wisely, effectively and efficiently invest its national resources to fulfil its commitments to children. The Plan 2005 is divided into 4 sections; and all categories of rights apply to all age groups, including before birth.

(1) Child Survival;
(2) Child Development;
(3) Child Protection; and
(4) Child Participation.

The guiding principles of the National Plan of Action for

Children, 2005 are: (a) To regard the child as an asset and a person with human rights; (b) To address issues of discrimination emanating from biases of gender, class, caste, race, religion and legal status in order to ensure equality; (c) To accord utmost priority to the most disadvantaged, poorest of the poor and least served child in all policy and programmatic interventions; and (d) To recognize the diverse stages and settings of childhood, and address the needs of each, providing to all children the entitlements that fulfil their rights and meet their needs in each situation.[113]

The Plan has identified twelve key areas keeping in mind priorities and the intensity of the challenges that require utmost and sustained attention in terms of outreach, programme interventions and resource allocation, so as to achieve the necessary targets and ensure the rights and entitlements of children at each stage of childhood.[114] These are: (a) Reducing Infant Mortality Rate; (b) Reducing Maternal Mortality Rate; (c) Reducing Malnutrition among children; (d) Achieving 100% civil registration of births; (e) Universalization of early childhood care and development and quality education for all children achieving 100% access and retention in schools, including pre-schools; (f) Complete abolition of female foeticide, female infanticide and child marriage and ensuring the survival, development and protection of girl child; (g) Improving Water and Sanitation coverage both in rural and urban areas; (h) Addressing and upholding the rights of Children in difficult; (i) Securing for all children all legal and social protection from all kinds of abuse, exploitation and neglect; (j) Complete abolition of child labour with the aim of progressively eliminating all forms of economic exploitation of children; (k) Monitoring, Review and Reform of policies, programmes and laws to ensure protection of children's interests and rights; and (l) Ensuring child participation and choice in matters and decisions affecting their lives.

Thus, the Government of India committed to dedicate the National Plan of Action for Children, 2005 to "The Children of India".

5.13. The Commission for Protection of Child Rights Act, 2005[115]

The Act provides for the Constitution of a National Commission and State Commissions for Protection of Child Rights and Children's Courts for providing speedy trial of offences against children or of violation of child rights and for matters connected therewith or incidental thereto.

(1) *The National Commission for Protection of Child Rights*: The Central Government constitute a body to be known as the

National Commission for Protection of Child rights to exercise the powers conferred on, and to perform the functions assigned to it.

(2) *State Commission for Protection of Child Rights*: A State Government may constitute a body to be known as the ....(name of the State) Commission for Protection of Child Rights to exercise the powers conferred upon, and to perform the functions assigned to, a State Commission.

(3) *Children's Court*: For the purpose of providing speedy trial of offences against children or of violation of child rights, the State Government may, with the concurrence of the Chief Justice of the High Court, by notification, specify at least a Court in the State or specify, for each district, a Court of Session to be a Children's Court to try the said offences.

6. GOVERNMENT PROGRAMMES AND SCHEMES

6.1. Integrated Child Development Services (ICDS)

This programme is a vehicle for achieving major nutrition, health, and education goals to nearly twenty-eight million children throughout the country (since 1975). A network of Anganwadi centers, literally courtyard play centers, provide basic health, nutrition and early childhood care and development services to address the interrelated needs of children below the age of six, adolescent girls, and expectant and nursing mothers from the disadvantaged communities.[116]

6.2. National Initiative for Child Protection (NICP)

This is a campaign initiated by the Ministry of Social Justice and Empowerment through the National Institute of Social Defense (NISD) and Childline India Foundation (CIF). National Initiative for Child Protection aims at building partnerships with the allied systems such as the police, the health care system, the judicial system, the Juvenile Justice system, the education system, the transport system, the labour department, the media, the department of telecommunications, the corporate sector, social workers, and elected representatives. National Initiative for Child Protection hopes to achieve this by using advocacy and creating awareness and by involving children in making decisions that will directly affect their lives.[117]

6.3. National Child Labour Project (NCLP) Scheme, 1988

The project is based on The National Child Labour Policy, 1987, and accordingly Ministry of Labour, Government of India has implemented the project since 1988 for rehabilitation of the child labour.

The National Child Labour Project (NCLP) was launched in 1988, in areas of high concentration of child labour. National Child Labour Project's are area specific, time bound, where priority is given to the withdrawal and rehabilitation of children engaged in hazardous occupations. The strategy of National Child Labour Project is to implement model programmes consisting of key elements such as:

(a) Stepping up the enforcement of the prohibition of child labour;
(b) Providing employment to parents of children;
(c) Expanding formal and non-formal education;
(d) Promoting school enrolment through various incentives such as payment of stipend; and
(e) Raising public awareness, survey and evaluation.

Presently, National Child Labour Projects are operationalised in 250 Districts spread over in 20 States of India such as Andhra Pradesh, Assam, Bihar, Chhattisgarh, Gujarat, Haryana, Jammu and Kashmir, Jharkhand, Karnataka, Madhya Pradesh, Maharashtra, Mizoram, Nagaland, Orissa, Punjab, Rajasthan, Tamilnadu, Uttar Pradesh, Uttaranchal and West Bengal.[118]

The project aims at withdrawing and rehabilitating children working in identified hazardous occupations and processes through social schools and finally mainstreaming them to be formal education system. Each special school provides for enrolment of 50 children. There is a provision of two educational instructors and one vocational instructor for every special school. A stipend of Rs. 100 per month is paid to each child and mid-day meals at the rate of Rs. 5 per child per day are also provided. Besides this, vocational training and health check-ups are essential components of the scheme.[119]

The target group for National Child Labour Project Scheme would be all children below 14 years of age and working in: (a) Occupations and process listed in the Schedule III of Child Labour (Prohibition and Regulation) Act, 1986; and (b) Occupations and processes which adversely affect their health and psyche. The programme components are: (a) To survey to identify children in hazardous occupations and processes; (b) Withdrawal of the children from the factory/work environment through awareness generation and enforcement of the Child Labour (Prohibition and Regulation) Act, 1986; (c) Rehabilitation of children withdrawn from work, through special schools established by the National Child Labour Project Society; and (d) Convergence with Sarva Siksha Abhiyan (SSA) of the Ministry of Human Resource Development and other developmental schemes of different departments of the Government of India and the State Government.[120] It also focuses on rehabilitation of children working in hazardous occupations and processes in the age group 9-14 years, is an important activity and a direct responsibility of the project authority. Project societies are required to set-up Child Labour Special Schools (Rehabilitation-*cum*-Welfare Centers) by encouraging voluntary efforts for imparting formal/non-formal education and vocational training. The children in the special schools are to be provided supplementary nutrition, stipend and health care services also. The entire project is required be implemented through a registered society under the chairmanship of administrative head of the district, namely, District Magistrate/Collector of the District. Members of the society can be drawn from concerned Government Departments, representatives of the Panchayat Raj Institution, NGOs, Trade Unions, etc.[121]

6.4. INDUS Child Labour Project

This project is also an infocus programme on the elimination of child labour. It is a technical co-operation project of the Government of India, Ministry of Labour and Department of Education and the United States Department of Labour, within the framework of a "Joint Statement on enhanced Indo-US Co-operation as elimination of child labour" signed on 31st August, 2000 by the Government of India and United States, briefly known as "INDUS". The project is being executed by International Labour Organisation, for which both the Governments are equally contributing.[122] The project recognizes that working children belong to specific sections of the population that continue to be marginalized. Therefore, it is the goal of the project to target marginalized populations of children in selected areas and to improve their attendance, performance and retention in education. The main components of the programme are: (a) Enrolment in public elementary education; (b) Withdrawal and provision of transitional education; (c) Strengthen Vocational Training (SVT); (d) Local Community Institution Buildings; (e) Strengthening public education of child workers; and (f) Social Mobilization.

Various sectors were identified as priority areas for action under the project. They are: Hand rolled Bidi/Cigarettes, Brassware, handmade bricks, Fireworks, Footwear (leather, rubber and plastic), Hand-blown glass bangles, Handmade locks, Hand dipped matches, Hand broken quarries stones, Hand spun or hand loomed silk thread, yarn and fabric.[123]

The project was practically implemented in some States of our country are; Madhya Pradesh, Maharashtra, Tamil Nadu and Uttar Pradesh from which five districts from each State have been chosen specifically in the above sectors. An important dimension in the implementation of project is: the existence of efficient, effective and sustainable system for monitoring the child labour situation; and to determine the extent of child labour, in general, as well as hazardous child labour.[124] The project structure is being organized at three levels, i.e. National Level, State Level and District Level.

6.5. Integrated Child Protection Scheme-ICPS (Eleventh Plan, 2007-2012)[125]

The Ministry of Women and Child Development, Government of India considered 'Child Protection' as an essential component of the country's strategy to place 'Development' of the child at the center of the eleventh plan'. The Integrated Child Protection Scheme is, therefore, proposed by the Ministry of Women and Child Development as a centrally sponsored scheme to address the issue of child protection and build a protective environment for children through Government-Civil Society Partnership. The main focus of the scheme is that, child protection is integrally linked to every other right of the child. Failure to ensure children's right to protection adversely affects all other rights of the child. Child protection is also closely linked to the achievement of the Millennium Development Goals (MDGs) and policy-makers have failed to see this connection or chosen to overlook it. The approach to Child Protection is, a comprehensive rights based approach; The cardinal principles of 'protection of child rights' and 'best interests of the child' form the fundamental basis for the scheme; Both prevention and protection are central to the approach; Mobilizing inter-sectoral response for reducing vulnerabilities and strengthening child protection and setting standards for care and services are important elements; to have Government Civil Society Partnership; and implementation through a decentralized structure. The Scheme aims at: expansion and improved Reporting and Redressal Mechanism; Improved institutional care; Quality Non-institutional and Alternative Care; Counseling and Family Support; Training and Capacity Building; Strengthening the knowledge base; and Child Tracking System including web-enabled child protection data management software and website for missing children. Some important Principles of Integrated Child Protection Scheme are: (a) child protection as a shared responsibility; (b) Reduce child vulnerability; (c) Strengthen families; (d) Promote non-institutional care; (e) Build inter-sectoral linkages and responsibilities; (f) Create a network of services at community level; (g) Establish standards for care and protection; (h) Build capacities of all stakeholders; (i) Provide professional child protection services at all levels; (j) Strengthen crisis management system at all levels; (k) Reintegrate with family and community; (l) Address protection of children in urban areas; and (m) Carry out child social audit.

6.6. National Resource Centre on Child Labour, 1993

The task of progressively eliminating child labour calls for an effective mechanism to provide inputs for policy formulations and program support. A modest beginning in this regard was made by setting up a Child Labour Cell in the V.V. Giri National Labour Institute (VVGNLI) in 1990 with the assistance of the Government of India and UNICEF. The increased pace of activities and emerging needs for various types of support by different agencies led to the up-gradation of the Child Labour Cell into the National Resource Centre on Child Labour (NRCCL), The NRCCL was set-up in March 1993 with financial support from the Ministry of Labour.[126] The objective of the centre is to endeavour to contribute to the attainment of the Government Policy of progressive elimination of child labour.[127] The centre is to assist the National and State Governments, NGOs, policy-makers and other social groups in the field of child labour through a research, training, technical support, advocacy, media management, documentation, publication and dissemination to various target groups towards progressive elimination of child labour in India. National Resource Centre on Child Labour has also been conducting orientation and sensitization programmes for personnel involved in child labour projects.[128] The National Resource Centre on Child Labour has built up an impressive database on child labour and is now assisting the Ministry of Labour in the implementation of child labour programs. Research and training are two other important activities of the National Resource Centre on Child Labour.[129]

7. CRITICAL ANALYSIS OF LAWS AND POLICIES

It is observed from the study of various Laws and Polices of the Government that, there is no nexus between the law and policies and they tend to work in isolations. For instance, The Right to Education is linked with the issues of Child Labour, Juvenile Justice, Child Marriages, Health and Nutrition, etc. The Policy perspectives relating to the children and childhood are not clear and the same leads to confusion. In pursuance of the Constitution (Eighty-sixth Amendment) Act, 2002, Right to Education Act, 2009 was enacted, which provides Education as a Fundamental Right of Children between six and fourteen, by which every child of this age is supposed to be at school. But the Child Labour (Prohibition and Regulation) Act, 1986 provides for regulation of the conditions of work of children below fourteen years in non-hazardous occupations and process. That means a child below the age of fourteen year can work as a labourer. The Persons with Disabilities (Equal opportunities, Protection of Rights and Full Participation) Act, 1995 is borrowed from the Education, Health, and Nutrition Policies and the children in need of Care and Protection under Juvenile Justice (Care and Protection of Children) Act, 2000. The present Criminal Laws do not address the cases of child abuse and needs clear legal definition for child sexual abuse. The National Policy on Children, 1974 is outdated, so it is to be revamped. So more child oriented and rights based policies are desired for their effective implementation. These require integrated and convergence approach for better protection of child and childhood and protection of their rights in the best interest.

8. CHILDREN'S RIGHT TO EDUCATION AND THE INDIAN CONSTITUTION

The Constitution of India came into force in January 1950, which contains provisions for survival, development and protection of children. These core ideas are incorporated both in Part III and Part IV of the Constitution, pertaining to fundamental Rights and Directive principles of state policy.[130] The Constitution of India recognizes the vulnerable position of children and their right to protection. Based on the Doctrine of "protective discrimination" Article 15(3) it guarantees that, nothing shall prevent the state from making special provision for women and children. Thus it is intended to give special attention to the children by making special laws and policies to safeguard the right of the children. Right to equality, freedom of speech and expression, protection of life and personal liberty, free and compulsory education and abolition of child labour and right against exploitation are enshrined in the Indian Constitution in Articles 14, 19(1)(a), 21, 21-A, 24, 39(e) and (f). The Government of India in its 10th Five Year Plan (2002 to 2007) emphasizes on Right-based approach, with regard to "survival, development and protection of children". Education imbibes values and wisdom. A man without education is a brute and there is no second opinion about it. Education seeks to build up the personality of the pupil by ascertaining a physical, intellectual, moral and emotional development.[131] Education of children is an important right of a child. The child who is physically, mentally or socially handicapped shall be given the special treatment, education and care required by his particular condition.[132] The child is entitled to receive education which shall be free and compulsory at least in the elementary stages. He shall be given an education which will promote his general culture and enable him, on a basis of equal opportunity, to develop his abilities, his individual judgment and his sense of moral and social responsibility and become a useful member of society. The best interest of the child shall be the guiding principle of those responsible for his educational and guidance. This responsibility lies in the first place with his patents. The child shall have full opportunity for play and recreation which should be directed to the same purpose as education. Society and the public authorities shall endeavour to promote the enjoyment of this right.[133]

The World conference on "Education for All" held at Jomtien in March 1990, marked the emergence of an International consensus that education is the single most vital element in combating poverty, empowering women, protecting children from hazardous and exploitative labour and sexual exploitation, promoting human rights and democracy, protecting the environment and influencing population growth.[134]

The framers of Indian Constitution have envisaged that within 10 years of the commencement of Constitution, steps should be taken to provide free and compulsory education for all children until they reach an age of 14. The right to education as a fundamental right gained momentum in *Mohini Jain's case.*[135] The Constitution bench of Supreme Court in the case of Unnikrishanan[136] ruled that right to education is a fundamental right that flows from the Right to life in Art. 21 of the Constitution, every child/citizen has a right to free education upto the age of 14 years and thereafter the right would be subject to the limits of the economic capacity of the state. This decision was upheld and confirmed by the 11 Judge Constitutional bench of the Supreme Court in *TMA Pai Foundation* v. *Union of India.*[137] In the year 2002, the Indian Constitution through its 86th Amendment Act, has made "Right to Education a Fundamental Right".[138] The State is obliged to/duty bound to provide free and compulsory education to all children of age 6-14 years in such manner as the State may by law determine. It was also provided that, it is the fundamental duty of a parent or Guardian to provide opportunities for education to his child between the age of 6 to 14 years.[139]

In view of the revolution made in the spectrum of education and in the light of Supreme Court Guidelines laid down in various cases and Constitution (Eighty-sixth Amendment) Act, 2002 which has made three specific provisions in the Constitution to facilitate the realization of free and compulsory education to children between the age of six and fourteen years as a fundamental right. These were: (i) Adding Article 21A in Part III (Fundamental Rights), (ii) Modifying Article 45, and (iii) Adding a new clause (k) under Article 51A (Fundamental Duties) making the parent or guardian responsible for providing opportunities for education to their children between six and fourteen years.[140]

8.1. The Right of Children to free and Compulsory Education Act, 2009: Salient Features[41]

The Act provides for free and compulsory education to all the children between the age of six to fourteen years.

(a) That every child has a right to be provided full time elementary education of satisfactory and equitable quality in a formal school which satisfied certain essential norms and standards;

(b) 'Compulsory Education' casts an obligation on the appropriate Government to provide and ensure admission, attendance and completion of elementary education;

(c) 'Free Education' means that no child, other than a child who has been admitted by his or her parents to a school which is not supported by the appropriate Government, shall be liable to pay any kind of fee or charges or expenses which may prevent him/her from pursuing and completing elementary education.

(d) It imposes duties and responsibilities upon the Appropriate Governments, local authorities, parents, schools and teachers in providing free and compulsory education; and

(e) To provide a system for protection of the right of children and a decentralized grievance redressal mechanism.

9. CONCLUSION

It is pertinent to give more emphasis on concept of child. It's evident that *child is an organic cell of the Society* and National Policies and Judicial decisions set a guidelines that *children are supremely important national asset.* This statement should be transformed into reality. In order to avoid confusion and dilemma, there should be a one standard age under the Constitutional Law, in legislations enacted by the Government and Government Policies and Plans. This needs integrated legislation on child, child rights instead of providing plethora of legislations. There is a need to have independent and autonomous body to deal with the multi-dimensional issues relating to children like education, health, nutrition, etc. at the Central level, State level and Local level to address the problems. There is also a need for change in the perceptions and attitude of the law enforcing agencies and general public.

Notes and References

1. *Gaurav Jain* v. *Union of India*, (1997) 8 SCC 114: AIR 1997 SC 3021.

2. Justice V.R. Krishna Iyer, "*Legally Speaking*", Delhi: Universal Law Publishing Co. Pvt. Limited, 2003, p. 186.
3. *Ibid.*
4. *St. Theresa's Tender Loving Care Home* v. *State of A.P.*, AIR 2005, S.C. 4375.
5. *Sheela Barse* v. *Secretary, Children Aid Society*, AIR 1987, SC 656, 659.
6. AIR 1986 SC 1873, see also The National Policy for Children.
7. Directive Principles of State Policy, Article 39 of Indian Constitution.
8. Asha Bajpai, *Child Rights in India—Law, Policy and Practice*, 2nd edn., New Delhi: Oxford University Press, 2006, p. 2.
9. *Ibid.*
10. *India Alliance for Child Rights*—2003 Citizens Alternative Review and Report on India's Progress Towards CRC Realisation, 2003, New Delhi, p. 78.
11. D.Venkateshwar Rao, *Child Rights—A Perspective on International and Nation Law*, New Delhi: Manak Publications, 2004, p. 24.
12. *Ibid.*, pp. 24-25.
13. Convention on the Rights of the Child Country Report, India, Feb. 1997. Department of Women and Child Development, Ministry of Human Resource Development, Govt. of India, New Delhi, 1997, pp. 17-18.
14. Rajvir S. Dhaka and Jagbir Narwal "Child Labour in the City of Rothak: A Study", *Nagarlok*, Vol. XXXVII, No. 1, Jan.-Mar. 2005, p. 39.
15. Article 21-A inserted by the Constitution (Eighty Sixth Amendment) Act, 2002, Sec. 2.
16. Substituted by the Constitution (Eighty-sixth Amendment) Act, 2002, Sec. 3; for "*Article 45 provisions for Free and Compulsory Education –The State shall endeavour to provide, within a period of ten years from the commencement of this Constitution, for free and compulsory education for all children until they complete the age of 14 years*".
17. Inserted by the Constitution (Eighty sixth Amendment) Act, 2002, Sec. 4.
18. UN Convention on the Rights of the Child 1989 was adopted by the General Assembly on 20th Nov. 1989 and came into force on Sept. 2, 1990.
19. The Census of India—2001.
20. Ss. 82 and 83 of Indian Penal Code.
21. Sec. 2(h), Juvenile Justice Act, 1986.
22. Sec. 2(K), Juvenile Justice (Care and Protection of Children) Act, 2000 (56 of 2000) received the Assent of the President on 30-12-2000, and Published in the Gazette of India, Ext., Pt. II, S. 1, dated 30-12-2000.
23. Sec. 2(a) and 2(d) of Child Marriage Restraint Act, 1929. Sec. 2(a) is substituted by Act No. 2 of 1978 w.e.f. 01-10-1978.
24. Sec. 2(a), The Prohibition of Child Marriage Act, 2006 (Central Act, No. 6 of 2007) received the assent of the President on Jan. 10, 2007 and Published in the Gazette of India, Ext., Part II, S. 1 dated 10th Jan. 2007.
25. Sec. 2(ii), Child Labour (Prohibition and Regulation) Act, 1986 (Central Act No. 61 of 1986), Published in the Gazette of India, extraordinary, Part II, Section 1, dated 23-12-1986, pp. 1-9.
26. Sec. 2(c) and 67 of Factories Act, 1948 (63 of 1948).
27. *Supra* note 11, pp 140-41.
28. Sec. 2(c), Mines (Amendment) Act, 1952.
29. Sec. 3, The Indian Majority Act, 1875.
30. Sec. 4(a): The Hindu Minority and Guardianship Act, 1956.
31. The Dissolution of Muslim Marriage Act, 1939.

32. The Indian Divorce Act, 1860.
33. The Parsis Marriage and Divorce Act, 1936.
34. Sec. 3 of The Apprentices Act, 1961.
35. Sec. 2(c) of Plantations Labour Act, 1951.
36. See, Merchant Shipping Act, 1958.
37. See, Karnataka Shops and Commercial Establishment Act, 1961.
38. See, Dangerous Machines (Regulation) Act, 1983.
39. Sec. 2(c) of The Orphanage and other Charitable Homes (Supervision and Control) Act, 1960.
40. See, Children Act, 1960.
41. Sec. 3, The Employment of Children Act 1938.
42. See, Motor Vehicles Act, 1939.
43. Sec. 361, Indian Penal Code.
44. See, Immoral Trafficking Act, 1956.
45. Sec. 2(b), Beedi and Cigar Workers (Conditions of Employment) Act, 1948.
46. Sec. 2(c), Minimum Wages Act. 1948.
47. Motor Transport Workers Act, 1961.
48. Sec. 3(b), Maternity Benefit Act, 1961.
49. See, Sec. 2(b), The Protection of Women from Domestic Violence Act, 2005 (Act No. 43 of 2005) received the Assent of the President on dated 13.09.2005, Published in the Gazette of India, Ext., Part II, S. 1, dated 14.09.2005 came into force w.e.f. 26.10.2006.
50. See, The National Plan of Action for Children 2005, working group on development of children for the Eleventh Five Year Plan (2007-12)—A Report, p. 24.
51. Sec. 2(c) The Right of Children for Free and Compulsory Education Act, 2009, (Central Act, No. 35 of 2009) received the Assent of the President on 26th Aug. 2009 came into force w.e.f. 01-04-2010.
52. Towards faster and more inclusive growth, an approach to the Eleventh Five-Year Plan, Planning Commission, Govt. of India, New Delhi, 2006, p. 17.
53. My name is Today-Children in News "Butterflies" Programme with street and working children, Vol. XVI, 2009, New Delhi, p. 70.
54. *Ibid.*
55. *Ibid.*
56. *Ibid.*, p. 71.
57. Vibhuti Patel, "Law Concerning Protection and Empowerment of Girls in India", *Legal News and Views*, Vol. 23, No. 8, New Delhi: A Social Action Trust Publication, 2009, p. 4.
58. *Ibid.*, p. 5.
59. *Ibid.*
60. *Supra* note 8, p. 5.
61. *Ibid.*, p. 30.
62. Praveen Jha, Pooja Parvati, "Right to Education Act, 2009: Critical Gaps and Challenges", *Economic and Political Weekly*, Vol. XLV, No. 13, Mar. 27-Apr. 2, 2010, Mumbai, p. 21.
63. *Supra* note 50, p. 33.
64. *Supra* note 62.
65. Dr. Savita Bhakhry, "*Children in India and their Rights*", NHRC, New Delhi, 2006, p. 45.

66. The State of the World's Children, 2005, UNICEF, "*Childhood under threat*", p. 1.
67. Subhash Sharma, "Trends, Causes and Consequences of Child Labour in India", *The Indian Journal of Public Administration*, April-June 2009, Vol. LV, No. 2, 2009, p. 221. Also *see* Edwards, M., "Policy Arena Children in Development", *Journal of International Development*, Vol. 8, No. 6, 1999.
68. Harish Umar, "Human Rights to Children: Agenda for Implementation", *Cochin University Law Journal*, 2000, p. 154. *See* also V.R. Krishna Iyer, *Jurisprudence of Juvenile Justice: A Preambular Perspective.*
69. *Supra* note 66, p. 3.
70. Article 39(e) of the Constitution.
71. AIR 1986 SC 1773.
72. C. Rajashekhar, *Social Revolution and the Indian Constitution – Interrelationship Between Fundamental Rights and Directive Principles*, New Delhi: Deep and Deep Publications, 1993, p. 48.
73. Article 45 of the Constitution.
74. Article 25, Universal Declaration of Human Rights, 1948.
75. *Bandhua Mukti Morcha* v. *Union of India*, (1984) 3 SCC 161 at p. 183, Para 10.
76. *In re* (1997) 10 SCC 549, at p. 533 Para 4.
77. (1973) 1 SCC 840 at p. 855, para 15.
78. *Campaign Against Child Labour*—ILO–IPEC Karnataka Child Labour Project - (Supported by the Govt. of Italy), pp. 12-13.
79. *Supra* note 65, p. 12.
80. *Ibid.*, p. 13.
81. *Ibid* p. 14.
82. *Ibid.*
83. *Ibid.*
84. *Ibid.*, p. 16.
85. *Ibid.*
86. *Supra* note, 66 p. 1.
87. *Ibid.*, p. 3.
88. *Ibid.*
89. *The Times of India*, 10th June 2003.
90. *M.C. Mehta* v. *State of Tamil Nadu*, Civil Writ Application No. 465 of 1986, dated 10.12.1996.
91. *Supra* note 8, pp. 6-7.
92. Resolution No. 1-14/74-CDD dated August 22, 1974.
93. *Supra* note 71.
94. *Supra* note 8, p. 11.
95. *Supra* note 50, p. 31.
96. *Supra* note 8, p. 343
97. *Supra* note 65, p. 28.
98. P.L. Mehta, S.S. Jaswal, "*Child and the Law*", New Delhi: Deep and Deep Publications, 1996, p. 70.
99. *Supra* note 8, p. 12.
100. Sudesh Kumar Sharma, "Child Labour: Problems and Prospects", *Cochin University Law Review*, 1999, p. 263.
101. Helen R. Sekhar, *Towards Combating Child Labour*, 2nd edn., Noida: V.V. Giri, National Labour Institute, 2005, p. 15.

102. *Supra* note 8, p. 12.
103. Ministry of Human Resource Development, Govt. of India, New Delhi, 1992, *See* also *supra* note 8, p. 13.
104. *Supra* note 8, p. 13.
105. *Ibid.*, p. XXIV
106. *Ibid.* p. 383.
107. *Supra* note 50, p. 30.
108. *Supra* note 8, p. 382.
109. Ministry of Human Resources Development, Department of Women and Child Development, New Delhi.
110. *Supra* note 50, p. 26.
111. *Ibid.*, p. 31.
112. *National Plan of Action for Children*, 2005, Govt. of India, Ministry of Human Resources Development, Department of Women and Child Development, New Delhi, 2005.
113. *Ibid.*
114. Department of Women and Child Development, Ministry of Human Resource Development, Govt. of India, New Delhi.
115. Received the Assent of the President on 20 Jan. 2006, and Published in the Official Gazette of India, extra, Part II, S.1. (Central Act No. 4 of 2006), came into force w.e.f. 15.02.2007 vide so 229(E) dated 15.02.2007.
116. *Supra* note 8, p. 28.
117. *Ibid.*
118. Helen R. Sekhar, *Child Labour: Situation and Strategies for Elimination*, Noida: V.V. Giri National Labour Institute, 2007. p. 93.
119. Children and Work-Annual Report, 2004-05 (Department of Women and Child Development, Govt. of India).
120. *Supra* note 117, pp. 93-94.
121. *Ibid.*, pp. 95-96.
122. M.P. Shrivastava, *Child Labour Laws in India*", Allahabad: Law Publishing House, 2006, p. 52.
123. *Supra* note 117, pp. 97-98.
124. *Ibid.*, p. 99.
125. *Supra* note 50, pp. 28-29, Department of Women and Child Development, Govt. of India, New Delhi.
126. "*Child Labour; Challenges and Response*", A status Report on Indian Initiatives towards the elimination of Child Labour, Noida: V.V. Giri National Labour Institute, 1996, p. 20.
127. *Supra* note 100, p. 20.
128. *Supra* note 118, p. 96.
129. *Supra* note 125.
130. See for detailed analysis of interrelationship between the two parts, *supra* note 72, p. 19.
131. *University of Delhi* v. *Ramanath*, AIR 1963 SC 1873.
132. Principle 5 of the UN Declaration on the Rights of the Child, 1959.
133. Dr. Bindu M. Nambiar, "Children and Human Rights", *Journal of Indian Legal Thought*, Vol. 5:149, M.G. University, Kottayam, 2007, p. 162.
134. Art. 7 of Universal Declaration of Human Rights, 1948, also known as World Declaration on "*Education for All*".

135. *Mohini Jain* v. *State of Karnataka*, AIR 1992 SC 1848.

136. *J.P. Unni Krishnan and others* v. *State of Andhra Pradesh and others*, AIR 1993 SC 2178 (1993) 1SCC 645.

137. AIR 1996, SC 2652.

138. Article 21-A of the Constitution.

139. Amendment Article 51-A of the Constitution by inserting clause (K) by Constitution (Eighty-sixth Amendment) Act, 2002, Sec. 4.

140. *Supra* note 62, p. 20.

141. (Central Act No. 35 of 2009) received the Assent of the President on 26th August 2009, came into force w.e.f. 01-04-2010.

3

Various Forms of Abuse of Children

"There is no trust more sacred than the one the world holds with children. There is no duty more important than ensuring that their rights are respected, that their welfare is protected, that their lives are free from fear and want and that they grow up in peace."[1]

1. INTRODUCTION

The National Policy for Children, 1974 declared that, "Children are supremely important national asset" and the same was approved in a celebrated case *Sheela Barse* v. *Union of India*.[2] The future well-being of the nation depends on how its children grow and develop. It is the duty of the State to look after every child with a view to assuring full development of its personality.

Protection of children from all forms of abuse and exploitation across the world is the need of the hour. Children face three-fold exploitation—of age, economic status and caste.[3] The future of Indian nation and prosperity of the people depend on the health and happiness of children and the care they receive from the family and society to grow up as good human beings and citizens. Their up bringing in a proper environment promoting their health, education and mental development is an important commitment.[4]

The Constitution of India mandates the state under Article 39 to ensure that "Children are not abused and that childhood and youth are protected against exploitation and against moral and material abandonment". Children are youngest, innocent and tender and hence they deserve the eldest care and concern.

Unfortunately, the children in India are subjected to various forms of abuse. The word 'abuse' is defined in *Black's Law Dictionary* as, everything which is contrary to a good order established by usage, departure from reasonable use, improper use, physical or mental treatment, deception. Thus the term "Child abuse" encompasses a broad and wide range of acts and maltreatment of Children. Various attempts to define child abuse have not achieved a consensus. There is also no consensus about its various forms, which can include child battering, extreme punishment, hard labour, emotional abuse, sexual abuse, including incest and exploitation, and abandonment.[5]

2. MAGNITUDE OF THE PROBLEM

There are few abuses which are universally condemned for violation of human rights. But in reality it is commonly practiced as child abuse. Centuries of experiences indicate that children have been subjected to physical, sexual and emotional abuse as well as neglect. The forms and dynamics of child abuse have undergone major change in recent years. The problem of child abuse is a clear replica of human rights violation and is a matter of worst forms of "child exploitation and abuse". Child abuse today does not only refer simply to physical, emotional, economic, substance abuse, sexual abuse and trafficking but also many other dimensions of violation of basic rights and non-fulfilment of the needs of the child.

India records 19% of the world children and 1/3rd of the country's population, i.e. 440 million children are below 18 years and nearly 40% of the children are in need of care and protection.[6]

It clearly shows the magnitudes of the problem.Children are considered as most disadvantaged and vulnerable section of the society. National Study on child abuse a study conducted by Prayas, indicates that it has covered 13 States of India with a sample size of 12,447 children, 2324 young adults in both rural and urban areas and 2449 stakeholders.[7] National Study on Child Abuse recorded its findings very exhaustively on various forms of abuse of children. They are:[8]

(i) Child Labour

With regard to child labour it includes children prematurely leading an adult like life. They receive low wages and work for long hours under conditions that are likely to damage their health as well as physical and mental development. Frequently they are deprived of meaningful educational and training opportunities besides remaining separated from their families. Out of 12,447 children covered under the study, almost 1/5th (19.7%) comprised children who were employed. Almost 1/10th

(9.8%) of the working children, work seven days for a week, with a somewhat lesser proposition (7.1%) reportedly working six days a week. Thus, only about 3 percent of the children were found to be working for five days a week or lesser still. This clearly reflects child labour being largely underpaid, over worked and exploited. As far as the nature of duties is concerned, nearly one-fourth (23.3%) of the working children, were found to be working as domestic help. A little more than one tenth (11.2%) of the employed children were found to be working in road-side tea-shops, eateries, etc. These are largely invisible domestic and other forms of child labour who have on 10th October 2006 been brought under the purview of the Child Labour (Prohibition and Regulation) Act, 1986.

About one-fifth (17%) of the working children were paid for the services they rendered, out of these, about one-tenth (9.3%) receive payment on monthly basis. Only 4.7% received their wages on a weekly basis and while a still lesser proportion (3.8%) received payment on daily basis. Only a small proportion (11.7%) of the working children reportedly like the jobs they were doing. According to the data, the highest percentage of children in domestic work was found in Bihar.

The percentage of children working in the agricultural sector and in other occupations like vending, shoe-shining. Lifting luggage on railway platforms, etc. were quite high in the States of Madhya Pradesh, Gujarat and Assam.

Regarding place of work of children, Study found that one third of the children (34.9%) worked at home. Their work patterns in case of these children include helping parents in house hold chores, assisting in farming and related jobs, working and hired labour through agents for factory owners, etc. Almost one-fourth of the children 23.5% worked in road-side shops: dabas, tea shops, cycle/scooter repair shops, etc. About one-fifth of the children (17.6%) were also found to be working in organised workshops. Further it was found that in the States of Bihar and Maharastra a large proportion of children worked in homes. In contrast, the States of Andhra Pradesh, Rajasthan, Uttar Pradesh and West Bengal, the number of children were highest in terms of employment in road-side establishments while in the States of Goa, West Bengal, Mizoram and Assam the percentage of children was highest *vis-a-vis* working in built-up shops.

Thus, the major findings of the National Study on Abuse of Children relating to child labour were: (a) of 12,447 children covered by the study, 19.7% are found to be at work. (b) only 17% of working children are paid for their work; and (c) among working children, 23.2% work as domestic help.

(ii) Physical Abuse

(a) 18.2% children reportedly suffered physical injuries by family members due to beating;
(b) 42.8% school going children reported facing corporal punishment; and
(c) 15.6% children suffered physical abuse by other than family members.

(iii) Emotional Abuse

(a) One out of five children suffers from high emotional abuse.
(b) 44.1% children reported that they were shouted at and humiliated by their own family members.
(c) The level of emotional abuse is seen to be the highest amongst young children (44.3%).
(d) Delhi, Assam and Madhya Pradesh are the States where emotional abuse is higher.

(iv) Substance Abuse

(a) 32.1% children report to have tasted any one of the substances like, alcohol, bhang, ganja, charas, heroin, smack, brown sugar, etc.
(b) The prevalence of substance abuse is distinctly lower among females (19.4%) than among males (43.9%).

(v) Girl Child Neglect

(a) Out of those girls with brothers (N=4138), 48.4% cases reported parents taking side of the brothers;
(b) one-third of the girls (32%) who had brothers, reported that their parents gave more love and attention to their brothers; and
(c) 44.8% of the girl respondents felt it was an advantage being a girl, though almost half of the total girl child respondents (N=5981) still wished they were a boy.

(vi) Sexual Abuse

(a) 27.9% children reported about adults trying to rub their private parts against children in crowded places;
(b) 30.2% children were shown dirty pictures and 4.5% have been photographed in nude;

(c) Every sixteenth child reported to having experienced intercourse (amounting to assault);
(d) Three out of every ten young adults admit that sexual abuse has been inflicted on them by close relatives; and
(e) Boys (52.9%) are as much sexually abused as girls (47.1%).

3. PROFILE OF CHILD ABUSE: SOCIO-ECONOMIC CIRCUMSTANCES LEADING TO CHILD ABUSE

Child abuse is a complex issue and a great threat and is a matter of serious concern. In majority of child abuse cases, "abuser" is either related to, known person or stranger or otherwise. It is very difficult to detect that culprit-Abuser for reasons best known either to the victim child or to their parents. None have guts to report that matter to anybody due to family prestige and reputation. In orthodox and conservative family the state of affairs is still worst and continued due to the family/ social disgrace. Child abuse-victim family prefer to resolve the matter privately rather reporting to Police, as they mean it as private matter and not a criminal one. According to the World Health Organisation "Child abuse or maltreatment constitutes, all forms of physical and/or emotional ill-treatment, sexual abuse, neglect or negligent treatment or commercial or other exploitation, resulting in actual or potential harm to the child's health, survival, development or dignity in the context of relationship of responsibility, trust or power". Parents/family poverty, single parent/no parent, etc. will force the child to be a child labour prohibited under the law[9] or to become child in conflict with law[10] and thereby become victim of abuse.

The problem of child abuse revolves around the complexities of conceptualisation and reporting of the problem since the abuser is someone close to the victim. To quote from the Indian Penal Code (Amendment) Bill, 1992.

> "That our heads bow in shame when it is learnt that a girl (child) has been raped (sexually abused) by a close relative of her own. She becomes the victim of her own trust on the relative (Saviour)".

The problems inherent in bringing child abusers to justice are, firstly, reporting of cases of child sexual abuse, secondly, problems in trial and proof, and thirdly, the competence and credibility of child witness.[11]

In *Sudesh Jakhu* v. *K.C.J.*[12], Justice Jaspal Singh laid down certain guiding principles and norms for conducting trial and taking evidence in child sexual abuse cases:

"The Magistrate should record the victim's statement in the same language as spoken by it, every effort should be made by the trial judge to lessen the ordeal of the victim when it is in the witness box by keeping a check on the prosecutor who might undervalue the child's feelings, handle the proceedings or ambiguous. The proceeding should be held in camera and the feasibility of giving breaks during questioning should be kept in mind, though such breaks need not be long, if the prosecution establishes to the satisfaction of the court that to obtain a full and candid account from the child witness, the use of a screen is necessary, the court may be inclined favourably to provide such a screen, etc".

The National Crime Record Bureau (NCRB) reported 14975 cases of crimes against children in 2005. Most subtle forms of violence against children such as child marriage, child labour—economic exploitation, practices like "*Devadasi*", tradition of dedicating young girls to God and Goddesses, genital mutilation in some parts of the country are often rationalised on grounds of tradition and culture.[13] Children from poor backgrounds are the key target groups, Ethnic Minorities, SCs, OBCs indigenous people, hill tribes, refugees and illegal migrants are the easy victims. Poverty, deprivation, natural disasters, inadequate educational and employment opportunities, economic disparities, erosion of traditional family systems, war of human rights are, *inter alia*, some of the factors responsible for the growth of this malaise in society.[14]

4. ABUSE OF CHILDREN—VARIOUS FORMS AND CATEGORIES

The child abuse include physical abuse, sexual abuse, substance abuse, emotional abuse, child labour, bonded child labour, child marriage, Juvenile Justice, child rag pickers, children in armed conflict, etc. and there are some categories of children who are abused and exploited namely, in a family environment, children in schools, children at work, children on the street and children in institutions.

4.1. Physical Abuse

"Physically abused child" means a child under 18 years of age, whose parents or other's concerned inflict upon the child physical injury or bodily harm, which includes beating, hitting, kicking, burning, or otherwise harming a child physically. According to a report about 18.2% children suffered physical injuries by family members due to beating and 15.6% children suffered physical abuse by other than family members. The UNICEF, Save the children and Government of India jointly conducted a survey in 2007 and found that 65% of school children in India are subjected to corporal punishment and virtually the schools and teachers still continue to follow the old saying, "spare the rod and spoil the child" which was a traditional wisdom.[15] Corporal punishment has been abolished through legislation or executive order in at least 17 States and Union Territories in India. It is due to tardy implementation that presents the major challenge. The Right of Children to Free and Compulsory Education Act, 2009[16] was enacted and under section 17, it bans all forms of corporal punishment and envisages disciplinary action against the guilty. The National Commission for Protection of Child Rights (NCPCR) held a public hearing in February 2008 at Chennai on all forms of torture of children in School and Hostels in Tamil Nadu. The Commission was shocked to record its findings that at least 10 school children had committed suicide after being subjected to various forms of corporal punishment and 8 had been raped.

4.2. Emotional Abuse

It is a humiliation of children, it is also known as verbal abuse, mental abuse and psychological maltreatment. It includes acts or failure to act by parents, care takers, peers, friends, relatives and others that have caused or could cause serious behavioural, cognitive, emotional, or mental distress/trauma. The emotional abuse can have more long lasting negative psychological effects than any other forms of abuse. Family members seldom realize the long-term implications of their humiliating behavior on children's psyche and life. Emotional abuse is humiliation of children and one study indicates that 44% children reported that they were shouted at and humiliated by their own family members including their mothers. Comparison amongst children is another kind of emotional abuse. The saddest part of making such comparisons is that it can lead to the development of unwarranted inferiority/superiority complexes which can further lead to the creation of warped personalities. Children were also found to have received considerably harsh treatment from their family members which is another kind of abuse of children.[17]

4.3. Sexual Abuse

The child sexual abuse is an exploitation and violation of human rights. It is a demoralization of the fiber of entire society. Children on street, children at work and children in Institutional care reported the highest incidents of sexual assault and most children did not report the matter to any one. Sexual abuse is an inappropriate sexual behavior with the child. It includes fondling a child's genitals, oral genital contact, forced vaginal or anal intercourse and making child fondle on adults genitals, sexual assault (intercourse, incest, rape and sodomy), exhibitionism and pornography.[18]

Sexual abuse of child is defined as any sexual relation between an adult and a child. Its legal definition includes child molestation, incest and rape. Child Sexual abuse is defined as the involvement of dependent child or adolescent in sexual activities with an adult in which the child is used as a sexual object for gratification of the older person's needs or desire, and to which the child is unable to give consent due to the unequal power in the relationship.[19]

The definition of sexual abuse of children is best understood when the problem is related to pedophilia. The term Pedophilia refers to any adult who habitually seeks the company of a child/children for the gratification of his/her sexual needs. The word pedophilia is derived from two Greek words "pedo" means "child"; and "philia" means "love for". The United Nations has also defined child sexual abuse as contacts or interaction between a child and an older or more knowledgeable child or adult (a stranger, sibling, or person in a position of authority, such as a parent or a caretaker) when the child is being used as an object of gratification for the older child's or adult sexual needs. These contacts or interactions are carried out against the child, using force, trickery, bribes, threats or pressure.[20]

Child sexual abuse, according to P.D. Mathew, includes employing, using, inducing or coercing, any child to engage in illicit and contact, and it also includes the use of children assisting with other persons to engage in explicit sex.[21]

There are four types of Sexual Abuse namely exposure which is viewing of sexual acts and exhibition, molestation, sexual intercourse on a chronic basis and rape in which there is acute assault intercourse. Rape can be of two kinds-first one is intra familial and extra familiar, i.e. rape by known person or person in authority and rape by a stranger. Child rape is a great social stigma, which shows complete degeneration of moral values in society. In some cases the victims of rape are not even accepted at home. The victim is either too traumatized by the experience or the parents, out of concern for their child's future, hush up the matter. The rapist knows that there is a high chance of his outrage against the minor not being discovered. This acts as a major motivating factor. Many victims do not go to the police out of fear of adverse publicity and unnecessary harassment. Apart from the delay or even absence of justice, the victims have to face similar incidence every now and then. When the victims do not find any safe place in society and do not see any future prospects, they enter into the den of prostitution.[22]

Thus, child sexual abuse is a dark reality. It has become a common phenomenon and majority of cases go unnoticed and unreported due to innocence of the victims, stigma attached to the act, tardy and insensitivity of the investigating and law enforcement agencies.

An adult who engages in sexual activity with a child is performing a criminal and immoral act which can never be considered normal or socially acceptable behavior. Articles 34 and 35 of Convention on the Rights of the Child provides right to protect the child from all forms of sexual exploitation and sexual abuse.

The Indian laws dealing with sexual offences do not address child sexual abuse and Indian Penal Code does not recognise child sexual abuse as an offence. A child sexual offender is booked under various other sections of the Indian Penal Code—Offences of rape (Sec. 375), outraging the modesty of woman (Sec. 354) and unnatural offences (Sec. 377). An act of child rape is a gruesome, and abhorring act, it leaves a permanent scar on the personality of the child, inhibiting growth and development. It instills fear, insecurity.[23] Rape defined under Indian Penal Code is very specific, providing remedy only to the women and there is a penal provision.[24] It does not include abuse on boys and the intercourse usually interpreted to mean with an adult. Due to the absence of clear provision to deal with child rape cases, there are 4,076 cases of rape of children reported in 2005.[25] Juvenile Justice (Care and Protection of Children) Act, 2000 does not address sexual abuse on children of both "Child in need of care and protection" and "Juvenile in conflict with law" under Section 23.[26] More so, Section 5 of the Immoral Traffic Prevention Act, 1969 prescribes punishment of not less than 7 years for inducing the child into prostitution. Indian Penal Code Section 354[27] covers outraging the modesty of women and not the girl child. This is a serious lacunae in the Criminal Law.

4.4. Child Prostitution

Child Prostitution is one of the worst forms of child labour. It means the use of child in sexual activities for remuneration or any other form of consideration. So this is another kind of abuse and exploitation of child for remuneration in cash or in kind usually but not always organised by an intermediary. However, child prostitution is inadmissible, it tantamount to exploitation and victimization of the child precisely, because it undermines the child's development. It is detrimental to the child both physically and emotionally and it violates the child rights.[28] The child prostitutes get infected with disease like Sexual Transmitted Diseases (STD) and even the HIV infection (AIDS). The United Nations Convention on the Right of the Child, 1989 defines child prostitution as sexual exploitation of a child below the age of 18 years for remuneration in cash or kind. It is also important to note that child prostitution, in present days, is very closely related to child pornography. The First World Congress held in Stockholm in 1996 against commercial sexual exploitation of children described child pornography as any visual or audio material which uses children in a sexual context. It consists of "the visual depiction of a child engaged in explicit sexual conduct, real or stimulated, or the lewd exhibition of the genitals intended for sexual gratification of the user".[29]

Besides, in 1999, the ILO adopted the Convention concerning Prohibition and in media Action for Elimination of Worst Forms of Child Labour which addresses among other issues, sale and trafficking of children, child prostitution and child pornography.[30]

Sexual trafficking and forced prostitution of children which is going on in certain areas shall be prevented and those unfortunate children should be properly rehabilitated. Most of the victims are girls between the age of 10 to 14 years. The operations of these notorious activities are quite complex. About 25% to 30% of prostitutes are estimated to be children. It is prevalent in an around tourist centers and in large cities as well as the areas where family-based prostitution traditionally practiced by some caste and communities. The potential areas are those where Devadasi/Jogin system is in existence. Enforcement of laws by Police in strict sense is very essential. Social action for creating awareness programme in the areas where Devadasi system is in existence is also required. Providing Education, rehabilitation and economic support will go a long way in tackling and eradicating this worst form.

4.5. Child Trafficking and Abuse of Child

Most children who are sold into sex trade by their parents either knowingly or unknowingly, mainly due to poverty. These children were kept in bondage by sex mafia. It is difficult for these children to escape, once they were trapped into this. Very often they were physically abused, beaten, burnt, tortured, and deprived of food, movement, etc. Children were trafficked from across the border and also from violence infested places. Sex tourism is on the increase.[31]

4.6. Substance Abuse

Drug abuse and drug trafficking has become a global phenomena. Various studies reveal that teenage children are falling prey to drug abuse knowingly or unknowingly. Substance abuse includes forcing or allowing the child to take or sell drugs or substances get involved in their smuggling or peddling or take alcohol or any other addictive drug or substances that retards and that may adversely affect the child's physical and mental well-being and growth.[32] There is a separate law dealing with substance abuse called the Narcotic Drugs and Psychotropic Substances (NDPS) Act, 1985. Article 33 of Convention on the Rights of the Child mandates to protect children from the illicit use of narcotic drugs and psychotropic substances and to prevent the use of children in the illicit production of and trafficking of such substances.

4.7. Child Marriage

Child Marriage is a social evil and its practice is not only abuse of child and exploitation but also a legal abuse. It stunts growth and development, particularly of the girl who is more vulnerable to domestic violence and sexual abuse. it also deprives the girl of her right to education and live with freedom and dignity. A comprehensive legislation known as The Child Marriage Restraint Act, 1929 was enacted during British India Government. This was also called as Sharada Act after the name of its architect. Way back in the year 1978, The Child Marriage Restraint (Amendment) Act, 1978 raised the minimum age of marriage from 18 to 21 years for boys and 15 to 18 years for girls although this Act is applicable to the whole country, it is inoperative in respect of communities, which have their own personal laws. Another drawback of this Act, is that it simply imposes restrictions on the solemnization of the marriage of the minors, but does not invalidate such marriages.[33] The new legislation, The Prohibition of Child Marriage Act, 2006,[34] is a secular legislation, which applies to all citizens of India, both within and beyond India. The legal age of consent for marriage is 18 years for female persons and 21 years for male persons. The violations of this legislation and offences under this Act has been made cognizable and non-bailable and empowered the courts to issue injunctions prohibiting solemnization of marriages in contravention of the provisions of this Act and any child marriage solemnized in contravention of an injunction order issued under this Act, whether *interim* or final shall be *void ab initio*. In relation to the age of the child in marriage and consensual sexual intercourse, the law is not certain.

As per the doctrine of "*doli incapax*" and under Sec. 82 of Indian Penal Code the child under 7 years of age is incapable for committing an offence and Sec. 83 of Indian Penal Code recognises that, a child above 7 years of age but below 12 years is capable of committing a crime if he/she has attained sufficient maturity of understanding to judge the nature and consequences of his conduct on that occasion.

Children above the age of 12 years are treated on par with adults in their ability to commit an offence. Therefore, a 13 year old can be held responsible for committing a murder and even rape, but is incapable of giving a consent for sex with another person of the same age.

The Law Commission has examined in detail the scientific and medical issues relating to child marriages in all respects, i.e. physiological and emotional and affects not only the parents to such marriage but also the household in which they stay. The Law Commission Panel said that "the age of marriage for both boys and girls should be 18 years as there is no scientific reason why this should be different". It also suggested mandatory registration of marriages within a stipulated period for all communities—Hindus, Muslims, Christians among others. In 2006, the Centre had notified a new Child Marriage (Prohibition) Law. But, a study by Centre for Social Research and National Institute for Public Co-operation and Child Development (NIPCCD) has found that 77 percent of marriages in Madhya Pradesh are, in fact, child marriages. In Rajasthan it was found to be 40 percent and in Uttar Pradesh, it was just over 37 percent. The survey conducted in the three states last year found that the practice of child marriage was deep rooted in the cultural heritage of the communities. "Most of the child marriages are reported from families where the broader community to which the family belongs indulges in practice", the Report released recently said. Communities like Meenas, Jats, Gurjars, Rajputs and Berwas among others were found to be following the practice of child marriage. In Rajasthan and Madhya Pradesh, it was found that even after marriage the girl lives with her parents till she attains puberty. It sent to marital homes on the day of the marriage.[35]

Further, The Law Commission candidly states that:

> "Child Marriage is thus child abuse and a violation of human rights of the child. It has an extremely deleterious effect on the health and well being of the child. It is a denial of child hood adolescence: it is a curtailment of personal freedom and opportunity to develop to a full sense of selfhood as well as a denial of psycho-social and emotional well-being and it is a denial of re-productive health and educational opportunities. The girl child is most affected and suffers irreparable damage to her physical, mental, psychological and emotional development.[36]

4.8. Child Labour: Abuse of Child

The practice of child labour is a hard reality. It is a cause and consequence of abuse and exploitation of children. The children are being exploited and forced into labour. Two main approaches defining child labour which consequently affects on the whole some personality of child are:

(i) Any labour force activity by children below a stipulated minimum age.

(ii) Any work, economic or not, that is injurious to the health, safety and development of children.

Hommerfolks, Chairman of United Nations Child Labour Committee has defined child labour as, "any work by children that interferes with their full physical development, their opportunities for a desirable level of education and of their need of recreation.

Thus child labour is any work undertaken by children below 14 years in such works which are injurious to their health and harmful to their proper development. The function of work in childhood is primarily developmental and not economic. Children's work, then as a social good, is the direct antithesis of child labour as a social evil.[37] Child labour is a abuse and exploitation of children and children pre-maturely leading an adult-like life. They receive low wages and work for long hours under conditions that are likely to damage their health as well as physical and mental development. According to a study on child abuse, out of 12,447 children, 19.7% are found to be at work. Only 17% of working children are paid for their work. Thus child labour is being largely underpaid, over worked and exploited.[38]

Children engaging in hazardous and non-hazardous labour have certainly continued to be exploited and abused. Large scale exploitation and abuse of children employed in domestic work and hotels are indicators of child labour and its abuse. On October 10, 2006 the notification issued by the Ministry of Labour, Government of India banned children from being employed as domestic servants, workers in Dhabas, Restaurants, Hotels, Tea-Shops, Resorts, Spas or other recreation centers.

Child labour and its exploitation has become a biggest challenge. On the problem of child exploitation High Court of Kerala in *Satyavan Kottarakkara* v. *State*,[39] held that, "exploitation of children in any form which has the tendency to exploit them either, physically, mentally or otherwise is objectionable. Any attempt in this direction should be put an end to achieve the goals enshrined by the Indian Constitution Makers, which are reflected in various provisions of the Constitution, namely, Article 21, 39, 41, 45 and 46...".

Practice of Child Labour causes health hazards. More so, working children suffer from the incidence of malnutrition and under nourishment. They are prone to become victims to the anti-social activities like black marketing, smuggling, theft, drug addiction, drug peddling, and prostitution even terrorist activities. Thus practice of child labour is cause and consequence for children to become "juvenile in conflict with law" and *vice-versa.*

The consequences of child labour are many-fold. A fundamental fact that has to be remembered here is that since children differ from adults in their physical and psychological attributes, a job that may not be hazardous to an adult may be highly hazardous for a child. A working child may be exposed to various things in the course of work including organic dusts, toxic chemicals, high temperatures that could have disastrous long-term consequences. Moreover, the term 'hazardous' should not be confined to physical hazard alone because they suffer more devasting psychological damage than adults from working and living in an environment in which they are oppressed or demigrated. In the context of Convention on the Rights of the Child, child labour is a violation of child's right to health, right to rest, leisure and play, right to optimal development, right to adequate standard of living protection from all forms of injury and abuse, etc. Besides, it is surely not in the best interest of the child which is one of the fundamental principles to be adhered to in all activities concerning children.[40]

4.9. Bonded Child Labour and Abuse of Child

Bonded Child Labour is inhumane and often dangerous and would certainly seem to qualify as a 'worst' form of child labour and is included as such in the 1999 Convention.[41] Parents of the child who are extremely poor consent to give their children in lieu of their debt taken from the land lord and their children are given as security.

Article 23 of the Constitution of India, prohibits the practice of debt bondage and other forms of slavery both modern and ancient as held in *Peoples' Union for Democratic Rights* v. *Union of India.*[42] The issue of bonded labour was raised in the Supreme Court in the form of Public Interest Litigations.

In the *Bandhua Mukti Morcha* v. *Union of India and others,*[43] the Supreme Court held that whenever it is shown that a labourer is made to provide forced labour, the Court would raise the rebuttable presumption that he is required to do so in consideration of an advance or other economic consideration received by him and he is, therefore, bonded labour. In *Neeraj Choudhary* v. *State of M.P.,*[44] Supreme Court held that the bonded labourers must be identified and released and on release they must be suitably rehabilitated. Any failure on the part of the State Government in implementing the provisions of the *Bonded Labour System (Abolition) Act,* 1976 would be violative of Articles 21 and 23 of the Constitution of India.

In a Bonded Labour System under which the debtor or his descendents have to work for the creditor and without reasonable wages or with no wages in order to discharge a debt. This system originated from the uneven social structure characterized by feudal and semi-feudal conditions. It is an outcome of certain categories of indebtedness, like customary obligations, forced labour, begar or indebtedness which have been prevailing for a long time involving certain economically exploited, helpless and weaker sections of society. They agree to render service to the creditor in lieu of debt. At times, several generations work under bondage for the repayment of a paltry sum, which had been taken by some remote ancestor, often at high rates of interest. The system is an infringement of basic human rights and a disgrace to the dignity of labour.

The factors that trigger-off bonded labour are: crisis and death in the family, natural calamity/accident, sudden loss of employment, cheating and loan design by money lender, non-sustainable expenses on wedding and other social functions, alcoholism, migration and trafficking.

Along with the Child Labour (Prohibition and Regulation) Act, 1986 and other labour laws, the following laws provide legal protection to bonded child labourers.

Salient features of the Bonded Labour System (Abolition) Act, 1976

The Act provides for the abolition of the system of any custom, agreements or instruments requiring any person to render any service as bonded labour void. The liability to repay bonded debt is deemed to have been extinguished from the date of commencement of the Act and the property of the bonded labour freed from mortgage. Civil prisoners stood freed as a consequence of the Act.

The law provides that (a) no suit or other proceedings shall be instituted in any Civil Court for the recovery of any bonded debt; (b) every attachment made before the commencement of the Act for the recovery of any bonded debt shall stand vacated; and (c) such movable property shall be restored to the bonded labourer.

The role of the District Magistrate is extremely important in view of the special sensitivity of the issue relating to bonded labour as under the Act, powers of a Judicial Magistrate are vested in the District Magistrate.

The definition of Bonded Labour System explained under Section 2 of the Bonded Labour System (Abolition) Act, 1976, is the system of forced labour under which a debtor enters or has or is presumed to have entered into an agreement with the creditor to the effect that he would render by himself labour or service for the benefit of the creditor for a specified/unspecified period, either without or nominal wages.

Thus, the bonded labour system is defined in section 2(g) as the system of forced, or partly labour, which a creditor extracts from a debtor by virtue of an agreement between the two. The Bonded Labour System (Abolition) Act purports to abolish all debt agreements and obligations. It is the legislative fulfilment of the Indian Constitution's mandate against begar and forced labour. It frees all bonded labourers, cancels any outstanding debts against them, prohibits the creation of new bondage agreements and orders the economic rehabilitation of freed bonded labour. The Act provides for imprisonment upto 3 years and fine upto Rs. 2000 to whoever advances any bonded debt. An offence under the Act may be tried in a summary manner. Every offence under the Act is cognizable and bailable.

Article 23 of the Constitution provides traffic in human beings and 'begar' and other similar forms of forced labour are prohibited and any contravention of this provision shall be an offence punishable in accordance with law. Article 39(a) provides that the citizens, men and women equally, have the right to an adequate means of livelihood; Article 39 (d) provides that there is equal pay for equal work for both men and women and Article 39 (e) provides that the health and strength of workers, men and women, and the tender age of children are not abused and that the citizens are not forced by economic necessity to enter avocations unsuited to their age or strength. Section 374 of Indian Penal Code deals with unlawful compulsory labour which says that whoever unlawfully compels any person to labour against the will of that person, shall be punishable with imprisonment of either description for a term which may extend to one year, or with fine, or with both.

Thus, the Bonded Labour System (Abolition) Act, 1976 has been enacted pursuant to the Directive Principles of the State Policy with a view to ensure basic human dignity to the bonded labourers and any failure of action on the part of the legislation would be the clearest violation of Article 21 apart from Article 23 of the Constitution.

4.10. Child Rag Pickers and Child Abuse

Child rag pickers are highly vulnerable to all kinds of child abuses and neglect, especially physical abuse, sexual abuse, and police abuse and so on. Growth of urbanisation has increased the number of dumping grounds to clean them. Here the role of child rag pickers becomes indispensable. Migrant groups are involved in this rag picking and they are subjected to all forms of exploitation. Due to significant family size, low earnings of the parents or below subsistence level, they force their children undertake ragpicking.

The people belonging to various social categories are involved in rag picking. But Scheduled caste households are the highest as compared to other social groups. So, rag picking is a kind of self-employment. Rag picking pays more than any other form of child labour in India, where every third child worker, an expert picker, can earn to Rs. 15 per day. In rag picking mostly boys between the age group of 8-14 years are employed. Some of the rag pickers are self-employed persons who pickup rag from the streets and bifurcate them and sell to the dealers who deal with such goods. Some of the rag pickers are employed by show owners who deals with plastic goods, tin products, etc. Thus, it is a most dangerous and hazardous occupation.[45]

Children who are involved in the process of rag picking collect mirror, glass, plastic, garbage and other waste including hospital wastes like; blood stained bandages, syringes, saline bottles, surgical wastes and lab wastes which endanger their health. This consequently, causes health and other hazards like injuries, Cough, Tuberculosis, stomach infections, skin diseases, etc. The sharp glasses lying in the garbage dump may injure their bare foot and injury may develop into festering wounds. Many of the garbage children die of curable diseases that go uncured.[46]

4.11. Juvenile Justice Administration and Child Abuse

Juvenile Justice Act is a comprehensive piece of legislation[47] to deal "Juvenile in conflict with law"[48] and "Children in need of care and protection"[49] for protection of such children and to secure speedy justice to child/juvenile and it is designed for reformative, rehabilitative and social re-integration of child. The Juvenile Justice Act is based on two philosophical objectives-parents patriae and individualised treatment. The parents' patriae doctrine allows the court to conduct the proceedings principally to determine what should be done in the best interests of the child and not as trials to determine Criminal guilt and give sentence. The individualised treatment doctrine views the disposition decision in view to inherently rehabilitate. It seeks to prescribe a treatment programme fitting the needs, personality, psychological development and social circumstances of a youth.[50] In *Bandela Aillaiah* v. *State*,[51] it was observed that: "The Juvenile Justice Law appears to be so emphatic and mandatory that no juvenile delinquent shall be tried for any offence charged against him or must be convicted or sentenced for such an offence. On the other hand, a special treatment should be given to him for his care and protection by way of correctional measures". But children often suffer neglect, abuse and violence in the administration of juvenile Justice. The very institution which is expected to protect the children is violating their rights. When the children in conflict with law were picked by the police, these children are frequently abused, tortured or ill-treated and their human rights are often disregarded. More often they are kept in degrading conditions at observation home without providing basic needs like food, dress, medical health care facilities, etc. and even custodial violence's are continued to inflict sufferings upon the juvenile offenders. In some Juvenile Justice Boards, juvenile cases are pending over 10 to 12 years and some juveniles have become adult, married and even got children. This shows inordinate delay in doing justice to the juveniles. Police cannot file charge-sheet of Juvenile offenders on time and in some cases they use to take 2 to 3 years to file charge-sheet, this in turn cause delay in disposal of the cases. The chairpersons of Juvenile Justice Board are over burdened with their regular court work and hardly, they have time to spend in Juvenile Justice Board. They conduct the proceedings without change of their mindset as usual and very passively rather actively. It is nothing but a mockery of justice and exploitation of Juvenile Offenders. This kind of conducting proceedings will not provide any opportunity to the Juvenile Justice Board to interact/discuss with the Juvenile Offenders parents for their rehabilitation. No co-operation, co-ordination, convergence between, Juvenile Justice Board concerned department, i.e. Women and Child Development, Police and Judiciary. There is wide gap between law in book and its practice in reality. There are nearly 4,992 Juvenile Offenders cases pending at Juvenile Justice Board in Karnataka State as on 31.01.2009.[52] Detention of Children in Jail/Prison would also leads to violation of Human Rights. The Supreme Court in *Sheela Barse* v. *Union of India*,[53] condemned and discouraged the detention of children below 16 years in jail, in a milestone decision. The Court observed:

> "It is a matter of regret that despite statutory provisions and frequent exhortations by social scientists, there are still a large number of children in different jails in the country...it is the atmosphere of the jail which has a highly injurious effect on the mind of the child estranging him from society and breeding in him aversion bordering on hatred against a system which kept him in jail. On no account should the children be kept in jail and if a State Government has not got sufficient accommodation in its remand homes, the children should be released on bail instead of being subjected to incarceration in jail".

'The National Commission for Protection of Child Rights (NCPCR) held an inquiry on 19th September 2009 and found that children living like 'animals' in Delhi boys home. No regular meals, dirty bed sheets, and rotten mattresses to sleep on contaminated water to drink, dingy toilets and filthy leaking rooms are provided to the children. Children cannot protest if they fall ill. If they do they are tortured. These children are treated like slaves; they cook for themselves in a dark, dirty kitchen; they clean their rooms and toilets and double up as waiters when visitors come to meet officials. The rooms they were living in were stinking and tube lights, fans and coolers in most of rooms were not functional. This clearly shows the miserable state of children and their exploitation in all levels.[54]

4.12. Children in Armed Conflict

The protection of children in armed conflict is a great challenge to the global world and is also a matter debatable under International Humanitarian Law. Children in armed conflicts will be forced to live in oppression and injustice and will be placed in fear of violence. The child affected by armed conflict is a matter of peace and security. The issue of children in armed conflict has been the political agenda according to Security Council Resolution.[55]

The concept of children in armed conflict is also an issue resolved under International Humanitarian Law which is applicable to them. Successive and sustained efforts have been made to put an end to the use of children as soldiers in violation of International Law—ILO Convention 182.

In the armed conflict of recent years, children have been the special targets and tragically also perpetrators of violence. The number of children who have been directly affected by armed conflict is enormous and unprecedented. During these conflicts, children have been maimed, killed or uprooted from their homes and communities. Children have been made orphans and have been subjected to exploitation and sexual abuse.[56] Children have been abducted and recruited as soldiers. War's impact on girls is particularly damaging to future generations.

The use of children as soldiers has become common. There is a growing evidence that some industries are responsible for fuelling wars that have resulted in horrific violations of children's rights.

Mal nutrition increases because of low food production and displacement, resources for social services are diverted into war effort; as health services deteriorate, infant and child mortality rates rise, the destruction of schools reduces access to education; and displacement separates families and deprives children of a secure environment. So to ensure the well-being of all children they deserve special attention and action.

4.13. Street Children and their Abuse

Children on streets are more vulnerable, exploitable and more prone to abuse. There is no one to safeguard their interests; they become easy prey to pedophiles. Street children live alone and therefore, become an easy target for unscrupulous elements and even many street children are sexually abused.

The UN has estimated that about 100 million children around the world are forced to live wholly or partially in the streets, although reliable figures are practically impossible to calculate. Many such children are among the 300 million who are subjected to exploitation, violence and abuse around the world, according to the same source. Most street children are to be found in poor countries in Africa, Asia, Latin America and the Middle East, although the problem is also acute in parts of Eastern Europe and the former Soviet Union. In its 2008 report on The State of the World's Children, the United Nations Children's Fund (UNICEF) lists a total of 60 priority countries for action on child survival and safety, of which almost two-thirds (38) are in sub-Saharan Africa. Although the actual numbers of street children in each region are unknown, an idea of the scale of the problem can be gained from social indicators such as primary school enrolment and the prevalence of child labour.[57]

According to the UN High Commissioner for Human Rights, India has the largest population of street children in the world—around 18 million, of whom nearly 2,50,000 live on the streets of Mumbai. Most of these children get by working as porters at bus or railway terminals. As mechanics in auto-repair shops, as vendors, as street tailors or as ragpickers.[58] Most children take to streets due to problems at home like poverty, an alcoholic father or an abusive mother, or due to the death of their parents". Street children find ways to earn and start living like adults. Those children have a distorted vision of freedom. Life of street children (boys) is very miserable. The railway platform is their permanent home. They start with begging and selling knick-knacks, and when they get no money, they turned to cry". In many cases these children are picked by criminals to run errands.[59] Seven out of 10 street children are abused, what is even more worrying is that none of these children come out in the open about their suffering. According to a nation-wide study undertaken by the Ministry of Women and Child Development in 2007, 53.2 percent children had faced one or more forms of sexual abuse. The study revealed that in 50 percent of the cases the abusers were persons known to the child or in a position of trust and responsibility and most children did not report the matter to anyone. The findings of the study point to a harsh reality: Despite their best efforts, parents are no longer able to protect their children from sexual predators, who in most cases have easy access to their homes.[60] Further the women and child development ministry has no database of street children, the target group of Integrated Scheme for Street Children (ICPS) Programme, a parliamentary committee has said, terming the findings as "surprising". The parliamentary standing committee on human resource development in its report said: "The committee is surprised to know that the ministry does not have any database on the street children in the country, the target group of the ICPS while analysing the scheme". The ICPS aims at providing shelter, nutrition, health care, education and recreation facilities to street children and seeks to protect them against abuse and exploitation. The panel in its report suggested that the ministry start preparing a database detailing the number of children on the streets and those benefiting from this scheme.[61]

A study on Street Children and Drug Abuse, done two years ago by R.Thilagaraj of the Madras University Criminology Department and Paul Sunder Singh of Karunalaya, an NGO, confirms these disturbing trends and 63.9 percent of street children interviewed in Chennai and Madurai said they had started sniffing solvents in order to "pass time". Over 22 percent confessed that they did to "keep themselves happy".[62]

4.14. Disabled Children—Differently Abled Children and their Abuse

Children and young people, with disabilities continue to be one of the most disadvantaged groups in all our societies. In fact, disability and its conceptualization are cultural and social constructs. Cross cultural literature on disability suggest that a broader view of society is needed to understand the cultural underpinnings and value system that dominate. It is now generally accepted that societal barriers place impediments in the way of persons with disabilities, preventing them from achieving their optimal levels. Disabled, thus, as a category are socially excluded and continue to be marginalized in our societies.

This exclusion is not a new phenomenon. Ever since the dawn of civilization, human society has been faced with the problem of disability. Children with defects were not cared for in pre-historic societies. Defects and mental illness in the good old days were considered the results of some kind of sin. The treatment meted out to them varied from age to age, civilization to civilization and culture to culture. The Spartans destroyed them by throwing them down, tumbling the mountain precipices; The Egyptian Pharaohs hanged their blind slaves from the branches of trees. The physicians and the scholars in ancient Greek and Roman Societies, made some efforts to treat and preserve the lives of the physically challenged and provided asylums. The renaissance brought a small change in earlier attitude. This was the state of affairs until the late eighteenth century and early nineteenth century.[63]

The situation in India was no better. The ancient India, however during the golden rule of *Ashoka*, the disabled received humane treatment. The first attempt at educating the disabled children were made in the last two decades of the 19th century with the establishment of - First school for hearing impaired in Mumbai in 1885, followed by the first school for the visually impaired in Amritsar in 1887. At present, there are more than 243 schools for visually impaired, 478 for hearing impaired and 604 for mentally retarded children. Vocational Rehabilitation Centre (VRC) has been set-up. National Institutes have started functioning. A three percent job reservation has been brought in and a special employment exchange has been set-up. National Awards, tax concessions, self employment schemes and sheltered workshops are available for the disabled. Establishment of District Rehabilitation Centre (DRC), Community Based Rehabilitation (CBR), Regional Research Training Centre (RRTC), National Information Centre for Disabled and Rehabilitation (NICDR) are among the other efforts made by the Government for the welfare of the disabled.[64]

In spite of all these efforts, societal attitude towards these children have not undergone any radical change. Ignorance about disability is widespread resulting in deep seated prejudice and about disability. Negative attitude dominate, and disability is thought of as a taboo and a stigma. Disabled children are often a terrible shock to their parents whose pride and self-esteem have a rude shock and they begin feeling inferior and built walls around them before they come to terms with the reality. Some curse the stars operative at the time of birth of the child, others attribute it to their 'sins' or bad 'karmas' in previous life. This is primarily due to the social construction of disability in our society. As such, these children because of their lower worth are denied the rights existing for the 'normal'. They remain enshrined in the ideologies of segregation, labeled and categorized according to the medical definition of their disability. Use of labels such as 'Mentally Retarded', 'Physically Handicapped', etc. put these children at disadvantage for no faults of theirs. Such a labeling has negative, stigmatizing effects which further accentuate their weaknesses. This labeling is thus disabling. Labeling human beings dehumanizes them. Their self-worth gets devalued and it reduces them to objects of pity, sympathy or even of patronage.[65]

The problem of these children lies not only in the limitations that they have but also in their feeling a 'sense of inadequacy' and 'insecurity' due to the attitude of rejection, isolation, and even ridicule by others around them. As a consequence, they feel unhappy and suffer from emotional disorders. They also, at times, show negative and aggressive behavior because of certain bodily disorders in them, such as anemia, blood sugar, hormone imbalance or neurological disorders, which contribute to their emotional, upsetting. Due to this, they find it difficult to adjust with their environment and develop certain personality disorders like lack of confidence, inferiority complex and often show tantrums to attract the attention of others.

Of late, the subject of segregation V. integration has generated many debates resulting in certain positive changes. The growing importance of the 'rights issue' was strongly stressed by disabled activists. Global initiatives on equalization of opportunity and education for all reinforced this. Rectifying the language used to describe the disabled in this regard has played paramount role. In an effort to dispel the stigma associated with the negative labels of the past the old language which labeled disabled people as 'lame', 'defective' 'crippled',' less fortunate', 'mentally retarded', 'epileptic', 'spastic', 'deaf and mute', all of which focused on their imperfections, was abandoned and replaced by the new language whereby children with disabilities were described in broader, more general terms such as children with special educational needs. The old language applied a mistaken model seeing difficulties within the individual child and disregarding the numerous facets in the external environment which disabled the child. This approach was regarded as a medical approach and known as the medical model. Today, the approach is a social one looking, instead, at all the barriers within the environment that can disable a person.[66] Our society is submerged in concerns of class, caste, gender and religion, which is highly detrimental to social change. Programs of poverty alleviation, caste and gender issues, and rural enlistment take a high priority, putting than disabled last on to list of development activity. The disabled are very much a part of these areas, but, mainly due to political weakness, they remain a neglected segment, kept out of the political and social framework of social policy and their social integration remain a dream to be realized. But there is a ray of hope and it calls for a revolution in the attitude of society. Civil society built on the dogmas of social justice and equal opportunity recognizes the weak, the needy and the helpless. This conforms to the spirit of the Constitution. We need to change ourselves into a society where people value each other despite differences and lest we forget that people with disabilities have a fundamental right to live and participate fully in the settings and programs in school, at home, in the workplace and in the community.

4.15. Missing Children and their Abuse

The term 'missing children' encompasses runaway kids, children who are abducted and those who get lost or separated from their families. But the single largest component contributing to these large numbers is runaway children between the age group of 10 and 18. While some leave home for trivial reasons like not wanting to study, others are forced to escape from what they say is a miserable existence. Many leave their homes to make a living or to escape abuse, while a large number fall prey to trafficking.[67]

The children may wander-off, be lured away by traffickers or kidnapped. If they are captured by traffickers, they may be used as forced labour, exploited sexually, sent to the Gulf countries as camel jockeys or child brides, pushed into begging rackets and drug peddling or become victims of the organ trade.[68] Not all children who are separated from their families are lost. Some times sick children are abandoned by their parents. Unable to afford the treatment, they leave their kids at temples hoping that God will look after them. A study conducted by Child Line Delhi, a helpline for kids shows that 33% of the total calls received between 2000-08 were about "missing children".[69] NGOs in the field categorize missing children in two ways. In the first category are those kids who are found to be without adult supervision and who cannot get home on their own. The second group is made up of kids whose parents have reported their disappearance. Between 2000-08 child-line got 6,330 calls from people who had located a "lost child" and 8,172 calls from parents looking for a missing kid[70].

A Committee on Missing Children was established by the National Human Rights Commission on February 12, 2007, to look into the issue. The Committee's Report noted that "despite the best efforts of the government, "countless children go 'missing' every year". It also "observed that the juvenile justice system too has failed to provide due care and protection to children"[71].

According to the National Human Rights Commission (NHRC), the New Delhi capital city has earned the dubious distinction of having the second highest number of missing children in the country. And it's due to the handicapped-policing system of the city. The report by the National Human Rights Commission (NHRC) emphasises that on an average 44,000 children are reported missing each year, out of which, as many as 11,000 remain untraced[72]

According to the Report, there are a number of problems, including abductions and kidnappings by family members, children who run away on their own or are forced to take that step due to compelling circumstances in their families. The list of missing children also includes those who face unfriendly and hostile environment and are asked to leave home or who are abandoned. Few children who are trafficked, smuggled or exploited for various purposes are among the missing lot. Delhi reported the highest percentage of such cases among children upto 15 years.

It was further reported that almost all girls under 10 years of age had been traced and there was no criminal activity linked to their disappearance. According to the report, ever since the introduction of computerisation of missing people's data in 2006, there has been a significant breakthrough in tracing missing people. The report highlights that before computerisations of missing person's data, the tracing out percentage of missing persons was about 25 percent, which has increased to 73.77 percent in 2006. As per the report 80 percent missing children were traced. However, some disagree[73]. A major problem lies in recording complaints. The police department does not have the right infrastructure to trace the missing children or even keep a record of them. The module that lodges the complaint of missing kids on the web is a long procedure. By the time it appears in the newspapers, the kid is either dead or back on his own. The report highlights that majority of these missing children are illiterate and had left their homes on their own for various reasons. Bajaj explains, "A majority of missing children belong to poor families from UP. These people come here in search of work and make their kids work for them. And when these kids go missing, none of the family members files a complaint, as they are not familiar with norms of this city. There is a serious lack of awareness and education in Delhi." While the fate of the children of Delhi stands questionable, the city must wake upto the pleas of these kids who are the assets of the country.[74]

If we go by the latest records, around 44,475 children go missing every year in India, out of which Mumbai alone witnesses an average of 4,182 missing children. And the numbers are rising. Startling though this figure is, the general populace, however, fails to notice the posters at railway stations and bus stops[75].

There are a number of NGOs who help trace missing children. One such organisation is Balprafulta, whose project—Talaash-was set-up exclusively for this purpose. Snehal Rane, the project coordinator at Balprafulta, says, "We believe that every child on the street is a missing child, and we try our level best to convince the child and the family to come together".

Project *Talaash,* which was initiated in the year 2002, already claims to have helped 1,744 children either by reuniting them with their families or by providing them with shelter. Then there are NGOs like *Saathi* and *Pratham,* which operate at railway stations that serve as hubs for runaway children. Volunteers are friend the child and try to extract as much information as possible about his family and home. The child is either produced before the Child Welfare Committee (CWC) or placed in shelter homes affiliated with the NGOs. A child produced before the CWC is usually sheltered in the government-run children's home till the parents are traced.[76]

Statistics show that between September of 2007 and 2008, 76,579 children went missing in India. Of them, 11,825 children have gone missing from Delhi alone.[77] Experts say that with numerous slums and a steady influx of migrants the poorer sections of the city are fertile hunting grounds for traffickers. Many kidnapped children are smuggled abroad to be married or work as domestic labour.[78] The NHRC committee report says that "complaints of missing children, by and large, are treated as any other non-cognizable offence and only an entry is made in the General Station Diary (GSD) that is followed by an enquiry".[79]

The term 'missing children' is not appropriate, explains *Satyarthi*, as its legal connotation does not comprehend the crimes that are generally involved. The National Human Rights Commission reported that 50,000 children went missing in 2005-06. Statistics naturally appear like the tip of iceberg, considering that a majority of poor families shy away from reporting cases involving their missing children. This for the fear of law, which holds them liable for pushing their children into labour.[80] As things stand, the two years of enforcement of amended Child Labour Protection Act, 2006 do not seem to have yielded much. Unconfirmed reports suggest millions of children are working under hazardous circumstances, missing from homes and untraceable.[81]

5. CONCLUSION

India is a developing country; socio-economic conditions prevailing in the society are strongly responsible for abuse of child in different forms. The problem of child abuse is deeply rooted in the socio-culture spectrums. High literacy and low literacy rate, both equally contribute to the problem of child abuse. This is a challenge to the civil society, which can be tackled by bringing attitudinal and behavioural change. Mindset of the people can be changed by imparting value based education and culture. Capacity building in children especially during abusive situations and school age children need to be sensitized to different forms of child abuse. Perceptions and attitudes of parents and people towards children be modified to understand the problem of child abuse.

NOTES AND REFERENCES

1. Foreword by Kofi A. Annan, Secretary-General of United Nations, *"In the State of World's Children, 2000"*.
2. AIR 1986 SC 1873.
3. India Alliance for Child Rights, *"India Every Rights for every child 2003 citizens alternate Review and Report on India's progress towards CRC Realisation in response to First periodic Report; 2001, Govt. of India submitted to the UN Committee on the Rights of the Child"*, 2003, New Delhi, p. 72.
4. National Plan of Action for Children, 2005.
5. Convention on the Rights, Country Report—India, Feb.,1997, Department of Women and Child Development, Ministry of HRD, Govt. of India, p. 77.
6. The Juvenile Justice (Care and Protection of Children) Act, 2000 (56 of 2000) Received the Assent of the President on 30-12-2000 and Published in the Gazette of India, Ext., Pt. II, S. 1. dated 30.12.2000.
7. Study on Child Abuse: INDIA 2007, Ministry of Women and Child Development, Govt. of India.
8. "National Study on Child Abuse", conducted by Prayas in collaboration with the

Ministry of Women and Child Development, GOI, supported by UNICEF and Save the Children Fund, UK, Executive Summary Report, 2005.

9. Child Labour (Prohibition and Regulation) Act, 1986.
10. Section 2, Juvenile Justice (Care & Protection of Children) Act, 2000.
11. Mamta Rao, *Law Relating to Women and Children*, 2nd edn., Lucknow: Eastern Book Company, 2008, p. 464.
12. 1998 *Cri.L.J.* 2428 (Del).
13. "*Crimes in India*", New Delhi: National Crime Record Bureau, Ministry of Home Affairs, Govt. of India, 2005.
14. *Supra* note 11, p. 463.
15. *Deccan Herald,* 14th August, 2009.
16. Received the Assent of the President on 26th August 2009; Act came force on 1.4.2010.
17. *Supra* note 8, pp. 12-13.
18. Vol. 1, Mar. (2008), *Mysore University Law Journal.*
19. Sadhana Gupta and Pankaj Kumar, "Child Sexual Abuse: A Socio-Legal Problem", Vol. 20, No. 6 (2006), *Legal News and Views*, p. 15.
20. UNICEF, 2001.
21. *Supra* note 11, and also *see* "Sexual Abuses of the Children and the Law", New Delhi: *Legal News and Views*, 1996.
22. *Supra* note 19, p. 16.
23. Krishnadas Rajagopal, "Child Rape is Gruesome, But Reform Offender: H.C", *The Indian Express*, New Delhi, 8 July 2008, cited in My name is Today, Children in News, "*Butterflies*", Vol. XVI, New Delhi, 2009, p. 76.
24. Sec. 376 of Indian Penal Code.
25. *Supra* note 13.
26. Sec. 23 of Juvenile Justice (Care and Protection of Children) Act, 2000.
27. Sec. 354, Indian Penal Code.
28. *Spirit of Human Rights*—A Manual of Gulbarga University, Gulbarga: Law Department, 2005.
29. *Supra* note 11, p. 463.
30. *Ibid.*
31. Dr. Bindu M. Nambiar, "Children and Human Rights", Vol. 5, 149 (2007), *Journal of Indian Legal Thought*, p. 158.
32. *Supra* note 8, p. 16.
33. D. Venkteshwar Rao, *Child Rights—A Perspective on International and National Law,* New Delhi: Manak Publications Pvt. Ltd., 2004, p. 147; See also Neel K. Sharda, *The Legal Economic and Social Status of Indian Children*, New Delhi: National Book Organisation, 1988, p. 39.
34. Received the Assent of the President on January 10, 2007 and Published in the Gazette of India, Extra, Part II, S. 1, dated 11th January 2007.
35. Chapter 3 of 205th Law Commission Report; *see* also Chetan Chauhan, "Despite Revised Law Child Marriage Still Common: Study", *The Hindustan Times,* Mumbai, 21 January, 2008, cited in *supra* note 23, p. 72.
36. Chapter 4 of 205th Law Commission Report.
37. Thomas Paul, "Child Labour Prohibition V. Abolition: Untangling The Constitutional Tangle", Vol. 50, 2 (2008), New Delhi: *Journal of Indian Law Institute*, p. 146.
38. *Supra* note 8, p. 7.

39. AIR 1997, Ker 133.
40. P. Pandiaraj, " Elimination Child Labour in India: Towards a glorious illusion ?" Vol. 8 (2006), *Indian Journal of International Law*, p. 88.
41. Convention concerning prohibition and immediate action for the elimination of 'worst' forms of Child Labour (ILO No. 182), adopted 17th June 1999 (Hereinafter ILO 1999 Convention).
42. Asiad workers case, AIR 1982 SC 1473.
43. 1984 2 SCR.
44. 1984 3 SCC 243.
45. Study Material, "*Successful Prosecution of Child Labour Cases for the Inspectors appointed under Section 17 CLPRA Act. 1986*", Bangalore: Department of Labour, Government of Karnataka, 2001, p. 15.
46. Helen R. Sekhar, *Child Labour: Situation and Strategies for Elimination*, Noida: V.V. Giri, National Labour Institute, 2007, pp. 44-46
47. Juvenile Justice (Care and Protection of Children) Act, 2000 received the Assent of the President on 30.12.2000 and Published in the Gazette of India, ext., Pt. II, S. 1 dt. 30.12.2000, see also Juvenile Justice (Care and Protection of Children) Amendment Act, 2006, received the Assent of the President on 22.08.2006 and Published on the Gazette of India ext., Pt. II, S. 1. dt. 23.08.2006.
48. Sec. 2(l) define, "*Juvenile in Conflict with Law*" means a Juvenile who is alleged to have committed an offence and has not completed eighteenth year of age as on the date of commission of such offence.
49. Sec. 2(d) define, "Child in need of care and protection" means a child:
    (i) Who is found without any home or settled place or abode and without any ostensible means of subsistence,
    (ia) Who is found begging, or who is either a street child or a working child,
    (ii) Who is resides with a person (whether a guardian of the child or not) and such person has threatened to kill or injure the child and there is a reasonable likelihood of the threat being carried out, or
    has killed, abused or neglected some other child or children and there is a reasonable likelihood of the child in question being killed, abused or neglected by that person.
    (iii) who is mentally or physically challenged or ill children or children suffering from terminal diseases or incurable diseases having no one to support or look after,
    (iv) who has a parent or guardian and such parent or guardian is unfit or incapacitated to exercise control over the child,
    (v) who does not have parent and no one is willing to take care of or whose parents have abandoned (or surrendered) him or who is missing and run away child and whose parents cannot be found after reasonable injury,
    (vi) who is being or is likely to be grossly abused, tortured or exploited for the purpose of sexual abuse or illegal acts,
    (vii) who is found vulnerable and is likely to be inducted into drug abuse or trafficking,
    (viii) who is being or is likely to be abused for unconscionable gains, and
    (ix) who is victim of any armed conflict, civil commotion or natural calamity,
50. Dr. B.B. Das, Sunanda Padhy, "*A Study of Objectives of Juvenile Justice Act, 2000*", cited in *supra*, note 12, p. 486.
51. 1995 *Cril. L.J.* 1083.
52. Workshop on Module Development for the Juvenile Justice Board Members under Juvenile Justice Act, 2000, sponsored by UNICEF held at ATI, Mysore, from 2nd to 4th Feb. 2009.

53. (1986) 3 SCC 596.
54. Chetan Chauhan, *Lost Innocence, The Hindustan Times*, New Delhi, 23 Oct. 2008 cited in *supra,* note 23, pp. 54-55.
55. *Supra* note 33, p. 93, *see* the Security Council, recalling the statements of its President on 29th June 1998.
56. Kofi A. Annan, Secretary General, U.N., "*We the Children—Meeting the Promises of the World Summit for Children*", p. 83.
57. "*100 Million Kids Live on Worlds Streets*", *The Hindustan Times*, New Delhi, 25, Mar. 2008 cited in *supra* note 23, p. 232.
58. Deepa Suryanarayan, "*Mumbai's children of a lesser God*", DNA, Mumbai, 25th July 2008 cited in *Ibid.*, pp. 233-34.
59. *Ibid.*, p. 234.
60. *Ibid.*, p. 233.
61. Ministry has no data base of Street Children, *The Asian Age*, New Delhi 2 May, 2008 cited in *ibid.*. p. 237.
62. Ramya Kannan, "Sniffing Solvents and Snuffing out Adolescence", *The Hindu*, Chennai, 20 Aug. 2008 cited in *ibid.*, p. 238.
63. Dr. Sapna K. Sangra, "*Disabled children—From Segregation To Integration*", *The Kashmir Times*, Jammu 6, June, 2008, cited in *ibid.*, pp. 189-90.
64. *Ibid.*, p. 190.
65. *Ibid.*
66. *Ibid.*
67. Humaira Ansari and Surekha, S., "*Missing*" DNA, Mumbai, 19 July 2008, cited in *Ibid.*, p. 60.
68. Shreya Roy Chowdhary, "When will these Children Return Home?" *The Times of India*, New Delhi, 14th Nov. 2008, cited in *ibid.*, p. 63.
69. *Ibid.*
70. *Ibid.*
71. *Ibid.*
72. Shruti Bodyal, "Figures of Missing Children Rise in City", *The Asian Age*, New Delhi, 13 Aug. 2008, cited in *ibid.*. p. 56.
73. *Ibid.*, p. 57.
74. *Ibid.*
75. *Supra* note 72.
76. *Ibid.*, p. 61.
77. *Supra* note 73.
78. *Ibid.*, p. 64.
79. *Ibid.*
80. Aditi Tandan, "Millions of Kids Still Working: Thousands Missing", *The Tribune*, New Delhi, 11th Oct. 2008, cited in *ibid.*, p. 52.
81. *Ibid.*

4

Evolution of Practice of Child Labour

I. INTRODUCTION

The child labour is a complex and a controversial issue. The existence and perpetuation of child labour is a challenge to the human society. It is really a curse and stigma upon the society; disgrace for the world of mankind, a malady which may destroy the economic backbone of a country. The practice of child labour would be an impediment in the way of human development in almost all the third world countries including India. The issue of child labour is one of major human rights issues and a highly emotive one. The problem of child labour in underdeveloped and developing countries is quite acute and abnormal and it is a global phenomenon which exists in almost all the countries of the world, but there is difference only in degree.[1]

In the past, child labour has been a part of the social organization in which all members contributed their labour to produce for the subsistence and survival.[2] In rural subsistence farming, the work of the child was formal part of labour, which was considered necessary for the reproduction of the system and value of labour taken as part of child's socialisation for reproduction of the labour power.[3]

The phenomenon of child labour is a symptom of the disease and a consequence of exploitative system, operating at the national and international levels, lopsided development, uneven resource of ownership, correlating of large scale unemployment and abject poverty among the nations.

The practice of child labour in India or in any country of the world is an age old phenomenon. In pre-industrial, agricultural society of India, children worked as helpers and earners in hereditarily determined family occupations under the benign supervision of adult family members. The work place was an extension of the home and work was characterised by personal informal relationships. The task and technology of that work involved was simple and non-hazardous.[4]

Prevalence of child labour in the different periods has marked the history and presents a vivid account of child's sad plight. It is imperative to trace the evolution of the problem of child labour in different periods and steps taken by the then society, and government which could be pertinent for the elimination of child labour.

2. CHILD LABOUR IN ANCIENT INDIA

Since ancient time, child labour existed in the Indian society in one form or the other. But the pattern of existence was to some extent different in ancient India. Then, the child labourers were regarded as 'child slaves'. Slaves of tender ages, may be less than eight years of age were purchased by the masters for rendering the low and dishonourable work. Slavery (Dasya) was one of the most pernicious practices that had been in existence since ancient times which was an affront to humanity and human dignity. By this custom some class of human beings were to be the owners and masters of some less fortunate human beings, and treated them as chattels. The children were treated similarly. During this period children of slaves were born as slaves, lived as slaves and died also as slaves, unless their master was pleased to release them from the clutches of slavery. Then the law-givers except *Kautilya,* were silent on this point and did little to abolish this inhuman practice of keeping child slaves.[5] *Mlechhas* were not only backward, but also uncivilized.[6] During that period child slaves could be purchased or sold like commodities. *Mlechhas* may sell or mortgage their own offspring, but an Arya shall never be subjected to slavery. Selling or mortgaging an *Arya*, who is not born a slave, by a kinsman is punishable by fine.[7]

Further, if an *Arya* child was sold or pledged with some one, then all the parties to the contract, including witnesses were liable to be punished and the degree of punishment was to depend upon the status of the parties.[8] *Kautilya* considered child slavery as degrading to make children work on such jobs and hence, prohibited the purchase and sale of slave children.

However, a humanist approach towards children was also recognised in Indian culture. Thus, ancient Indian Jurisprudence emphasised that there could be no real gift or sale of one's child and unjustified parting with the child was unlawful. Kautilya prescribed that it is the duty of the village elders to ensure proper development of the infants. The collectivism of joint family life provided shade of protection to them and the ultimate protection of the child and its personality came from king because of the precept that king is fountain of strength to the weak.[9]

Kautilya realised that children were not physically fit to do ignoble work and rendering such work by them was considered in-human and degrading. So he strictly prohibited the purchase or sale of slave children of less than 8 years of age. [10] Although Kautilya was not in favour of employment of children, still they were employed in large scale in agriculture and domestic services. During Ancient India, children were exploited by their employers and the wages were paid to them was very low. There was no definite form of payment of wages. It was paid either in cash or kind, as such then barter system was practiced.

Labour legislation of the Dharmashastra shows that public conscience was alive to the fundamental inequality in distribution of wealth because these protective laws were themselves derived from ancient tradition. The economic status of the slaves, hired labourers and unskilled was worse.[11]

There was a harsh social reality of child's condemned life. Prior to the nineteenth century, there was a considered notion to treat child as human chattel. The child was human property of the parents and owed them total subservience. The parents enjoyed an absolute right to the child's services and earnings and full control over the child's person and property.[12]

Further, child labour was existing in ancient India in the form of slavery. Slavery was common in the past. The adult male and female slaves who worked in their masters houses and children born to them were owned by the masters. The children of such slaves and bonded families were also owned by the masters. The masters obviously did not rear them just for the sake of rearing. As soon as they grew up either they were sold to other slave owners or made to work in their masters houses and fields as menials and cowheards. In the primitive slave-holding stage of history the slaves were the chief source of labour and income. The process, however, continued till the advent of the industrial era, which freed from personal slavery to the feudal lords, but, enslaved them to capitalist means of production.[13]

Aryans arrived to India as invaders who introduced the disastrous '*varna*' system which provided the wherewithals. In the '*varna*' system the '*shudraas*' were given the lowest of the low status in social hierarchy. It is the men, women and their children who basically provided the 'upper' social exploiter strata with surplus product. So, one can infer from such past operation of social system that, the children of the '*shudraas*', slaves and other conquered groups were obviously made to work for their victorious masters and exploiters.[14]

Henry Maine, ancient scholar and jurist stated that, in the earliest period of history, the patriarchal system was in existence in all societies belonging to Indo-European stock, Romans and the Hindus. As such, the eldest male parent—the eldest ascendant was absolutely supreme in his household. He had complete sway over all the persons; male, female, children, their property, cattle, slaves, etc. The flocks, slaves and herds of the children were that of the father and law to them was parents word.[15]

To some extent, the obligations of these parents, in many cases, involved in working for the land lords on very low wages, which forced their children to work with the same land lords at their home as bonded labourers, because to repay· or minimise debts borrowed by their parents.[16] Children, however, helped their parents in household activities and family crafts. They learnt the skills by observing and participating in such activities.[17]

Thus, it was usual in the olden days to own children as slaves and bonded workers. The children born to slaves were treated by their owners as potential workers, and the children thus owned either worked and served their masters or were sold to others. Besides, children were most docile section of the workforce. The economic vulnerability of their parents and exploitative motive and profiteering greed of their masters who owned the means of production, together provided the most fertile ground for exploitation of children of deprived and dis-inherited workers.[18]

Thus, it is evident that, children were engaged in agricultural sector and exploited by land lords and child labour in ancient India was very common and could be witnessed in different occupations where they were engaged by the rich landlords to carryout activities directly or indirectly related to their agricultural sector.

3. CHILD LABOUR IN MEDIEVAL PERIOD

During the medieval period child labour was prevailing in India. Increasing pressure on land led to fragmentation of holdings and growing families had to look beyond personal cultivation for subsistenence. A class of landless labourers became wide spread in society. They had to work as bonded labourers for owners having large holdings. These labourers used their children to help in their economic activities and children were required to help them in rendering their traditional crafts or family occupations at the young age.[19] Later on in Moghal period, child had no freedom of his own, his condition was quite miserable, and his condition was no better than a slave. Ain-I-Akbari,

Bernier's Travels reveal that, children were frequently mortgaged and sold like movable properties[20] and this was a regular practice in that period. They were victims of haves and were always exploited to their selfish cause.

The labour market was composed of labourers and of slaves. Then slavery was rampant and had become the order of the day. The Decree of Akbar of 1594 A.D. ordains that, 'A father or a mother might, if, forced by hunger and extreme misery, sell their child and afterwards when they had the means to pay, might buy it back again from servitude.[21]

The Moghal Emperor, Akbar the Great, during his reign when canabilism was practiced near to his capital, suggested and granted permission to hypothecation of children, in the situation of famines and unavoidable crisis.[22]

In the province of Sylhat (Bengal), it was the custom and practice for people of those parts to make eunuch of some of their sons and give them to the Governor in lieu of payment of revenue (mal-wajibi). This custom had been adopted in the provinces and every year some children were ruined and cut-off from procreation. King Jahangir strictly prohibited and ordered for abolition of this abominable custom and traffic in young eunuch.[23]

The position of child labour during the period of Jahangir did not improve, as the supply of child labour was more than demand and the demand was restricted mainly to the capital. Even the workmen (labourers) and children were not allowed to follow any occupation other than their fathers. They were whipped if they raised their voice. The slavery was encouraged by the king and his Omrahs mainly for two reasons. First, slave met a real demand which was then existed and second the king enjoyed the monopoly of slaves. He made some money by trafficking in slaves and was himself royally served.[24]

From the above, it is clear that, child labour in Medieval India was quite rampant and rulers encouraged it with an intention to make only traffic in child slaves. The child labour was found in the form of child slavery and rulers did not made any sincere efforts to abolish this practice due to their selfish ends and there by exploited the children.

4. CHILD LABOUR IN MODERN ERA

Child labour became an important issue during British India. In Pre-capitalist societies and even in India, children were employing guild and trade occupations. In these societies their workplace was an extension of the home and work relationship was informal in nature. Children were allowed to work in family environment in a non-hazardous and easy work. Work was a central aspect of their socialization and training.[25] This conception, however underwent a dynamic change on the advent of capitalism in the industrialization during the 18th century and child labour began to be designated as a social problem.[26] The new economic forces unleashed by capitalism destroyed the family based economy, a large number of labour is displaced due to mechanisation of agriculture—the farmers were alienated from their home-based work place. They became wage-earning labourers. Extreme poverty created a situation and forced the child, who had to be introduced in the labour market. [27] Moreover, the uneven development of industrialization gave new turn to the history of mankind and brought a change in the overall socio-economic order. As a result of uneven development of industrialization, the family-based economy was destroyed and large number of people were converted into wage-earning labourers, consequently children were forced to earn wages not only for themselves but for their families as well. The work-place was separated from the family environment and industrialization exposed children to unhealthy environment. The working hours were quite long, i.e. from morning to night, but earnings were very low. This resulted ultimately to restrict the children's ability to grow and develop into a mentally and physically sound adult.[28] There was no sponsored scheme available to provide family allowances to enable poor parents to give adequate diet to their children which forced them to join industrial establishment. Giving education was not compulsory and it was ignored upto certain age limit of child which also makes children to accept occupations even at a tender age.[29]

Near the middle of 19th century, the mechanised large scale production came into existence. During that time State regulations were lacking over the conditions of employees in any industry. The employers were free to bargain with labour. Therefore, the labour in this country was exploited by the employers for their benefit. Many children were employed in cotton and jute mills and coal mines, they were even employed for underground work.[30] With the advent of factory organisation, some public attention was drawn towards the existing evils of child labour in spite of active opposition for the employers.

Then, first protective legislation for child labour was enacted in 1881. This was known as the Indian Factories Act, 1881. The Act provided some protection to the children preventing employment of children under 7 years of age in factories and also in two separate factories on same day, secondly, by limiting their working hours to 9 hours a day and thirdly, by making it compulsory to provide 4 holidays in a month and rest intervals to the children. Lastly, the Act made provisions for safety, such as fencing of dangerous machines. However, this Act, covered only factory employing 100 or more persons. The evils continued due to lack of enforcement machinery. There was no adequate coverage and no attention was given to the agriculture and unorganised sectors of industries consequently child labour continued as a means of cheap labour.

According to the recommendations of the Factory Commission, which was appointed by the Government of India in 1890, in the year 1891, the Indian Factories Act, was enacted with a view to increase the age of the working children. The lower age was extended from 7 to 9 years. The upper age also exceeded from 12 to 14 working hours were reduced from 9 to 7 hours per day. The children were not allowed to work at night. Inspite of the little reformations made for the protection of children, exploitation of the children increased because attention was not paid due to the deficient provisions of the Act, and also due to inadequate enforcing machinery.

The history of Modern era reveals that, condition of working children in mines was very bad. In 1901, about 5,000 children who were working were below 12 years, this perhaps made the government to bring Mines Act. In 1901 Mines Act was passed which prohibited the employment of child below 12 years of age in mines. The Chief Inspector of Mines was empowered by the Act, to prohibit the employment of children to certain place, if he was satisfied that the employment conditions were dangerous to children's health and safety. This defective position was continued because no improvement was made to the provisions of this Act till the next Mines Act.

Children were forced to work day and night in factories because the employers started to use electric power in their factories which had adversely affected the children due to the selfish attitude of the employers, as there was no improvement reported inside the factories. So, to overcome these situations and not to leave the matter in the hands of the employers, the Government appointed Freer Smith Committee in 1906 and a Factory Labour Commission in 1907 to make enquires on labour conditions in factories. Therefore, a new Factory Bill was introduced in 1909 which was enacted into law in 1911.

The significance of the Factory Act, 1911 lies in the fact that it reduced the working hours of the children in factories to 6 hours a day. It also prescribed that child workers should have in possession a certificate of age and fitness for employment. The children were not allowed to work at night, i.e. between 7 pm and 5.30 am and they were also prohibited in certain dangerous processes.

The history of child labour law found little improvement under the Indian Factories (Amendment) Act, 1922, which was enacted to give effect to the International Labour Organisation Convention on the minimum age for admission for children into employment, hours of work and night work of young persons and women. The scope of factory was extended to cover any premises where 20 or more persons were employed and mechanical power was used. The local governments were empowered to extend the provisions to any premises where 10 or more persons were employed. Under this Act, child was defined as a person who had not completed his 15 years of age. The children under 12 years were prohibited to enter into labour market. The children were required by this Act to have a medical certificate as to their age and physical fitness for the employment. Their working hours were fixed by this Act to 6 hours a day with an interval of half an hour to the children employed for more than five and half hours. The inspectors were empowered to enquire from children a certificate of re-examination for continuing work. This Act, also prohibited the employment of women and young person under 18 in certain processes. Some minor changes in this Act, were introduced by an amendment in 1923.

Even the then existing Mines Act was found inadequate in providing protection to child labourers. So a new Mines Act, 1923 was enacted which prescribed the hours of work according to International Labours Organisation Convention. This Act, fixed the working hours for the above ground work at 60 hours in a week, and for underground at 54 hours a week. It raised the minimum employment age from 12 to 13 years. Three years later, the Indian Factories Act, 1911 was further amended in 1926 for some administrative purpose. After 2 years the Mines Act, 1923 was amended for regulating the hours and working conditions in mines. Again in 1931, the Indian Factories Act of 1911 was further amended to bring certain minor changes for administrative purpose. This Act, imposed certain penalties on the parents and guardians for allowing their children to work in two separate factories on the same day. Provincial Governments were empowered under this Act, to make certain Regulations for taking precautions against fire. In the same-year Indian Ports (Amendment) Act, 1931 prescribed minimum age of 12 years for the employment of children in the handling of goods in ports. The year 1931, was also important in the Indian legal history because, in this year the Report of Royal Commission on Labour was published. This Commission was appointed under the compulsion of intensive agitation to improve the condition of labour, to investigate and report on the existing conditions of labour in industrial undertaking and plantations; and on the health and standard of living of the workers in British India. This Commission found that the children as young as five years were employed to work for 10 to 12 hours daily for very low wages. They were not provided with adequate meals, interval or weekly rest. Therefore, the Commission recommended that children under 15 should not be allowed to work as adult without a certificate of physical fitness. It also recommended the fixation of maximum working hours for children at 5 hours a day. It further recommended to limit the spread over for children at 7½ hours, and to prohibit work by children between 7 pm and 5.30 am.

To regulate the employment of plantation workers, the Government of India, enacted the Tea District Emigrant Labour Act, in 1933. There was a provision relating to children under the Act, which required that, no child under 16 shall be employed and immigrated to the district unless accompanied by his parent or adult relative on whom the child is dependent. In 1933, one more step was taken by the Government to prevent the exploitation of child when Children (Pledging of Labour) Act, 1933 was enacted on the recommendation of the Royal Commission on Labour. The main aim of this Act, was to eliminate the evils arising from the pledging of the labour of young children by their parents for a loan or an advance amount.

The Factory Act was completely modified by incorporating significant recommendations of Royal Commission on Labour. A new consolidated and amended Act was enacted in 1934, which came into effect from 1st January, 1935. This Act was meant to prohibit the employment of children under 12 years. The children between 15 and 17 were defined as adolescent. The maximum working hours for children between 12 and 15 years were 5 hours a day.

The Indian Mines (Amendment) Act, 1935 regulated the working conditions and hours of work in mines. This Amendment prohibited the employment of children under 15 years of age in mines. Further it laid down that, the adolescent, i.e. the young persons between 15 and 17 years could be employed in underground work as adult, on the production of a certificate of physical fitness issued by recognised medical authorities. The working hours for such workers, according to this amendment, were 10 hours a day and 54 hours a week for above ground work and 9 hours a day and 54 hours a week were fixed for underground work.

The Factories Act, was subsequently amended by Factories Amendment Act, 1935 and Repealing and Amending Act, 1937 which did not alter the general provisions of the Act. Way back in the year 1938, an important legislation concerning children, i.e. the employment of Children Act, 1938 was enacted in order to prevent the evils of employment of children in workshops which were not covered under Factories Act. The provisions of this Act, continues even now. This Act also prohibits the employment of children under 15 in Railway and port.[31] Subsequently by the amendment of above Act in 1939, the children under 12 are prohibited to work in workshops connected with beedi making, carpet weaving, cement manufacturing, cloth printing, dyeing and weaving, manufacture of matches, explosives, and fireworks, mica cutting and splitting shallac manufacture, soap manufacture, training and wood cleaning.[32]

During the modern era, i.e. before independence, much efforts had been made by bringing various legislations, along with their suitable amendments relating to the employment of children in various sections, but the same failed to achieve its goal for the elimination of the evils of child labour. The labour investigation committee, in its report in 1946 pointed out that, the main cause of this was the inadequacy of the inspecting staff to enforce the provisions of law.

Further, it was realised that, before independence, though discussion had taken place and opinions were sought about various aspects of child labour, nothing significant was done to abolish the system. It was on the contrary, argued that, banning of child labour could be detrimental to the interest of working children. For employers, the pet argument had been that, they were providing employment to the children, otherwise they could have starved and with them their families too.[33]

5. CHILD LABOUR AFTER INDEPENDENCE

Child labour is a common occurrence in India. Today their numbers exceed those of any other country. Independence ushered in a new era for children, the survival, development and protection of children has become a major goal of the Government and it fall either in the concurrent or in the state list. After Independence of India the first drastic step took by the Government was to bring an amendment to the Factories Act in 1948, which raised the minimum age for entering into employment in factories to 14 years. A new section was added which specifies that, the provisions of chapter, dealing with employment of young persons, are in addition to and in-derogation of the employment of Children Act, 1938.[34] The minimum age of admission to the employment in workshops was also raised from 12 to 14 by an amendment to the Employment of Children Act, 1938. Regarding the verification of child's age, in case of dispute between employer and inspector, provisions were introduced in 1949 under the Employment of Children Act.[35]

On 26th January, 1950, the people of India having constituted India, into a Sovereign, Democratic, Republic, adopted the Constitution on the same day, promised a new era based on freedom, equality, fraternity and justice for all citizens of the country. It recognised that political freedom by itself was not enough and therefore, gave priority to the achievement of "social and economic" justice. Children were given low priority during the pre-independence period in India. It was only after Independence that, the founding fathers of the nation became aware that employment of children is one of the manifestations of the pervading poverty in the country and realised the nation's responsibility towards children, their education, protection and development.[36] Thus, the framers of the Constitution deemed it necessary to make special provisions for the protection of working children. They are embodied under Article 15(3), Article 21, Article 24, Article 39(e) and (f) and Article 45. These constitutional mandates clearly focus its vision on preventing exploitation and protection of the children. The Constitution laid down various special protective measures for protection of children to prevent exploitation.[37]

The International Labour Organisation Convention relating to night work of young persons was responsible for an Amendment in 1951 in the Employment of Children Act, (1938) which prohibits the employment of children between 15 and 17 years at night in Railway and port. The employers were required to maintain register for children under 17 years.

The First Five Year Plan (1951-56) took a comprehensive review of resources and needs of children. Health, nutrition and education of children were identified as special areas of concern. In 1954, the Factories Act was further amended by the Factories (Amendment) Act, 1954 to prohibit the employment of adolescent under 17 at night.[38] Night means, under this Act, a period of 12 consecutive hours which include hours between 10 pm to 7 am. Again, the children under 15 are prohibited to be engaged or carried to sea to work in any capacity in any ship, except in certain specific cases by an Act known as Merchant Shipping Act which was passed in 1958.

The Government of India passed the Protection of Civil Rights Act, 1955 and ratified the International Labour Organisation Convention No. 5 of 1919 on minimum age of work in industry. In 1961, two important Acts were passed in order to provide a legal protection to children. One, the Motor Transport Workers Act, 1961, prohibits the employment of children under 15 in Motor Transport undertakings.[39] Second, the Apprentice Act, 1961, provides for regulating and controlling of trainees.[40]

The Second Five Year Plan (1956-61) aimed at stabilizing the child welfare system and Third Five Year Plan (1961-66) increased emphasis on intersectoral coordination of services for children. The Third Plan also recognised that the child was a human being with special needs.

An important step was taken in 1966, to protect children working in beedi industries by enacting Cigar Workers (Conditions of Employment) Act, 1966, which prohibits the employment of children under 14 in any industrial premises.[41] Young persons between 14 and 18 are also prohibited to work at night between 7 pm and 6 am.[42]

The Fourth Five Year Plan (1969-74) focussed on development of a package of basic minimum services for children. In the history of labour movement, Government of India had constituted First National Commission on Labour, in 1969, under the chairmanship of P.B. Gajendragadkar, J. to study and review the conditions of labour since 1947. The Commission found that, child labour persisted in varying degrees in the unorganised sectors such as small plantations, restaurants and hotels, cotton ginning, carpet weaving, stone breaking, brickiln, handicrafts and Road building. To regulate the labour of unorganised sector as observed, the Government of India passed a legislation known as Contract Labour (Regulation and Abolition) Act, 1970. This Act having a comprehensive coverage of all the establishments and contractors employing 20 or more workers in the whole of India. There was no specific provision relating to child work, so, many children could be seen in building the houses, roads, etc., under contractors.

In order to fulfil the mandate of the Indian constitution provided under Article 39(e) and (f), Government of India introduced and adopted the National Policy of a Children in 1974.[43] It sets out a policy frame work and measures aimed at providing adequate service and protection for children. The policy has recognised that, "the nation's children are supremely important asset and declared that the nation is responsible for their nurture and solicitude." So it is the duty of the state to look after the child with a view to ensuring full development of its personality. The policy has spelled out several measures to be adopted and priorities to be assigned to children's programmes with a focus on areas like child health, child nutrition. The policy has also provided for setting up of a National Children's Board to focus attention on child welfare and child development. It also emphasises the importance of free and compulsory education for all children upto the age of 14 years and to take measures for protecting children against neglect, cruelty and exploitation with regard to employment of children. The policy has laid down that "no child under 14 years shall be permitted to engage in any hazardous occupations or be made to undertake heavy work".

The Fifth Five Year Plan (1974-79) saw a shift in focus from child welfare child development where in emphasis was laid on further integration and coordination of services. In 1975, the Government ratified the International Labour Organisation Convention number 123 of 1965 relating to minimum age for underground work. In 1976, the Bonded Labour System (Abolition) Act was enacted. In response to the decision of the United Nation's declaring 1979 as the International Year of Child, the Ministry of Labour, Government of India, New Delhi had set-up a 16 member committee on Child labour under the chairmanship of Shri M.S. Gurupadaswamy in February 1979 to look into the causes leading to and the problems arising out of the employment of children in organised and unorganised sectors and requested the committee to (a) Examine the existing laws, their adequacy and implementation, and suggest corrective action to be taken to improve implementation, and to remedy defects; (b) Examine the dimensions of child labour, the occupations in which children are employed, etc., and suggest new area, where laws abolishing/regulating the employment of children can be introduced; and (c) Suggest welfare measures, training and other facilities which would be introduced to benefit children in employment.[44] But it can be seen that there was no reference to suggest ways and means of abolition/prohibiting child labour in all employments.

The Committee on Child Labour, after an in depth study of the problem of child labour in the country came to the finding that "Child labour involves the use of labour at its point of lowest productivity, hence it is an inefficient utilization of labour power. Child labour represents pre-mature expenditure rather than saving". It concluded: "the argument that employment of children increases the earnings of the family and keeps children away from mischief is misleading. It glosses over the fact that child labour, stunts their physical growth, hampers their intellectual development and by forcing them into the army of unskilled labourers or blind alley jobs condemns them to low wages all their lives. Child labour is economically unsound, psychologically disastrous and physically as well as morally dangerous and harmful.[45] It was also observed by the Gurupadaswamy Committee that "Labour becomes an absolute evil in the case of child, when he is required to work beyond his physical capacity, when hours of employment interfere with his education, recreation and rest, when the wages are not commensurate with the quantum of work done and when the occupation he is engaged endangers his health and safety.[46]

During the Sixth Five Year Plan (1980-85) the problem of working children and their welfare simultaneously received attention of the planners for the first time under the plan and appropriate programmes were undertaken to improve the health, nutrition and educational status of working children.

The Gurupadaswamy Committee submitted its report to the Government of India putting greater emphasis on all round development of a child including his education, health and regulation of the employment of children in the Indian industries. In response to the report of Gurupadaswamy Committee, in the year 1981, the

Government has set-up the Central Child Labour Advisory Board to review the implementation of existing laws concerning child labour.

The National Children's Fund 1979 was created during the International Year of the Child under the Charitable Endowment Fund Act 1980, which provides financial assistance to voluntary agencies for implementing programmes for the welfare of children including rehabilitation of destitute children.

The Seventh Five Year Plan (1985-90) was a milestone in the history of child labour. In view of the various recommendations made by Committees[47] and to prohibit the engagement of children in certain other employment and to achieve this goal and to achieve the mandate provided under Article 24, and Article 39(e) and (f), parliament enacted the Child Labour (Prohibition and Regulation) Act, 1986 which came into force on 23rd December, 1986.[48] Legislative history in India had made a long journey since 1981 by progressively extending legal protection to the working children. Provisions related to child labour and various enactments have concentrated mainly on aspects such as minimizing working hours, increasing minimum age and prohibition of employment of children in occupation and processes detrimental to the health and welfare of children of tender age.[49] The Employment of Children Act, 1938, which was the first enactment on child labour, was repealed by Child Labour (Prohibition and Regulation) Act, 1986.

The Government of India has formulated the National Policy on Child Labour in August 1987. The policy focuses mainly on three welfare aspects of the child, firstly, on the enforcement of child labour; secondly, on the families of child labourers to avail the benefits of welfare and development programmes made for this purpose; and thirdly, to take up projects in the areas of child labour concentration.[50] The basic goals of the policy were to rehabilitate the children withdrawn from employment and reduce the incidence of child labour in the areas of high concentration of child labour. It focuses on improving health condition for child labour and introducing anti-poverty programmes like IRDP and NREP.

In pursuance of National Child Labour Policy, 1987, Ministry of Labour, Government of India, implemented the National Child Labour Project in 1988 for the rehabilitation of child labour. The project was launched in areas of high concentration of child labour. At present more than 250 National Child Labour Projects (NCLP) are undertaken working in different districts, spread over in 20 states of India.

In the wake of the 1990 World Summit for Children, the Government of India adopted a National Plan of Action for Children in 1992.[51] Reports submitted by the Government on the issues, to some extent recorded some positive changes in the situation in India.

The Government of India ratified United Nations Convention on the Rights of the Child, 1989 on 11th December, 1992. The Convention on the Rights of the Child is the most complete statement of child rights ever made and an innovated documents and First U.N. Human Rights instrument which aims to create and balance between the rights of children and those of the parents/adults responsible for their survival, development and protection of children.

During the Eighth Five Year Plan (1992-97), on 15th August 1994, Government has announced programme to eliminate child labour in hazardous employment by 2000. Subsequently, the National Authority for Elimination of Child Labour constituted on 26th September 1999 to lay down policies and programmes for elimination of child labour. Further the enforcement of Child Labour (Prohibition and Regulation) Act, 1986 was strengthened. The Eighth Plan specifically recognised the girl child as an important target group. Another very important legislation, enacted by the Government of India in this plan period was the Persons with Disabilities (Equal Opportunities, Protection of Rights and Full Participation) Act, 1995 that came into force in February 1996.

6. CHILD LABOUR ON THE THRESHOLD OF NEW MILLENNIUM

At the dawn of the new millennium, Government of India brought various legislations and made amendments to the existing laws

Juvenile Justice (Care and Protection of Children) Act, 2000 was enacted by repealing Juvenile Justice Act, 1986. The Census of India 2001 has recorded its major statistical data on children and child labour. During the Tenth Five Year Plan (2002-07) emphasis was given on a Right based approach with regard to survival, development and protection of children. In the year 2002, the Indian Constitution through its (86th Amendment) Act, has made Right to Education a Fundamental Right to provide free and compulsory education to all children in the age group of 6-14 years. The important components of this Amendment are (1) Adding Article 21A in part-III [Fundamental Rights]; (2) Modifying Article 45 [Directive Principles of State Policy]; and (3) Adding a new clause (k) under Article 51A [Fundamental Duties) making the parent or Guardian responsible for providing opportunities for education to their children between 6 and 14 years.[52]

The Government of India has set-up The Second National Commission on Labour in 2002, which has recommended the repealing of the existing Child Labour (Prohibition and Regulation) Act, 1986 suggested a new model Act as Child Labour (Prohibition and Rehabilitation) Act, "To Prohibit Employment of children in all employments and to regulate employment of children where permitted".

The Government of India has adopted National Charter for Children 2003 on 9th February, 2004 to emphasise its commitment to children's right to survival, development and protection, and in order to see that no child remain hungry, illiterate or sick. The Government has formulated the National Common Minimum Programme (NCMP) 2004 to protect the rights of the children, strive for the elimination of child labour and to ensure facilities for schooling and extend special care to the girl child. The National Plan of Action for Children 2005 was introduced in the parliament to provide a road map for steps be taken for improvement in the lives of Indian Children.[53] The National Plan of Action stressed on child survival, development, protection and participation. The major initiatives undertaken by the Government of India was enactment of the Commission for Protection of Child Rights Act 2005[54] which provides for the constitution of a National Commission and State Commission for Protection of Child Rights and Children's Courts for providing speedy trial of offences against children or of violation of child rights and for matters connected therewith or incidental there to.

The Juvenile Justice Act, 2000 was modified by Juvenile Justice (Care and Protection of Children) Amendment Act, 2006 to protect the best interest of children and deal them with child friendly approach.

To address the situation of child labour, specially with regard to large scale exploitation and abuse of children employed in domestic work and hotels, etc. The Ministry of Labour, Government of India on 1st August, 2006 added certain occupations to the list of hazardous occupations; like domestic servants, workers in dhabas, restaurants, hotels, tea shops, resorts, spas or other recreational centers. This notification came into effect on 10th October, 2006.

During 11th Plan Period (2007 to 2012) the Ministry of Women and Child Development, Government of India considered 'Child Protection' is an essential component of the countries strategy to place "Development of all the child at the centre of the eleventh plan". So, Government proposed Integrated Child Protection Scheme-(ICPS) to address the issue of child protection and build a protective environment for children through Government-Civil Society partnership.

After a long debate and deliberation, very recently Government of India in order to respond to the directions issued by Supreme Court of India and to achieve the objectives of the constitution, Constitution (Eighty-sixth) Amendment Act, 2002, brought an enactment, 'The Right of Children to Free and Compulsory Education Act, 2009'[55] which provide for free and compulsory education to all the children for the age of six to fourteen years.

7. CONCLUSION

Right from the ancient period to present day, the problem of child labour has been in existence and perpetuated in one or the other form, due to several socio-economic and political factors. Prior to independence of India the menace of child labour was not subjected to effective legal regulation. However, in the post-independence era, due to the human rights orientation the child labour was considered abominable and various legal provisions have been made to abolish/regulate child labour. New Policies and new laws have been adopted to deal with child labour.

NOTES AND REFERENCES

1. Umesh Sahoo, "Child Labour in Surath Textile Industry," *Social Change*, Vol. 20, No. 3, September 1990, p. 20.
2. N. Mitra, "The Slave Children of Mandsour", Sunday 8, 19th December, 1980, pp. 10-17.
3. *Ibid.*
4. P. Ishwara Bhat, *Law and Social Transformation*, 1st edn., Lucknow: Eastern Book Co., 2009, p. 610.
5. J.C. Kulshresta, "*Child Labour in India*", 1978, p. 48.
6. Kautilya Arthashastra, Part III, Chapter 13, Prakaran 65,
7. M. Rama Jois, *Legal and Constitutional History of India*, Vol. 1, Bombay: N.M. Tripathi Pvt. Ltd., 1990, p. 307
8. *Supra* note 6.
9. *Supra* note 4, pp. 606-07.
10. *Supra* note 6.
11. Radhakrishna Chaudhary, *Economic History of Ancient India*, 1982, p. 146.
12. S.J. Stoljar, *Children, Parents and Guardians*, 4, INT'L, Ency. of Company Law, pp. 16-35.
13. M.H. Rehman, Kanta Rehman, S. Mehraj Begum, *Child Labour and Child Rights: A Compendium*, New Delhi: Manak Publications, 2002, p. 4.
14. *Ibid.*, pp. 4-5.
15. Dr. S.N. Dhyani, *Jurisprudence: A study of Indian Legal Theory*, 1985, p. 70.
16. See Lai Ah-Eng., "The Little Workers: A study of Child Labour in Small Scale Industries of Penang.", Vol. 13, No. 4, (1982) *Development and Change*, pp. 565-70.
17. Manju Gupta, "*Child Labour: A Harsh Reality*", Child Labour in India, 1987, p. 1.
18. *Supra* note 13, p. 6.
19. *Supra* note 17, p. 2.
20. Dr. Panth, *Economic History of India under the Moghals*, 1990, p. 64.
21. Al-Badayuni, *Murtakhabir-Tawarikh*, Vol. II, p. 404.
22. *Supra* note 11, p. 66.
23. P.L. Mehata, S.S. Jaswal, *Child Labour and the Law*, New Delhi: Deep and Deep Publications, 1990, p. 26.
24. *Supra* note 11, p. 131.
25. *Supra* note 23, p. 27.

26. Elias Mendelievitt, "Child Labour", Vol. 8, No. 5, ***International Labour Review***, 1979, p.212.
27. *Supra* note 17.
28. *Supra* note 11.
29. *Ibid.*
30. *Supra* note 5, p. 1.
31. Section 3(i), The Employment of Children Act, 1938.
32. *Ibid.*, Section 3(iii).
33. *Supra* note 13, p. 5.
34. Section 68 of the Indian Factories Act, 1948.
35. *Ibid.*, Section 70(2).
36. Helen R. Sekhar, *Child Labour Legislation in India: A Study in Retrospect and Prospect*, Noida: V.V. Giri National Labour Institute, 1997, pp. 1-2.
37. See Chapter VIII infra.
38. Section 70 of Factories Act. 1948.
39. Section 21, Motor Transport Worker's Act, 1961.
40. Preamble to the Apprentices Act, 1961.
41. Section 2(b), The Beedi & Cigar Workers (Conditions of Employment) Act, 1966.
42. *Ibid.*, Section 25.
43. Resolution Number 1-14/74-CDD dated August 22, 1974.
44. See the Government of India, Report of the Committee on Child Labour, 1979, p. 55.
45. See the Report of the Committee on Child Labour (Gurupadaswamy Committee Report, 1979) at p. 10, Thomas Paul, "Child Labour-Prohibition V. Abolition: Untangling The Constitutional Tangle", Vol. 50, No. 2, April-June (2008), ***Journal of Indian Law Institute***, pp. 146-47 and also see P. Ishwara Bhatt, *Law & Social Transformation in India*, 1st edn., Lucknow: Eastern Book Company, 2009, p. 610.
46. *Ibid.*, p. 9.
47. The National Commission on Labour, Gurupadaswamy Committee on Child Labour, 1979.
48. Published in the Gazette of India, Extraordinary Part-II, Section–I, dated 23.12.1986, pp. 1-9.
49. Awards Digest, Vol.XX, Nos. 7-12, *Journal of Labour Legislation*, *see* also Asha Bajpai, *Child Rights in India*, New Delhi: Oxford University, 2009, p. 163.
50. Suresh Kumar Sharma, "Child Labour: Problems and Prospects", ***Cochin University Law Review***, 1999, p. 263.
51. Ministry of Human Resource Development, Government of India, New Delhi, 1992.
52. Praveen Jha, Pooja Parvathi, "Right to Education Act, 2001: Critical Gaps and Challenges", Vol. XLV, No. 13, March-April (2010), *Economic and Political Weekly*, p. 21.
53. National Plan of Action for Children, 2005, Government of India, Ministry of Human Resource Development, Dept. of Women and Child Development, New Delhi, 2005.
54. Received the Assent of the President on 20th January, 2006 and Published in Official Gazette of India, Extra., Part-II, S. 1 (Central Act, No. 4 of 2006) came into force w.e.f. 15.2.2007.
55. (Central Act N. 35 of 2000) received the Assent of the President on 26th August, 2009 came into force w.e.f. 01.04.2010.

5

Concept of Child Labour and Factors Leading to Child Labour

I. INTRODUCTION

Children are the most tender, gentle and fragile one and needs to be handled and protected with immense care and delicacy. The welfare of the entire community, its growth and development depends on the health, strength and well-being of its children. The prosperity and development of any country would certainly depend upon 'human development' or the well-being of its people in general and children in particular, than the development of their military or economic strength or the splendour of their capital cities and public buildings. In order to protect and secure human Rights of the children, Universal Declaration of Human Rights, adopted way back in 1948, had proclaimed that childhood was entitled to special care and protection. The UN Convention on the Rights of the child, adopted in 1989, proclaims in Article 6, that every child has the inherent right to life and that the state parties shall ensure to the maximum extent possible the survival and development of the child.

Article 32 of the Convention on the Rights of the Child mandates that the State parties to recognise the right of the child to be protected from economic exploitation and from performing any work that is likely to be hazardous or to interfere with the child's education, or to be harmful to the child's health or physical, mental, spiritual, moral or social development. The Government of India has ratified United Nations Convention on the Rights of the Child in December 1992 and undertakes to initiate measures to progressively implement the provisions of Article 32. Various Constitutional provisions, hundreds of legislations, policies and programmes have been brought into protect the "best interest" of children.

Since centuries child labour is prevailing across the World and it is a Universal problem, its practice in any society is violation of human rights as it is barbarous, illogical, inhuman and degrading the ethos of the children. Thus the child labour is not only a social evil but it is a stigma on the childhood and exploitation of the children.

2. MEANING OF THE CHILD LABOUR

Sri V.V. Giri, former President of India characterises that, child labour is an "economic practice" and "social evil".[1] Firstly, 'economic practice' signifies employment of Children in gainful occupations with a view to adding to the total income of the family. Secondly, 'social evil' refers to, character of the jobs in which children are engaged, the danger to which they are exposed and the opportunities of development of which they have been denied. In the present situation children are denied even their basic and fundamental needs. Children are innocent, vulnerable and dependent, and they are unable to understand their rights as such, during their formative age they are prone to exploitation. Thus, child labour has become a hard reality and global phenomena. The two main approaches which define child labour are: (1) Any labour force activity by children below a stipulated minimum age, and (2) Any work, economic or not, that is injurious to health, safety and development of children.

Kulashresta says that the 'Child Labour' is at times used as a synonym for 'employed child' or 'working child' whereas Gray Rodgers and Gay standing have classified[2] child labour into four categories which include: (1) Domestic work; (2) Non-domestic work and non-monetary work; (3) Bonded Labour; (4) Wage Labour.[3] Child Labour is done by any working child who is under age specified by the law. The word, 'work' means full time commercial work to sustain self or add to the family income. Child labour is a hazard to a child's mental, physical, social, educational, emotional and spiritual development. Broadly any child who is employed in activities to feed self and family is being subjected to "child labour".[4]

Technically the term 'child labour' is used for children occupied in profitable activities, whether industrial or non-industrial. It is especially applicable for activities which are detrimental to their physical, psychological, emotional, social and moral developmental needs. It has been researched and proved that the brain of a child develops till the age of ten, muscles till the age of seventeen and his lungs till the age of fourteen. To be more specific, any activity which acts as a hazard for the natural growth and enhancement of these vital organs, can be considered harmful for natural human growth and developments and termed—'child labour'.[5]

According to Committee on Child Labour, "Child labour" broadly defined as that segment of child population in work either paid or unpaid.[6] The term child labour is defined as the work which deprives children of their childhood, their potential and their dignity, and that which is harmful to their physical and mental development.[7]

Homer Folks, the Chairman of the United Nations Child Labour Committee, defined child labour as "any work by children that interferes with full physical development and their opportunities for a desirable minimum level of education of their needed recreation".[8]

According to ILO's comprehensive definition of child labour, "Child Labour includes children prematurely leading adult lives, working long hours for low wages under conditions damaging to their health and to their physical and mental development, sometimes separated from their families, frequently deprived of meaningful education and training opportunities that could open up for them a better future".[9]

In Encyclopaedia of Social Sciences (1959) Child labour has been defined, "When the business of wage earning or of participation in itself or family support conflicts directly or indirectly with the business of growth and education, the result is child labour. The function of work in childhood is primarily developmental and not economic.[10] Children's work, then, as a social good, is the direct, antithesis of child labour as a social evil.[11]

The 'Operation Research Group' based in Baroda—India, defines a child labour that "A Working Child is one who was enumerated during the survey as a child falling within the five to fifteen age bracket and who is at remunerative work, may be paid or unpaid, and busy in any hours of a day within or outside family".[12]

Article 24 of the Constitution accepting the fact of prevalent child labour in India provides that "no child below the age of fourteen years shall be employed in work in any factory or mine or engaged in any other hazardous employment".

The Committee on Child Labour provides, "child labour involves the use of labour at its points of lowest productivity; hence it is an inefficient utilisation of labour power. Child labour represents premature expenditure rather than saving". It concludes that "the argument that employment of children increases the earning of the family and keeps children away from children is misleading. It glosses over the fact that child labour stunts their physical growth, hampers their intellectual development and by forcing them into the army of unskilled labourers or blind alley job condemns them to low wages of their lives...Child labour is economically unsound, psychologically disastrous and physically as well as morally dangerous and harmful".[13]

"Child Labour" according to an elected representative of the people, is no longer a medium of economic exploitation; it is necessitated by economic compulsions of the parents and in many cases that of the child himself. They work because they must, for their own survival and that of their families. Therefore, any attempt through legislation will not be successful.[14]

3. THE CONCEPT OF CHILD LABOUR

The concept of child labour is complex in its nature. The word 'child labour' is a combination of two components, i.e. 'child' in terms of his chronological age, and 'labour' in terms of its nature, quantum and income generating capacity.[15]

The word 'labour' is a controversial concept to define, especially in the context of child labour, child work and child labour often used synonymously. However, all work is not bad for children because some light work, properly structured and regulated, is not child labour. This implies that work which does not detract from other essential activities for children such as leisure, play and education are not child labour. 'Child labour', therefore, is the work which involves some degree of exploitation namely, physical, mental, economic and social and therefore, impairs the health and development of children.[16] It is pointless to try and distinguish between child labour and child work or between hazardous and non-hazardous employment. Work that is seemingly non-hazardous for adults becomes hazardous for children because they have no negotiating power.[17] With regard to the conceptual and definitional problems concerning child labour there are two schools of thought. According to the first school known as abolitionist school, education should be made a fundamental human right of every child in 5-14 age group, and any child who is out of school should be treated as a potential working child. They feel that elimination of child labour and attainment of compulsory primary education are two sides of the same coin and one cannot be achieved without achieving the other. According to them, the distinction between hazardous and non-hazardous work is immaterial.[18] According to the second school known as reformist school, child labour is a 'harsh reality', which means, given the socio-economic conditions of India (like poverty, unemployment and illiteracy) it is impossible to root out the problem of child labour altogether. They feel that elimination of child labour should be viewed as a long-term goal to be achieved progressively. Hence, they advocate a dual approach of prohibition of child labour in hazardous work and regulation of it in non-hazardous work.[19]

4. FORMS OF CHILD LABOUR

Children work in three sectors of the economy:[20]

(a) The Agrarian Sector

The agrarian sector in India is characterised by poverty, illiteracy, unemployment, highly skewed distribution of land-ownership, traditional modes of production, prevalence of old customs and traditions, system of usury, etc. Several forms of child labour such as invisible, migrant, bonded, etc. emerge from this sector, which encompasses such time-consuming activities for boys as looking after animals, gathering wood and fodder, sowing and reaping, protecting fields from pests, weeding, etc. For girls, the activities are milking animals, cooking, and looking after younger children. The rural child is working child and work is a fundamental part of his or her existence, irrespective of whether it is non-monetary. It also, therefore, means that education is a casualty for such a child.

(b) Industrial Sector

Industrial sector is a growing level of urbanisation as a result of migration from rural to urban areas and from smaller towns to bigger cities, where industries are being set-up. Another feature is the dispersal of industries into family-based units. This again causes the emergence of various forms of child labour, such as invisible, wage-based child labour working under conditions of acute exploitation in the industries, children of marginalised families working as self-employed children or under-wage employment in the services sector.

(c) Service Sector

The services sector actually has a certain overlap with the industrial sector. A majority of children in this sector are self-employed because its very nature provides relief from direct supervision. It also provides autonomy and freedom of control over resources. Such children are found to be working both in the urban as well as rural areas. In this sector, child labour can take such forms as invisible, self-employed or under wage-based employment, with children changing jobs at regular intervals. This is particularly true in urban areas.

The UNICEF has classified child work into three different categories:[21]

(i) Within family in which children are engaged without pay in domestic/household tasks, agricultural/pastoral work, handicrafts/cottage industries, etc.

(ii) With the family, but outside the home in which children do agricultural/pastoral work which consists of (seasonal/full time) migrant labour, local agricultural work, domestic service, construction work and informal occupations, e.g., laundry/recycling of waste—employed by others and self-employed.

(iii) Outside the family in which children are employed by others in bonded work, apprenticeship, skilled trades (carpet, embroidery, brass/copper work), industrial/unskilled occupations/mines, domestic work, commercial work in shops and restaurants, begging, prostitution and pornography.

Each Form of child labour has its own peculiar features, which are in the forms of domestic labour, agriculture labour, migrant labour, bonded labour, wage-based labour, self-employed labour and invisible labour.

4.1. Elements of Child Labour

Child labour involves one or more of the following elements:[22] (1) Work by very young children, (2) Long hours of work on a regular full-time basis, (3) Hazardous working conditions (Physically and mentally), (4) No or insufficient access, attendance or progress in school, (5) Abusive treatment by the employer, and (6) Work in slave like arrangements (bonded labour).

5. FACTORS LEADING TO CHILD LABOUR

The Indian problem of child labour is not a result of any single isolated factor. It is a multi-dimensional problem that involves various reasons contributing to it in a variety of ways. Some of the factors contributing and responsible for prevalence and perpetuation of child labour are: continued poverty, illiteracy and ignorance of poor parents, population explosion—large family size, low family income, the tradition of making children learn the family skill, lack of political will and weak/tardy enforcement of laws, un-employment/under-employment, migration, absence of provision for universal compulsory primary education, etc.[23] Thus, the problem of child labour is acute and multi-dimensional. The Government of India has conceded the existence of child labour as "harsh reality".[24] The debate about whether child labour should be banned or regulated is not new. It surfaced in 1985, when the Government of India claimed that 'child labour was a harsh reality' and found it more prudent to regulate rather than ban it; the Child Labour (Prohibition and Regulation) Act, 1986—an Act without teeth and innumerable loopholes—was passed.[25]

Child labour has been in existence since time immemorial in one form or the other. In pre-industrial era children used to help their parents in family work, farm operations or family occupations. Even in the post-industrial era, it was existing on account of its cheapness and profitability of its employment.[26] P.A. Sangma, former Lok Sabha Speaker, says 'child labour practice was only a symptom of a more deep-seated disease of a complex nature'. Across the globe, to a less or greater degree, visible or invisible, admittedly or otherwise child labour exists.[27]

Child labour is a complex socio-economic and universal phenomenon. It is the need of the hour to find out the causative factors leading to child labour in a scientific, rationalist, and pragmatic approach. It has been accepted that the intrinsic nature of the worst form of child labour is bearing on socio-economic and other multiple causes. It is a mixture, of both illiteracy and poverty. The problem of child labour is the symptom of the disease which is widespread due to exploitative structure, lopsided development, iniquitous resource ownership with its co-relates of large scale of unemployment and abject poverty among the countries. The existing international economic order perpetuates this 'harsh reality' because powerful multi-national corporations operate and use child labour directly or indirectly, to maximise profits and minimise costs. The poor third world countries faced with acute foreign exchange crisis permit and encourage export of goods using cheap and vulnerable child labour in the hope of improving their foreign exchange reserves and balance of payments crisis. Indian carpet industry, lock industry, gem and precious metals, etc. are examples. It is true that extreme poverty and employment force the poor to send their children to work as a part of their survival strategy. Greed for profit and desperate competition for markets in the developed world encourage employers to use child labour for economic advantage. Lack of firm commitment to the goal of eradication of child labour results in a haphazard and ineffective intervention from the government which is quite conducive to the interest of M.N.G. and other vested interests.[28]

There are various socio-economic and cultural factors which force children into work and these factors can be broadly classified into supply side factors, refer to the conditions under which families are engaging children in work, i.e. families force them to send their children for work. Demand side factors refer to the preference of employers for employing children.

5.1. Poverty.

Poverty is the womb of all illness. In addition, poverty is a double edged weapon in that the poor victim of illness loses his daily winning capacity as well making him/her poorer at the end of the day.[29]

Poverty as an extreme human condition has always evoked immense social interest.[30] Poverty is a single major cause of child labour; this is a major contributing factor and has many dimensions. The Institution of Public opinion conducted a survey in 1969, which showed that 41.2 percent of Indian population was under poverty line. Half of these belonged to the Scheduled Caste and Tribes. In village a vast majority of agriculture labour belongs to these communities.[31]

A Seminar on the subject organised by National Institute of Public Co-operation and Child Development, New Delhi on November 25 to 28, 1975 also came to the conclusion that, millions of families were below poverty line and they had to deploy their children in the labour market in order to eke out a bare subsistence.[32]

The phenomenon of child labour clearly demonstrates vicious cycle of poverty and unemployment. Poverty is the main reason for which the children are forced to work. Their income is necessary for the survival of their family members and also of themselves.[33] Poverty is most often supplemented by other socio-economic factors to expose the child to manual jobs.

Millions of people in this country live in a state of abject poverty, without food, shelter, employment, health care and education. According to a UN Report, "1/5th of the population in a developing country, like ours, are hungry every night, 1/4th do not have access to basic amenities like drinking water; and 1/3rd live in a acute poverty".[34] According to the Human Development Report, 2005, every hour 1200 children die, one crore children every year do not live to see their 5th birthday.[35]

Another important factor for the perpetuation of child labour is the rising rate of dropouts from school of children of the poor families. The high rate of dropouts is invariably a consequence of poverty. In most places, schools are situated in very remote areas and are not accessible to a sizable population. There was lack of infrastructure facilities like building, equipments, furnitures, teachers, staff, drinking water, toilets, etc. Pathetic conditions in school education system hold little attraction for children. In rural areas schools and classes do not run regularly due to the absence of teachers frequently. Schooling of children becomes burdensome for the poor families and economically expensive and more so schooling the children deprives them of the income that accrues from child labour. The poverty alleviation programmes launched by Government through NGO's are not properly implemented and its benefits do not reach the real, needy and deserving sections of the society, consequently children are economically exploited.

Most traditional families believe that a child is born to them to earn more for family. The child is considered as just another source of income and traditional business families in fact put the child into the business rather than send them to school. Under the protext of training them, they make them work long hours, sometimes resorting to physical torture in case the child makes mistakes.

Rampant unemployment and underemployment of parents who force their wards to some odd jobs to supplement the meagre income. Thus, whenever the family is in need to fulfil its basic needs like food, clothing and shelter, it is inevitable for the members and compelled to support the family income, by pressing the children to work and earn wages. The rural landless poor and urban destitutes send their boys and girls for wage earning.

There is another argument which advocates that, poverty is a cause but often "perceived poverty" is a cause for child labour. If the poverty was the only cause of child labour all children from poor families would have been working as child labour. Incidence of child labour is rare than the incidence of poverty. Poverty and child labour thus always begets each other and tend to reinforce. Thus, child labour is not only an economic compulsion of poor families, it is also the consequences of extreme social and economic exploitation.[36] Poverty of the households may be due to several factors:

(a) Inadequate income of the family,
(b) Unemployed adults;
(c) Absence of scheme for family allowances; and
(d) Large family, etc.

Poverty and lack of education are the two primary reasons for the ever growing social malice of child labour. Parents in the poverty zone give birth to money-making machines, and not children. They earn more on the streets from begging. Then as they grow they make beggars and eventually send them to employers. Thus children living in poverty are deprived of many of their rights: survival, health and nutrition, education participation and protection from harm, exploitation and discrimination. Hence, poverty deprives children of their rights.[37]

Those who are at the bottom of poverty line are supposed be in abject poverty and the economists and planners often plead for a determined attack to reduce their misery. Often in their enthusiasm to make Five Year Plans attractive, the planners fail to distinguish between schemes realistic radicalism and political opportunitism.[38]

5.2. Illiteracy and Ignorance

Illiteracy and ignorance is the bane for the society. Even after 60 years of Independence, Indian people are continued to lead a dark life. As far as literacy is concerned, India is lowest ranked in the world. As per 1991 Census literacy rate is 52% and as per 2001 Census it is 64.8%, —Male Population is 336,533,716—75.3%, Female Population is 224,154,081—53.7% and Rural literacy is 58.7% and Urban literacy it is 79.9%. Kerala State records highest literacy rate of 90.9% and Bihar records lowest literacy of 47%.

The higher rate of illiteracy shows the ignorance of parents, so they push their children to work force which is a supply factor and contributory cause for child labour. Parents do not think better future of their wards. Especially rural/migrated parents, tribal and people staying in slum areas do not understand their responsibilities and hence children are deprived of their right to education and development.

There is a very close nexus between child labour and illiteracy and they go hand in hand and each one supports the other. Same studies have revealed that most of the child labourers are either total illiterate or partial illiterate and their parents are illiterate. No study has ever found a child labour coming from an educated family. Greed for money, and gross ignorance on the part of the parents in not sending their children to school is a sad commentary and condemnable. Adam predicted that, 'Child labourers today will be the paupers tomorrow, they are the boys and girls who will grow up without either formal schooling or knowledge of trade, sooner or later their youthful energies exhausted, they will become dull stiffless and driftless.[39] Thus, illiteracy and ignorance of the parents and their attitudes towards educating the child is an important factor contributing to child labour.

Due to ignorance, parents of working children often have little faith in the quality of education available to them and may perceive little use in schooling where prospects of better paid employment after several years of education remains uncertain.[40]

Impoverished and illiterate parents are of the view that more children means more hands to work to bring extra money. Due to illiteracy of the parents/guardians the importance education has not yet been realised and appreciated by them. Parents are also ignorant about the facilities and assistance providing to children by the Government for helping them to acquire free education in child labour school funded under National Child Labour Project and UNICEF. Illiterate and ignorant parents do not understand the need for wholesome proper physical, cognitive and emotional development of their child. They are themselves uneducated and unexposed, so they don't realize the importance of education for their children.

Due to high degree of illiteracy and ignorance of the parents, the children are deprived of getting proper counselling for building up their future career and at the same time of economic necessity, the children move into the job market to eke out their subsistence.[41]

5.3. Population Explosion and Large Family Size

In a developing country like ours, every thing is regulated by population. Population explosion is an important and major factor for the problem of child labour. Parents due to their ignorance believed that children are God Gifted, great human resource and continued to go on increasing the family size is a misconception and they understand that more children means more income, they generate. Consequently, large family size is burdensome and liability for them especially for poor, to tribal backward families. These people are ignorant to provide basic resource like better quality of life, education, health care facilities, etc. and progressive development of their children has been a myth for them.

There is no effective family planning programme in India and no check on birth control which leads to poverty and parents due to poverty are forced to send their children to work and thereby parents cannot fulfil needs and aspiration of children and some children run away from house, some will become delinquent and develop bad habits.

Thus, parents are forced to send little children to hazardous job for reasons of survival, even when they know it is wrong. Monetary constraints and the need for food, shelter and clothing drives their children into the trap of premature labour. Over population in some regions creates paucity of resources. When there are limited means and more mouths to feed, children are driven to commercial activities not provided by their development needs.[42]

Population Statistics

According to 1971 Census, population of India was 548 million and in 2001 it was 1028.70 million. By the turn of 2016 the population is expected to reach 1264 million. Such a massive increase in numbers will affect economic development and require massive inputs for social services, civic amenities and infrastructure development.

Child population records 398,306,000 and interpretation of 2001 Census figures of the National Labour Institute indicate that, out of 203 million children between the ages of 5 and 14, 116 million are in schools, 12.6 million are in fulltime employment and the status of 74 million is unknown. Most, if not all, of the 87 million, not in school, do house work on family farms, work along side their parents as paid agriculture labourers, work as domestic servants, or are otherwise employed.[43]

5.4. The Tradition of Making Children Learn Family Skills

Most traditional families believe that a child is born to them to earn more for the family. The child is just another source of income and traditional business families in fact put the child into business rather than send them to school. Under the pretext of training them, they make them work for hours, sometimes resorting to physical torture in case child makes mistakes.

There is a myth that child labour is necessary to preserve traditional arts and crafts. Children bonded to families or who are hired labour are never taught the actual craft. Learning of a particular art or craft by children within their families, as part of their socialization, should be integrated with their education. Children should not be sacrificed at the altar of preserving traditional art.[44] There is another argument which advocates that work equips the children with skills for the future is a contributory factor to child labour.

The tasks allotted to child labour are simple and repetitive such as labelling, filing, rolling, fetching and carrying. "Skill" is misnomer when applied to the back breaking toil and drudgery children engage in. The hard, physical labour, exposure to the elements like dust, toxic, fumes and chemical solutions damage children's health irrevocably, shortening their life span and impairing their development. Research shows that 95% of the children do not continue in the same jobs when they are either adolesent or adult. Worse many of the sectors employing child labour forcefully eject such individuals who have crossed their age of childhood.[45]

The proviso annexed to Sec. 3 of Child Labour (Prohibition and Regulation) Act, 1986 is often and invariably misused, which keep the occupation, work or process that is carried on by the occupier with the aid of the family out of the preview of the Act. The intention of the Act is to exempt a family enterprise in which all or several of the members of the family are involved. Thus, proviso is abused by employing children in respect of families and work experience acquired by children.[46]

5.5. Unemployment and Underemployment

Child labour is as much the cause as consequence of adult unemployment and underemployment. It supplements and buttresses the family income. Child labour is not only a subsidy to industries but a direct inducement for payment of low wages to adult workers. The entrance of the children into the labour market reduces the opportunities of employment for the adult and lowers the bargaining power of adult workers. Child labour involves the use of labour as its point of lowest productivity. Hence, it is an insufficient utilisation of labour force. The argument that employment of children increases the earnings of the family and keeps children away from mischief is misleading. Infact, the practice of child labour deprives children of educational opportunities, minimises their chances for vocational training, affects their physical growth, hampers their intellectual development.[47]

The employment of children adversely affects not only the employment of opportunities of others, forcing many to remain jobless in the present age but also considerably lowers the rates of their wages. The Report of Committee on Child Labour accepted the above caption. It at once supplements and buttresses the family income,[48] child labour increases the unemployment among the adults and reduces their income and on the other hand the unemployment and low wages of adults force them to put their children to work in order to boost the family income. Thus, child labour simultaneously increases and reduces the family income, but in reality it reduces rather increases that income. Thus, child labour is both a cause and consequence of both adult unemployment and underemployment. Some studies and experts observed that, if children are eliminated from the labour market in India, employment opportunities for atleast 20 million adult unemployed workers would be increased.[49]

5.6. Weak and Tardy Enforcement of the Child-related (Child Labour) Legislation

Although plethora of legislations have been enacted for prohibition of child labour, but due to certain lacunae, shortcomings and week and defective enforcement mechanisms, the practice of child labour is on increasing trend. The Child Labour (Prohibition and Regulation) Act is intended to regulate child labour rather abolish. Proviso of Sec. 3 is abused by the employers/vested interests. Various studies show that enforcement of child labour legislation faces a number of critical problems.

The Child Labour (Prohibition and Regulation) Act is a social legislation, benefiting and protecting the core rights of children and for obvious reasons, social legislations are difficult to enforce and implications of enforcement are deep rooted and complex. The enforcement agencies do not understand the spirit of the law for which it is enacted. Neither the employers of child labour nor the enforcers, nor the parents understand child labour as an undesirable thing. Since the practice of child labour is interlinked with unorganized sector, its enforcement is difficult one, as the units do not possess licence and registrations, employers will not maintain records of child workers and consequently enforcers cannot prosecute the employers. Inspectors[50] are not trained, conversant with child psychology and problems. So their insensitive approach leads to increase of child labour cases.

Prosecution of cases as against the employers are very less. Even if they are prosecuted Inspectors are unable to produce evidence and courts rely on production of evidence. Thus, employers taking the benefit of doubt in majority of cases go scoot free. There is no co-ordination between Labour Department and prosecution and Judiciary. Due to the human weakness, Inspectors could be properly managed by the employers. Many employers, especially from small units, are often let-off because; they claim that the children were their family members. The proviso to Sec. 3 of Child Labour (Prohibition and Regulation) Act helps them in this claim. In larger units, the employers generally claim that the children had come to meet their parents or to provide lunch to their parents and were not working there.[51] Thus, there is no evidence that the child was working in the premises and courts let-off the employers. Violation of this legislation is not a cognizable offence and burden of proof rests on the prosecution, hence it is difficult to prove.

There is a strong reason for failure of prosecution due to lack of evidence relating to the age of the child. The child's age has to be proved in the courts. Usually, in rural places the children do not have a birth certificates[52] and some schools/institutions will issue a fake/bogus certificates showing upper age of the child in order to escape from prosecution. Therefore, there is no reliable evidence to prove the age of the child. In such cases Inspectors are required to get the child medically examined at the cost of the employer. Due to strict compliance of this procedure, there is a delay in filing of cases.

In very few cases, courts convict the employer just by imposing a fine, but in very rare case convict the employer by imprisonment. Thus, courts tend to pass lighter sentences in child labour matters. This is also due to the insensitivity of the Judiciary. The implementation of child labour legislation is entrusted to Inspectors of Factories/Labour Department. These Inspectors are over burden and enforcement of the Child Labour (Prohibition and Regulation) Act is not their priority/ agenda. The reasons best known commonly, there is rampant corruption in the enforcement machinery. Caste factor and class bias are also negative indicators for non-prosecution of employer. No accountability upon the enforcers nor they have punished under law. Due to absence of checks and balances, there is every reason for encouragement and sustenance of child labour.

Another reason for non-availability of evidence and failure of prosecution is that Inspectors are required to draw panchanama (mahazar) for prosecution of employer and instructed to get two witnesses preferably adjoining owners of shops who may not be willing to stand as witness and they do not want to spoil their cordial relation with the neighbouring employers and even when Inspectors force them to sign as witness, they simply sign and subsequently become hostile and in some cases stranger witnesses will not respond for the prosecution of employers.

Failure to provide required infrastructure to the enforcement people also promotes for continuation of child labour. Insufficient strength of Inspectors and not providing training/orientation for Inspectors in order to sensitise them to the complex problem of child labour leads to increase of child labour. Even concern department fail to provide stationeries, hand books, course materials and support and security, etc. to the enforcers.

5.7. Migration and Child Labour

There is a close nexus between migration and child labour and migration is one of the major contributory factors to child labour. Migration refers to the movement of workers from one place to another. There are various factors responsible for migration of parents and children. Again poverty, large family size, with low family income and non-availability of work in the village compels the parents to migrate to urban areas. The adverse financial position of parents compels them to borrow from the village moneylender who charges high rate of interest on the loans advanced to the villagers and a pressure from the side of moneylender to repay the debts is likely to compels the parents to send their children to earn, since no work is available in the villages.

Due to liberalisation, privatisation and globalisation and scientific, technological advancement and development in industries, Village handicrafts no longer continued and attraction of city life and comparatively higher income opportunities are reasons for migration of parents to cities. Consequently, parents due to the economic compulsion induce their children to work at the nearest area of the city or send them to sub-urban places. Debts and financial liabilities, economic compulsion and to seek better employment, to learn technical work and no work at the place of origin were the factors leading to migration and migrant children work and earn concentrating mainly on constructions and in service sectors, domestic works, etc. and some child labourers work as, hawkers, shoeshine boys, balloon sellers, flower vendors and some migrant children are beggars, ragpickers, etc. When the family head or others move to urban cities, such parents make with their children and they face the problem of lack of shelter, hunger, unemployment, etc. which forces the children to join the labour force. So migration is both push as well as pull factor for child labour

5.8. Employer's Preference for Child Labour

It is one of the demand factors for causation and perpetuation of child labour. The most important objective of the employer is to earn more profit on limited expenditure. Employer perfectly knows that child labour is cheap and adult labour is expensive. Hence he prefers to employ child labour rather than adults by payment of low/minimum wages and displacing the adults from labour market. He prefers to employ child labour as children are innocent, docile, disciplined and sincere and don't have any union and cannot question the authority of employer.

Employer knows that economic compulsion of the families of having extreme poverty. They watch out for exploiting the parental economic compulsion and knows that children of backward families are more tolerant can be put on difficult jobs for long hours, even on low wages. Secondly, they have understood the productive quality of children who do not raise grievances pertaining to their working conditions.[53]

It is a employers' greed/avarice to exploit un-unionised disciplined child workers who work for long hours and for lower wages to make more profit at the cost of health and strength of children. There is also another reason that children work faster and have 'nimble fingers' needed in certain types of work especially for making knots in carpets than the adults.

Anker and Melkas have given following reasons for employer's preference for child labour:[54]

(A) Awareness and Innocence

(i) More docile and less troublesome.
(ii) Greater willingness to do repetitive, monotonous work.
(iii) More trustworthy and innocent, so less likely to steal.
(iv) Less absenteeism (none if bonded).
(v) Do not form trade union

(B) Tradition

(i) Tradition of hiring child labour by employers.
(ii) Traditional occupations have children working along side parents.
(iii) Social role of employer to provide jobs families to families in the community.
(iv) Employers need labourers. Children are available and ask for jobs so why not higher child labour

(C) Physical Characteristic

(i) Better health as young, health is not spoiled by work.
(ii) Irreplaceable skills (though this notion is not true in fact).

5.9. Defective Legislation, Law, Policy, Plans and Programmes

Equally this factor leads to perpetuation of child labour because of lacunae in laws, policy and plans do not address the burning problem of child labour. Art. 24 of the Constitution[55] intended for abolition of child labour whereas Sec. 3 of Child Labour (Prohibition and Regulation) Act, 1986[56] is designed to the regulation of child labour rather than prohibition. Thus there is a contradiction between each other and leads to confusion and ambiguity. Further, Sec. 3 of the Act prohibits and Sec. 6 of the Act regulates the conditions of work of children, again there is ample scope for child labour. Further the proviso annexed to Sec. 3 of the Act is often and invariably misused which keep the occupation, work or process that is carried on by the occupier with the aid of the family, out of the purview of the Act. This proviso is abused by employing children.

The Second National Commission on Labour has also not recommended complete ban on the employment of children altogether. It has only stressed on providing universal education as means to tackle the problem of child labour. The Commission has therefore, recommended the repealing of the existing Child Labour (Prohibition and Regulation) Act, 1986 with a new model Act, "To prohibit the employment of children in all employment and regulate employment of children where permitted".[57] This recommendation is clearly contradictory as once the employment of children is prohibited in all employments the question of regulation does not arise.

There is no provision for rehabilitation of rescued child in Child Labour (Prohibition and Regulation) Act. It does not say what should happen to the child labourer once the employer is prosecuted. Due to defective and unsuitable plans and programs of development particularly on educational policies, objectives are not met successfully. Most of the schemes whether poverty elimination or literacy campaign do not fulfil the local needs of the people and schemes meant for them being not fit for their socio-economic and cultural environment are not fruit bearing.[58]

Under National Child Labour Project, child labour enforcement drive-raids are not periodically conducted and lack of convergence among the various departments which have to play their vital role leads to prevalence of child labour. Neither elected representative nor higher officials of the department take part in the enforcement drive. The object of the National Child Labour Project is rehabilitation of rescued child labourers at child labour school. Any legislation for totally prohibiting child labour amount to hardships to the poor parents and their children's unless they are rehabilitated or their families are provided alternative source of income. Most of rehabilitation programmes today aim at improving the working environment of the child and are hence helping to perpetuate this evil. The ultimate aim ought to be the abolition of child labour and all governmental programmes must work towards fulfilling this objective, child labour should not be under the jurisdiction of the Ministry of Labour. As the rehabilitation programme comes under Education Department, Health Department and Rural Development, etc. Co-ordination among these Departments is often a major hurdle. Therefore, a child labour should be under the Ministry of Welfare because it should be better suited to deal with the problem in its various dimensions. Land reforms programmes should be strictly implemented. Land to the landless must be provided, as most of the families of child labour are landless. Government of India continued to add few more occupations and processes in the list of existing prohibited ones[59] and increasing the number of child labour projects under the National Child Labour Project[60] is nothing but a mockery. It is an indicator of increase and aggravating the problem of child labour just like increase in establishment of police stations, which shows the increase in the commission of crimes and increase of hospitals signifies increase of diseases respectively. It seems, at present Government has no intention to ban the practice of child labour atleast in the near future.

5.10. Low Educational Attainment

"Child labour is the enemy of child education". Proclaims Krishna Iyer J., "The right to life, which includes the right to education and development, interdicts child labour which not only risks life opportunity for growth but also denies those freedoms and facilities sans which a child is condemned to midgetry, moronism and penury of creativity.[61]

Our education system perpetuates the domination of the privileged few over the entire society, while the children of poor people forced to remain uneducated. A child which is supposed to be at school but, due to poverty poor children are forced to work. Therefore, it is rightly said that "all children who are out of school are child labourers". After a ceremonial ruling laid down by the Constitution Bench of Supreme Court in the case of *Unnikrishnan* v. *State of Andhra Pradesh*[62] that the right to education is a fundamental right that flows from the right to life in Art. 21 of the Constitution, every child/citizen has right to free education upto the age of 14 years. This Judgment was upheld and confirmed by the 11 Judge Constitution Bench of Supreme Court in *TMA Pai Foundation* v. *Union of India.*[63] Government of India in 2002 amended the Constitution by 86th Amendment.[64] In pursuance of this in August 2009, Parliament has enacted Children Right to Free and Compulsory Education Act, 2009 which also suffers with certain infirmities and thereby depriving children from the benefit of education which leads to child labour.

Jomtein marked the emergence of an International consensus that, education is the single most vital element in combating poverty, empowering, protecting children from hazardous and exploitative labour and sexual exploitation, promotion of human rights and democracy, protecting the environment and influencing population growth.[65]

6. CONCLUSION

The phenomenon of child labour is multi-dimensional complex problem and deep rooted in the socio-economic fabric of the society. So it may not be wise to rely on one single approach to deal with it. There are many factors responsible to this complex problem, so a comprehensive integrated approach is required to tackle and combat child labour. This can be done only by bringing attitudinal change, and social awareness and rigorous campaign against the problem of child labour. Thus, it requires honest effort and strong commitment and support from all concerned.

Notes and References

1. P.L. Mehta, S.S. Jaswal, *Child Labour and The Law,* New Delhi: Deep and Deep Publications, 1996, p. 13.
2. P.K. Padhi, "*Child Labour: Yesterday, Today and Tomorrow*", Journal Section Lab. I.C., 2004, p. 177 cited in Kulashresta, J.C., "*Child Labour in India*", 1978, p. 1.
3. *Ibid.*, cited in Rodgers Gray and Standings gay; "Economic Roles of Children in Low Income Countries", *International Labour Review,* 120(1), Jan.-Feb. 1981.
4. http:/www.childlabour.in/what is child labour.htm *visited* on 10.27.2009 p. 1.
5. http:/www.childlabour.in/child labour the real situation .htm *visited* on 10.27.2009, p. 2.
6. *Supra* note 1, also *see* Committee on Child Labour, 1979, p. 8.
7. Initiating a Child Labour Free Work Culture, An Employer Obligation, Karnataka Labour Department Records (2004).
8. *Supra* note 1.
9. Francis Blanchard, "*Child Labour*", ILO, 1983, pp. 3-4.
10. Archana Mehendale, "*Elimination of Child Labour—A Study of the Role of Law and Non-Governmental Organizations from a Perspective of the Rights of the Child*", Bangalore: National Law School of India University, 1997, p. 2.; also *see* Encyclopaedia of Social-Sciences (1959), p. 413.
11. Thomas Paul, "*Child Labour-Prohibition* v. *Abolition*: untangling the Constitutional Tangle", Vol. 50 (2008), New Delhi: *Journal of Indian Law Institute*, New Delhi, April-June 2008; No. 2, p. 146 also *see* the Report of the Committee on Child Labour, p. 10 (Government of India) Gurupadaswamy Committee Report, 1979.
12. Jain, Mahaveer, *Child Labour in India—A Select Bibliography*, Noida: National Labour Institute (1995), p. 12.
13. *Supra* note 11, pp. 146-47.
14. *Ibid.*, p. 159, also *see*, Lok Sabha debates, Seventh Session (8th Lok Sabha), Vol. XXIII, No. 22, Cols. 329, 331 (Dec. 3, 1986).

15. P.P. Jayanti, "Child Labour: A Socio-Legal Study", Vol. I (1998) *Kerala University Journal of Legal Studies*, Department of Law, University of Kerala, Tiruvantapuram, p. 143.
16. *Ibid.*, p. 145.
17. Neera Burra, *"Child Labour: it's a Reality tale"* The Indian Express December 18, 2007 New Delhi, *see* also Association for Development (AFD), *News Letter Issue*. XXIX, October-December 2007, Delhi, p. 6.
18. S. Pandiaraj, *"Elimination of Child Labour in India: Towards a glorious illusion"* ? Vol.46, (2006), *Indian Journal of International Law*, *see* also Laxmidhar Mishra, *Child Labour in India*, New Delhi: Oxford University Press, 2000, p. 18.
19. *Ibid.*, p. 19.
20. Helen R. Sekhar, *Child Labour Legislation in India—A Study in Retrospect & Prospect*, Noida: V.V. Giri National Institute of Labour, 1997, pp. 13-15.
21. *Ibid.*, p. 15.
22. *Supra* note 11, *see* also Anker and Melkas, *"Economic Incentives for Children and Families to Eliminate Child Labour"*, 32 (ILO, 1996)
23. D. Venkateshwar Rao, *Child Rights—A Perspective on International and National Law*, New Delhi: Manak Publications Pvt. Ltd., 2004, p. 5.
24. *Ibid.*, *see* also *Gurupada Swamy Committee Report on Child Labour* (1979), Ministry of Labour, Government of India.
25. *Supra* note 17.
26. *Supra* note 23.
27. Sheela Srivastava, "Child Labour as a Socio-Economic Problem in India" cited in Mahaveer Jain, Sangeeta Saraswal, *"Elimination or Empowerment-Child Labour from Different Perspectives"*, New Delhi, p. 4.
28. Tapan Kumar Sandilya and, Shakeel Ahmed Khan, *Child Labour: A Global Challenge*, New Delhi: Deep and Deep Publications Pvt. Ltd., 2006, p. 21.
29. Prof. B.N. Hegde, "Hungry Mouth's Day", Vol. 55, No. 12 (2007), Mumbai: *Bhavan's Journal Bharatiya Vidya Bhavan*, p. 37.
30. Polly Vizard, Review by Prof. B.B. Pande, "Poverty and Human Rights—Sen's Capability Perspective", Vol. 5 (2006), New Delhi: *Journal of National Human Rights Commission*, p. 191.
31. C.K. Shukla, S. Ali, *Child Labour: Socio-Economic Dimensions*, New Delhi: Swaroop and Sons, 2006, p. 178; *see* also Institute of Public Opinion, Monthly Commentary on Indian Economic Conditions, December 1973.
32. National Institute of Public Co-operation and Child Development (NIPCCD – Seminar Recommendations).
33. *Supra* note 29, p. 63 and also *see* Jain and Chand (1979).
34. Dr. Justice A.S. Anand, Article on "Neglect of Economic and Social and Cultural Rights—A Threat to Human Rights", Vol. 5 (2006), New Delhi: *Journal of the National Human Rights Commission*, p. 14.
35. *Ibid.*
36. Dr. Bindu M. Nambiar, "Children and Human Rights", Vol. 149 (2007), *Journal of Indian Legal Thought*, M.G. University, Kottayam, p. 157.
37. The State of the World's Children, 2005—Childhood under Threat, UNICEF, p. 17.
38. *Supra* note 29, p. 31.
39. *Supra* note 31.
40. Draft Declaration and Agenda for Action of the National Consultation and Child Labour, Delhi, 4-5 August, 1997.
41. *Supra* note 28, p. 14.

42. http://www.childlabour.in/causes of child labour .htm.
43. H. Kamalakar Halambi, Sanjiv Kumar, "*Hand Book for the Orientation of Employer's Organization Members and Office Bearers and Elimination of Child Labour*", International Labour Organization, ILO-IPEC—Karnataka Child Labour Project (Funded by Government of Italy), New Delhi, 2008, p. 56.
44. *Ibid.*, p. 80.
45. Proviso to S. 3: Provided that nothing in the section shall apply to any workshop wherein process is carried on by the occupier with the aid of his family or to any school established by or receiving assistance or recognition from Government.
46. Asha Bajapai, *Child Rights in India—Law, Policy and Practice*, New Delhi: Oxford University Press, 2003, p. 173.
47. *Supra* note 23, pp. 7-8.
48. *Supra* note 11, p. 152, *see* also Report of the Committee on Child Labour (1979), p. 9.
49. *Supra* note 28, p. 67.
50. Under Section 17 of CLPRA Act, Inspectors are appointed and they are deemed to be public servants.
51. *Supra* note 46, p. 179 and also *see* Meera Gupta, "Special Problems of Enforcement of Child Labour Laws and Regulations", Vol. XX, Nos. 7-12, *Awards Digest; Journal of Labour Legislation*,
52. *Ibid.*, p. 181.
53. A.N. Singh, *The Child Rag Pickers*, Socio-Economic Perspectives and Intervention Strategies, 1996, p. 26.
54. M.H. Rahman, Kanta Rahman, S. Meharaj Begum, *Child Labour and Child Rights—A Compendium*, New Delhi: Manik Publications, 2002, p. 18.
55. Article 24 of the Indian Constitution states that "No child below the age of 14 shall be employed to work in any factory or mine or engaged in any other hazardous employment".
56. Sec. 3 of the Child Labour (Prohibition and Regulation) Act, 1986 (61 of 1986), "No child shall be employed or permitted to work in any of the occupation set forth in Part A of the Schedule or in any workshop wherein any of the process set forth in Part B of the Schedule is carried on, provided that nothing in the section shall applied to any workshop wherein any process is carried on by occupier whether with the aid of his family or to any school established by or receiving assistance or recognition from Government".
57. The Report of Second National Commission on Labour 1967 (2002), No action has ever been taken by the Government on this Recommendation of the Commission.
58. *Supra* note 28, p. 66.
59. The Ministry of Labour and Employment, Government of India, on the advice of the Technical Advisory Committee issued a notification, prohibiting the employment of children below 14 years in service sector including domestic labour w.e.f. October 10, 2006.
60. Under this policy the Government has now 250 projects in 21 States.
61. *Supra* note 11, p. 171.
62. (1993) I SCC 645.
63. AIR 1996 SC 2652.
64. Article 21A of The Indian Constitution, "The State shall provide free and compulsory education to all children of the age 6 to 14 years in such a way as the State may, by law, determine".
65. Sheeba Pillai, "Right To Education And The Fishing Community In Kerala", Vol. 1 (2008), *Mysore University Law Journal*, p. 95.

6

International Instruments Regulating Child Labour

'Every child has the right to be protected from economic exploitation and from performing any work that is likely to be hazardous or to interfere with the child's health or physical, mental, spiritual, moral or social development.'[1]

I. HISTORICAL PERSPECTIVE

Child labour is a universal problem and is prevailing across the world whether it is developed, developing and under developed country. Long ago, countries basically had no concern for children and their rights. It is significant to make a mention that, factory system in England abused child labour force and were employed and made them to work for long hours from the age of 8 years. Children who were forced to work at the machines for a long time, used to sleep and get rolled into them along with cotton bales.[2]

The history of rights of child can be traced back to mid-nineteenth century with the publication of an article in June 1852 by Slagvock, titled "The Rights of the children", followed by Kate Kliggins "Childrens rights" in 1892. Gradually there was shifting of working conditions of children and the legal position of children in England began to change with the introduction of factory laws, which concentrated on the amelioration of the working conditions of employees especially children.[3] The International childrens' rights movement has been traced to the work of the British born Eglantyne Jebb, who founded SCIU in Geneva in 1919.[4]

In the year 1923, for the first time International attention was drawn concerning the situation of children when the Council of newly established NGO "Save the Children International Union" adopted a five point declaration on the rights of the children.

Prior to the 19th century child was the human property, chattel of the parents, the parents enjoying an absolute right over the child's services and earnings and total control over the child's person and property. Hence, concept of the rights of the child was never recognised prior to the 19th century. The International law for the first time recognised the importance of the rights of the child in 1924. The Geneva Declaration, 1924 and following it the United Nations Declaration of the rights of the child 1959, have proclaimed the child to be the most privileged ward of humanity; when they stated that "Mankind owes to the child, the best it has to give". Legal evolution brought substantial improvements in the area of Children's Rights.[5]

2. PRE-UNITED NATIONS INSTRUMENTS

2.1. The Geneva Declaration of 1924

The Geneva Declaration or the 1924 Declaration of the Rights of the child which was adopted by the League of Nations was the first Convention in which the Rights of the child were considered. It conferred upon men and women of all nations the following obligations:

(1) The child must be given the means needed for its normal development.

(2) The child that is hungry should be fed; the child that is sick should be helped; the erring child should be reclaimed; and the orphan and the homeless child should be sheltered.

(3) The child must be the first to receive relief in times of distress.

(4) The child must be protected against every form of exploitation.

(5) The child must be brought up in the consciousness that its best qualities are to be used in the services of its fellow men.

The 1924 Declaration was based on relief-oriented approach. The attitude was that the child in difficulty should receive help. The brutality experienced during the First World War had prepared mankind to appreciate the position of the weak in times of distress. There should not be hungry, sick or an orphan or homeless child who is not cared for.

An erring child should not be treated as a criminal but should be rehabilitated. All means should be provided for the material and spiritual growth of the child so that he grows upto appreciate the human life and contributes to the well-being of the mankind. But Right to economic or political freedom was absent from the catalogue of the children. The Declaration was only an expression of good will that the mankind felt towards the future and the very existence of a civilized World, and represented a feeling that children are part of the "sacred trust of civilization".[6]

2.2. The UN Charter, 1945 and Human Rights

The Members of the United Nations affirmed their faith in fundamental human rights and the dignity worth of the human being in various provisions of the charter. It is to be noted that the dignity and worth of the human being stated there also includes children.[7]

3. THE UNITED NATIONS INSTRUMENTS

3.1. Universal Declaration of Human Rights, 1948

The General Assembly of the United Nations adopted the Universal Declaration of the Human Rights on 10th December 1948,[8] proclaimed UDHR as a "Common standard of achievement for all peoples and all nations". The Declaration proclaims, "All Human beings are born free and equal in dignity and rights. They are endowed with reason and conscience and should act towards one another in a spirit of brotherhood".[9] It recognizes the inherent dignity and equal and inalienable rights of all human beings as the foundation of freedom, justice and peace in the World. It embodies more measures to protect the children, throughout a "common standard" of achievement for all people and all nations was adopted. It provides that, every one is entitled to all the rights and freedoms set forth in this Declaration without any distinction of any kind. Naturally the standard set forth includes children.

Article 25(2) of the Universal Declaration of Human Rights says that: "Motherhood and Childhood are entitled to special care and assistance. All children whether born in, or out of, wed lock shall enjoy the same social protection".

Article 26(1) of the Universal Declaration of Human Rights more focused that every one has the right to education, and that education shall be free and compulsory upto elementary and fundamental stages and Article 26(3) says that, parents have a prior right to choose the kind of education that shall be given to their children.

The Universal Declaration of Human Rights is an elaboration of

UN Charter obligation relating to human rights and recognizes, that every person to be free from inhuman and degrading treatment—slavery, slave trade, etc. Inspite of the recognition of human rights long back, a child labourer is deprived of such rights.

3.2. The UN Declaration of the Rights of the Child, 1959

The adoption of the Declaration of the Rights of the child by the General Assembly of the UN on November 20, 1959 was indeed a very important event as regards the international recognition of the right of the child. The General Assembly affirmed that the child has the right to enjoy special protection and to be given opportunities and facilities to be able to develop in healthy and normal manner. The Declaration contained 10 principles, being of comprehensive nature which formed code for the well-being of every child. The 1959 Declaration expanded the 5 principles of the Geneva Declaration to 10 basic principles. There was no reference to bind the Members-States for their implementation. The child only remained as an object of concern, rather than a person with self-determination.

To give legal force to the provisions of the Universal Declaration of Human Rights, The United Nations adopted two International covenants on Human Rights.

(A) International Covenant on Economic, Social and Cultural Rights, 1966[10]

There are 31 Articles incorporated in the covenant. Articles 10, 12 and 13 of the covenant refer to the needs of the children. In response to Rights laid down in Articles 25 and 26 of United Nations of Human Rights, Articles 10, 12 and 13 have framed as covenant on Economic, Social and Cultural Rights. Article 10(3) of the ICESCR provides that, "special measures of protection and assistance should be taken on behalf of children and young persons without any discrimination for reasons of parentage and other conditions. Children and young persons should be protected from economic and social exploitation. Their employment in work harmful to their morals or health or dangerous to like or likely hamper their normal development should be punishable by law. States should also set age limits below which the paid employment of child labour should be prohibited and punishable by law". Thus, children and young persons are to be protected from economic and social exploitation. Their employment in hazardous work which is harmful to health or dangerous to their life and likely hamper their normal development and should be made punishable by law and states are under an obligation to observe and implement it. It also insists state parties to set age limits for employment.

Article 12 of the ICESCR recognises the right of everyone to the employment of the highest attainable standard of physical and mental health.

Article 13 of ICESCR provides that state parties to this covenant recognise the right of everyone to education and that education shall be directed to the full development of the human personality and the sense of its dignity and strengthen the respect for human rights and fundamental freedoms. Article 13(2) is intended to achieving the full satisfaction of this right:

(a) Primary Education shall be compulsory and available free to all;
(b) Secondary education in its different forms, including technical and Vocational; Secondary education shall be made generally available and accessible to all by every appropriate means and in particular by the progressive introduction of free education;
(c) Higher education shall be made available equally to all, on the basis of capacity, by every appropriate and in particular by the progressive introduction of free education;
(d) Fundamental education shall be encouraged or intensified as for as possible for those persons who have not received or completed the whole period of their primary education; and
(e) The development of a system of schools at all levels shall be actively perused, an adequate fellowship system shall be established, and material conditions of teaching staff shall be continuously improved.

(B) The International Covenant on Civil and Political Rights (ICCPR), 1966[11]

This Covenant consisting of VI Parts with 53 Articles. Article 24 provides in respect of children:

(1) Every child shall have, without any discrimination as to race, colour, sex, language, religion, national or social origin, property or birth, the right to such measures of protection as are required by his status as a minor, on the part of his family, society and the state;
(2) Every child shall be registered immediately after birth and shall have a name; and
(3) Every child has the right to acquire a nationality.

According to Article 24, every child has the right to protection by its family, society and state. The Human Rights Committee extended Article 24 to extreme forms of child labour and stated that, every possible social and economic measure should be undertaken to prevent forced labour and prostitution.[12]

3.3. The United Nations General Assembly adopted another Declaration on Social Progress and Development in 1969

Part I of this Declaration, which focusing on the concept of family as a basic unit of society, observed that the growth and well-being of its members, particularly children and youth, should be assisted and protected. Part II provides for the protection of the rights of the child.

3.4. Declaration on the Protection of Women and Children in Emergency and Armed Conflict in 1974

Which provides for prohibition of attacks and bombings on civil population inflicting incalculable suffering specially on women and children who are the most vulnerable members of the population.

3.5. International Year of the Child, 1979

The UN General Assembly decided on 21st December 1976 to observe the year 1979 as the International Year of Child with the following objectives:[13]

(a) To provide a framework for advocacy on behalf of children and for enhancing the awareness of the special need of children on the parts of decision makers and the public.

(b) To promote recognition of the fact that programmes for children should be an integral part of economic and social development plans, with a view to achieving, in both the long-term and short-term, sustained activities for the benefit of children at the National and International level.

The International Year of the Child, 1979 was observed as the 20th Anniversary of the adoption of the 1959 Declaration on the Rights of the Child. It was marked by activities, at national, regional and international level, for the improvement of life of the children. UNICEF has provided with the essential leadership. In India during the International Year of Child, Nov. 14, Jawaharlal Nehru's Birthday was declared as Universal Children's Day. India is the only country in the world, which celebrates birthday of its Prime Minister as Children's Day.

3.6. UN Convention on the Rights of the Child, 1989

The Declaration of 1959 prompted the UN Human Rights Commission to constitute a working group of representatives of the UN Commission to draft a Convention on the Rights of the Child. The Convention, drafted by the UN Commission on Human Rights and adopted by the General Assembly on 20th November 1989, came into force on 2nd September 1990 and India became party to the Convention on 11th December 1992 and has now being ratified by 191 countries at the end of 2000, but USA and Somalia have not ratified the Convention. But USA however has signed convention, thereby showing general support for Convention on the Rights of the Child and it did not intend to take actions, which would in fact disregard Convention on the Rights of the Child principles.

The Convention on the Rights of the Child is really a "*Magna Carta*" and it is a Bible for children and it is a most important human rights document focusing and concentrating on children. The Convention on the Rights of the Child is the most complete statement of child rights ever made. It is the guiding principle of Convention on the Rights of the Child to protect best interest of child as mandated by it. It is indeed an innovative document in overall human rights theory and practice. In fact, it is the first United Nations Human Rights instrument since the Universal Declaration of Human Rights which brings together as inextricable elements of the life of an individual human being, the full range of civil and political rights, and economic, social and cultural rights. The Convention on the Rights of the Child treats children as complete individuals rather than as elements in an economic or socio-political system. The Convention aims to create balance between the rights of children and those of the parents or adults responsible for their survival, development and protection. This is achieved by according children the right to participate in decisions concerning them and their future. It is thus, a holistic document, for each Article is intertwined with the others. The Rights defined in the Convention are interdependent as none of the articles can be dealt in isolation.[14] The Convention is a set of international standards and measures intended to protect and promote the well-being of children in society. The Convention contains 54 Articles, and it provides civil, political, social, economic and cultural rights of every child, and out of 54 Articles 41 relate specifically to the rights of children. These rights are:

(a) *The Right to Protection*: It includes freedom from all forms of exploitation, abuse, inhuman or degrading treatment, and neglect including the right to special protection in situations of emergency and armed conflicts.

(b) *The Right to Development*: It includes the right to education, support for early childhood development and care, social security, and the rights to leisure, recreation and cultural activities.
(c) *The Right to Participation*: It includes respect for the views of the child, freedom of expression, access to appropriate information and freedom of thought, conscience and religion.
(d) *The Right to Survival*: It includes the right to life, the highest attainable standard of health, nutrition and adequate standards of living. It also includes the right to a name and a nationality.

Thus Convention on the Rights of the Child is the first globally binding treaty protecting childrens' civil, political, economical, social and cultural rights with regard to problem of child labour in India. Convention on the Rights of the Child addresses:

(1) To find out the extent of incorporation of the provisions of Convention on the Rights of the Child concerning child labour into the legislation and policies of India.
(2) To find out whether there remains any gaps in India's legal regime *vis-a-vis* the obligations arising out of Convention on the Rights of the Child.[15]

Among other Rights that Convention on the Rights of the Child accords to children, the following are the relevant and important ones in the context of child labour. They are:

(1) Article 6 recognizes Right to Life, Survival and Development.
(2) Article 19 mandates to protect the child from all forms of physical and mental violence, injury or abuse 10/07/2011, neglect or negligent treatment, maltreatment or exploitation including sexual abuse.
(3) Article 24 provides the right to the child to the enjoyment of the highest attainable standard of health and to facilities for the treatment of illness and rehabilitation of health. It directs the state parties to strive to ensure that no child is deprived of his/her right of access to such health care services.
(4) Article 27 recognizes the right of every child to a standard of living adequate for the child's physical, mental, spiritual, moral and social development. It direct the parents or

others responsible to ensure child development. It directs the state parties to take appropriate measures to assist parents and others responsible for the child to implement this right and shall in case of need provide material assistance and support programmes, particularly with regard to nutrition, clothing and housing.

(5) Article 28 recognizes the right of the child to education with a view to achieve this right progressively and on the basis of equal opportunity, and to make primary education compulsory and available free to all. It directs to encourage the development of different forms of secondary education, general and vocational education available and accessible to every child, and state parties to take measures for introduction of free education and offering financial assistance in case of need. It further directs to encourage regular attendance at schools and the reduction of drop-out rates. It mandates to promote and encourage international co-operation in matters relating to education, in particular with a view to contribute to the elimination of ignorance and illiteracy throughout the world and facilitating access to scientific and technical knowledge and modern teaching methods.

Article 32 of the UN Convention on the Rights of the Child, 1989 prohibits practice of Child Labour and recognises the rights of the child to:

(i) be protected from economic exploitation and performing any work that is likely to be hazardous; or
(ii) interfere with his education; or
(iii) be harmful to the child's health or physical, mental, spiritual, moral or social development. It mandates every state party to;
  (i) provide for a minimum age or minimum ages for admission to employment;
  (ii) provide for appropriate regulation of the hours and conditions of employment; and
  (iii) provide for appropriate penalties or other sanctions to ensure the effective enforcement of the above article, i.e. (Art. 32).

The International Labour Organisation is also opposed to child labour in situations where children are disadvantaged educationally and socially where they work in conditions that are exploitative to their health.

The significance of the Convention on the Rights of the Child lies in the fact that it has revolutionized the concept of the rights of the child by introducing two elements—

(i) First, it has widened the perspective of the rights of the child not by treating him as mere beneficiary of special protection and assistance but rather as an active person possessing certain rights.

(ii) Secondly, for the effective implementation of the rights contained therein, the convention laid down certain measures, such as the obligations of the states parties to respect and ensure the rights set forth in the present convention to each child within their jurisdiction, their obligation to provide information to both adults and children regarding the rights of the child and their obligation to publicize their reports on the implementation of rights of child.[16]

3.6.1. Procedure for the Implementation of the Convention

The states parties to the Convention undertake under Article 44 paragraph 1, to submit Report to the Committee on the Rights of Child through the Secretary-General of the United Nations on measures they have adopted to give effect to rights recognised in the Convention and on the progress made there to and Reports should indicate practical difficulties they faced and Committee suggest remedies.[17]

State parties are required to submit their first report within two years of the entry into force, of this Convention and every five years thereafter.[18] In total the Convention on the Rights of Child does not have a time limit nor does it have an expiry date.

Article 45 provides that for the effective implementation of the Convention and to encourage international co-operation, the Committee may invite specialized agencies, UN organs and the UNICEF to be represented at the consideration of implementation of such provisions as they would fall within their respective mandates.[19]

One of the main drawbacks of the Convention is that nowhere does it hold states responsible for failure to implement the children's rights they have accepted as a matter of obligation. Since there are no concrete steps laid down for the states to implement and ensure the rights of the children made for, there is a scope for making criticism for its partial/total failure of implementation of children rights. The words

"Appropriate measures" used in various Articles of Convention on the Rights of the Child is a vague expression and hence responsibility cannot be fixed on such state.[20] There is no accountability on states for their performance of their obligation. There is a need to empower the Committee to take cognizance against such states to provide Justice to the citizens.

3.7. Declaration on Survival, Protection and Development of Children: World Summit for Children, 1990[21]

The World Summit for Children was convened at United Nations Head-Quarter, New York on 30th September 1990. It was convened at the initiative of Canada, Egypt, Mali, Mexico, Pakistan and Sweden. More than seventy world leaders gathered in 1990 and made "A Solemn Commitment to give high priority to the rights of children, to their survival, protection and development" and to adopt the Plan of Action for implementing the World Declaration for survival, protection and development of children.

The 1990 World Declaration on the Survival, Protection and the Development of Children provide that, children are entitled to Joy and Peace, playing, learning and growing which are necessary for the harmonious development of children. But there are many children who face various problems and suffer in their very childhood. The Declaration lays down 10 point programme for the protection of the rights of the children and improvement in their lives. It aims to have programme for reducing illiteracy and promoting educational opportunities for all children.

A Plan of Action for implementing World Declaration on the survival, protection and development of children in 1990 was drawn having three parts namely: (a) Introduction, (b) Specific Action for child survival, protection and development, (c) Follow-up actions and monitoring.

Thus, as the needs and problems of children vary from place to place, community to community, "The Plan of Action" dealt with the "common aspirations". While addressing the World Summit for Children in 1990 J. Perez de cuellar, the former Secretary-General of United Nation's said: "As we look at the world's social and economic landscape, we marvel at the extraordinary advances that have been made in civilization as a whole yet with all this we also see that children continue to be the most vulnerable segment of society. Two set of anxieties are to be addressed, one arises from the global social crisis which robs children of emotional shelter and the most sustenance that they need. The other cause of distress is the poverty that stalks the larger part of the world and that denies children enjoyment of their rights. To this are added effects of conflicts internal and external. One in two among the eight million refugees in the world is a child".[22]

The World Declaration on the survival, protection and the development of children, 1990 and the follow-up plan of action made a promise to end child labour practices and protect the child. [23]

3.8. Outcome Document Titled "A World Fit for Children"

Adopted by the United Nations General Assembly special session on children held in May 2002 (6th Plenary Meeting, 10th May 2002) The Document contains the goals, objectives, strategies and activities to be undertaken by the member-countries for the current decade.

3.9. World Conference on Human Rights—The Vienna Declaration and Programme of Action, 1993

The world conference on human rights reiterates the principle of "First call for children" and in this respect, underlines the importance of major National and International, especially those of the United Nations Children's Fund for promoting respect for the rights of the child to survival, protection, development and participation.

It also mandates to take measures to achieve universal ratification of the Convention on the Rights of the Child by 1995 and the universal signing of the World Declaration on the survival, protection and development of children and Plan of Action adopted by the world summit for children as well their effective implementation. The world conference on Human Rights urges states to withdraw reservations to the Convention on the Rights of the Child contrary to the object and purpose of the Convention or otherwise contrary to International treaty law.

The world conference on Human Rights urges all states, with the support of International Co-operation, to address the acute problem of children under especially difficult situations. Exploitation and abuse of children should be actively combated, including by addressing their root causes. Effective measures are required against female infanticide, harmful child labour, sale of children and organs, child prostitution, child pornography, as well as other forms of sexual abuse.[24]

3.10. Second World Children Congress on Child Labour Delhi, 2005[25]

First children's World Congress on Child Labour was held in 1993. The Second World Children Congress on Child Labour and education was held in New Delhi from 4th to 8th September 2005, which was organised by Global March Against Child Labour and hoisted by its core partner in India, Bachpan Bachao Andolan. Children from 30 different countries with children from India attended the Congress. Objectives of the Congress was to provide Justice to the children, who were denied, the Visa and could not participate in the First Children's World Congress 1993, giving them a platform to share opinions, experiences and ideas and to learn from one another and empowering them in the process to emerge as the leaders in the struggle against child labour. Another objective is to formulate a children's Plan of Action to implement the Declaration made by the children in the First Children's World Congress 1993 and to strengthen, broaden and consolidate, a world wide child and youth movement against child labour through the establishment of a strong network and to remind Govt. to fulfil their promises to ratify and implement ILO conventions 182 and 138.

Lastly, to urge International organisations to increase their support to programmes aimed at eradicating child labour, poverty reduction, achieving universal, free and quality education for all children.

Thus, The Vienna Declaration 1993 addressed the root cause of child labour and encouraged combating exploitation and abuse of children. It also stressed the need for necessary measures to eliminate child labour.[26]

4. SPECIALISED AGENCIES OF THE UNITED NATIONS

There are specialized agencies of United Nations whose functioning is of great relevance to the protection and rights of the child. They are International Labour Organization (ILO), United Nations Educational, Scientific & Cultural Organisation (UNESCO), United Nation's Children Emergency Fund (UNICEF), South Asian Association for Regional Co-operation (SAARC) and World Health Organization (WHO), etc.

4.1. International Labour Organisation (ILO)

ILO is an inter-governmental agency, established by Peace Treaty of 1919 for promotion of Industrial peace and social justice. Its structure is tripartite and includes representatives of Governments, employers and workers.[27] The basic principles of the ILO are: (i) Labour is not a commodity. (ii) Freedom of expression and of association is essential to continued progress. (iii) Poverty any-where constitutes a danger to prosperity everywhere. (iv) Workers and employers enjoying equal status with Governments and join with open discussion and take democratic decisions which can be carried to the promotion of the common welfare. The significant feature of ILO is its constitution of organization which comprises not only the representation of the Member-States, but also of the workers and employers. The Tripartite system of partnership has made the organization one of the most representative and democratic in the real sense of the term. It is the policy and objective of ILO to abolish child labour. It is a time taking process, but it is intended to make beginning in making the "world free from child labour". Its objective based on the convention that, "child-hood should be consecrated not to work but to education and development, that child labour. Often jeopardizes children's possibilities of becoming productive adults. and that child labour is not inevitable...its elimination is possible when the political will-exists".

The ILO standards conventions and recommendations were designed to improve working and living conditions of the workers. It has done commendable work to achieve social-justice for the workers. In the field of International Legislation, International Labour Code is a significant achievement.

ILO is committed to the abolition of the worst forms of child labour and gradually other forms also. This is the first child labour convention, which prohibited the work of children under the age of 14 in industrial establishments. The protection of the child against exploitations in employment is one of the major concerns of this Convention.

ILO has moved totally 19 Conventions out of which

(a) 10 Conventions are related to minimum age for employment of children.
(b) 5 Conventions concerned with medical examination of children to decide the fitness for employment.
(c) 3 Conventions are related prohibition of night work for children.
(d) 1 Convention with regard to total prohibition of worst forms of child labour.

The basic objective of ILO's Conventions was to provide certain norms and standards for the well-being of the working children. Thus, ILO so far in the interest of children all over the world has adopted 19 Conventions and 17 recommendations.

(1) Minimum Age (Industry) Convention, 1919;
(2) Night Work of Young Person's (Industry) Conventions, 1919;
(3) Minimum Age (Sea) Convention, 1920;
(4) Minimum Age (Agriculture) Convention, 1920;
(5) Minimum Age (Trimmers and Stockers) Convention, 1921;
(6) Medical Examination of Young Persons (Sea) Convention, 1921;

(7) Minimum Age (Non-Industrial Employment) Convention, 1932;
(8) Minimum Age (Sea) Convention (Revised), 1936;
(9) Minimum Age (Industry) Convention (Revised), 1937;
(10) Minimum Age (Non-Industrial Employment) Convention, (Revised), 1946.
(11) Medical Examination (Sea-Farers) Convention, 1946;
(12) Medical Examination of Young Persons (Industry) Convention, 1946;
(13) Medical Examination of Young Persons (Non-Industrial Occupation) Convention, 1946;
(14) Night Work of Young Persons (Non-Industrial Occupations) Convention, 1946;
(15) Night Work of Young Persons (Industry) Convention, 1948;
(16) Medical Examination of Young Persons (Under Ground Works) Convention, 1965;
(17) Minimum Age (Under Ground Works) Convention, 1965;
(18) Minimum Age Convention, 1973; and
(19) Worst Forms of Child Labour Convention, 1999.

Out of 19 Conventions, one of them is for effective abolition of child labour.[28] The global financial crisis could push an increasing number of children, particularly girls, into child labour according to new report issued by the ILO. It has been released to mark the world day against child labour on June 12.

4.1.1. ILO's Worst Forms of Child Labour Convention, 1999 (No. 182)

On 17th June 1999, the 87th session of the General Conference of the International Labour Organisation (ILO) adopted a Convention and accompanying Recommendation concerning the prohibition and elimination of the worst forms of child labour.[29] So far 163 countries have signed this Convention. The adoption of this Convention represents a significant strategic shift in the international campaign against child labour. The intention of this Convention is to target certain forms of child labour for prioritized action. The Convention defines as 'child' all persons under the age of 18. Nations which ratify the Convention promise to "take immediate and effective measures to secure the prohibition and elimination of the worst forms of child labour as a matter of urgency".[30]

"The worst forms of child labour" defined in the Convention include:

(1) Bonded or forced child labour;
(2) Compulsory military recruitment of children;

(3) Participation in the commercial sex industry through prostitution and pornography;
(4) Use of children in the drug trade and other illicit activities; and
(5) Hazardous work.

Thus, the Convention defines "worst form of child labour" as all forms of slavery or practices similar such as the sale and trafficking of children, debt bondage serfdom and forced or compulsory labour, forced or compulsory recruitment of children for use in armed conflict, use of child for prostitution, production of (pornography), use in illicit activities, etc.

This Convention also defines "hazardous work" as work which exposes the children to physical, psychological or sexual abuse, work underground, under water, at dangerous heights, closed places, with dangerous machines/tools, work in unhealthy atmosphere, long hours, during nights, etc.

The Convention requires ratifying states: [31]

(1) To work on the implementation programmes of action for the elimination of the worst forms of child labour as a priority.
(2) To establish appropriate mechanisms for monitoring the implementation of the Convention.
(3) To take time bound measures for prevention of child labour.
(4) To provide adequate support for the removal of children from the worst forms child labour, effort for the rehabilitation of the child labour and proper guidance, so that the children get access to free basic education or vocational training.
(5) Calls for International co-operation or assistance in the efforts to make its provisions really applicable.

4.1.2. Minimum Age Convention, 1973 (No. 138)[32]

The Convention 138 was adopted by the ILO at its first session in 1973 and 149 countries have signed this Convention. This is the most comprehensive ILO Convention on the child labour issue and calls for fixing minimum ages for admission to work or employment. This Convention demands for a National Policy designed to ensure effective and gradual abolition and elimination of child labour. The Convention lays down the basic principle, that the minimum age for admission to employment or work should not be less than upper age limit of compulsory education and in any case should not be less than 15 years.

It also provides flexibility in the minimum age for employment for countries which are less developed in educational facilities and such countries can fix minimum age as 14 instead of 15 in the initial stage and gradually increase the same. The Convention also suggests that the minimum age for hazardous work should be 18. It also suggests that the minimum age should not be static; it should be progressively raised to a higher level corresponding with the full physical, mental and spiritual development of young persons.[33]

The ILO has reiterated that it considers the term 'child labour' to include violations of the standards of the 1973 Minimum Age Convention. Since these standards permit full time employment by minors as young as 14 in developing countries, allow some minors to be involved in hazardous employment under certain circumstances and permit children as young as twelve to be engaged in formal part time employment.[34] Work that does not interfere with education (light work) is permitted from the age of 12 years. Light work has a different definition under Convention 138 and is allowed from 12 years. The word hazardous is confusing and is left out here. The Convention 138 (Article 7) provides light work is work from the age of 12 which is:

(1) Not likely to be harmful to their health or development; and
(2) Not such as to prejudice their attendance at school, their participations in vocational or training programmes approved by the competent authority or their capacity to benefit from the instruction received.[35]

Thus, according to Convention 138, child labour refers to children working in contravention of the above standards and involves children below 12 years of age working in any economic activities, and those aged 12-14 years engaged in non-hazardous fulltime work, those under 18 engaged in hazardous work as determined by national legislation and all children engaged in other worst forms of child labour.

4.1.3. Minimum Age Recommendation, 1973 (No. 146)

This calls on States to raise the minimum age of employment to 16 years. Though it is not legally binding, but it compels member states to initiate action on this Convention No. 138 and these recommendations are regarded as the most comprehensive international instruments and statements on child labour.

4.1.4. ILO's International Programme for the Elimination of the Child Labour (IPEC)

The International Programme for the Elimination of the Child

Labour is global programme launched by the ILO in Dec. 1991. India was a first country to join it in 1992 when it signed a Memorandum of Understanding with the ILO. The long term objective of IPEC is to contribute to the effective abolition of child labour.

Its immediate objectives are:[36]

(a) Elimination of the capability of ILO constituents and Non-Govt. Organisations to design, implement and evaluate programmes for Child Labour Elimination;
(b) To identify interventions at community and national levels which could serve as models for replication; and
(c) Creation of awareness and social mobilization for securing elimination of child labour.

At the International level, IPEC has a Programme Steering Committee consisting of representatives of the ILO, the donors and participating countries. At the National level in India, there is a National Steering Committee of which the Labour Secretary is the Chairman. This is a tripartite body, in its composition with representation from the NGO's as well. There is National programme co-ordinator based at New Delhi who co-ordinates IPEC work between the Ministry of Labour, the agencies receiving assistance and ILO Head Quarters.

Two pillars of ILO/IPEC approach in its direct programme have been:

(a) The economic empowerment of the household at risk.
(b) Making education accessible and meaningful to the children concerned.

Further, the IPEC[37] is the technical co-operation programme on child labour in the world. In more than 70 countries ILO/IPEC inspires, guides and supports national initiatives to eliminate child labour.

The aim of IPEC is to work towards progressive elimination of child labour by strengthening national capacities and policies to address the child labour problems and creating world-wide movement to combat it.

Priority target groups for IPEC are:

(1) Bonded child labourers;
(2) Children in hazardous working conditions and occupations; and
(3) Children who are particularly vulnerable.

The support is given under this programme to organizations to develop and implement measures which aim at preventing child labour, withdrawing children from hazardous work and providing alternatives and improving working conditions and livelihoods.

The important activities of IPEC are:

(1) Motivating a broad spectrum of partners to acknowledge and act against child labour;
(2) Carrying out the situation analysis to find out quantitative and qualitative attributes of child labour to create awareness on the problem; and
(3) Promoting development and application of protective legislation and preventive and rehabilitative policies and programmes, etc.

IPEC is moving forward with several projects in the country, one of the projects is Karnataka Child Labour Project.

4.2. United Nations Education, Scientific and Cultural Organisation (UNESCO)

UNESCO is a specialized agency of the United Nations. The Constitution of the United Nations Education, Scientific and Cultural Organisation (UNESCO) was adopted by the London Conference in Nov. 1945 and entered into effect in Nov. 1946. According to 1 of its Constitution, UNESCO's main functions are to collaborate in the work of advancing the mutual knowledge and understanding of people through all means of mass communications, giving fresh impulse to popular education and the spread of culture, maintain and or increase and, diffuse knowledge and encourage the teaching and understanding of science. UNESCO focuses on four major programmes: (a) Education, (b) Natural, Social and Human sciences, (c) Culture, and (d) Communications.

4.3. United Nations Children's Emergency Fund (UNICEF)

The UNICEF is not legally a specialised agency as it was created by the UN General Assembly in 1946 as one of its subsidiary bodies.[38] At the beginning stage it focussed to provide large scale emergency relief to the child victims of World War II with 3 years duration. But later on UNICEF's mandate was extended indefinitely and expanded to include children in the developing world.

UNICEF acknowledges the need to tackle the problem of child labour in order to implement the Conventions on the Rights of the Child and achieve the goals for improving the conditions and well-being of children. UNICEF's objectives are:[39]

(1) To promote compulsory primary education as the fundamental strategy for the elimination and prevention of child labour;
(2) To advocate revision and enforcement of child labour legislation and to strengthen monitoring systems;
(3) To assist Central and State Governments to develop and implement programmes and an action plan for the withdrawal and rehabilitation of child labour; and
(4) To promote convergence of all sectoral and developmental programmes on "at risk" families.

During the year 1965, UNICEF was awarded the Noble peace prize in recognition that the well-being of today's children is, inseparable from the peace of tomorrow's world. The UN General Assembly entrusted the UNICEF with the responsibility of co-ordinating all activities relating to the International year of the children in 1979.

UNICEF has played a prominent role in emergencies. It has a four pronged emergency approaches.[40] They are:

(a) Preventive actions through which the acute threat or risks to children are identified, monitored and eliminated or reduced by addressing root causes;
(b) Readiness measures, which will ensure that emergency assistance will be effective, timely and appropriates;
(c) Emergency assistance, through the provision of a range of goods and services in the midst of a crisis necessary to assure the survival, protection and essential developmental needs; and
(d) Rehabilitation and recovery assistance to help victims towards physical, social and psychological recovery.

State of World Children's Report, 2006 from UNICEF points out that, half the world's under nourished children live in South Asia.[41]

According to the recent State of Worlds Children Report prepared by UNICEF, children of the poorest households in rural areas are the most likely to be engaged in labour as they are most vulnerable. It is also important to note that, child labour is made possible by the social and cultural sanctions that it continues to receive so that we can move towards not only eliminating poverty and ensuring access to education but also making child labour culturally and socially unacceptable.[42]

4.4. South Asian Association for Regional Co-operation (SAARC)

SAARC is not a specialized agency of the UN but is a regional organization, which works one behind the other, i.e., with the UN. SAARC is regional organization which comprises seven countries, Bangladesh, Bhutan, India, Maldives, Nepal, Pakistan and Sri Lanka. These countries' geography indicates resources and cultural environment, share common religions and historical traditions and linkages with antiquity or the ancient days. The common history and difficult socio-economic realities have inevitably touched the lives of the majority of children in all countries of the region.

The idea of regional co-operation in South Asia was first mooted around November 1980. After consultations, the Foreign Secretaries of the seven countries met for a first time in Colombo in April 1991 and thereafter identified 5 broad areas for regional co-operation. They are Agriculture, Rural Development, Telecommunication, Meteorology and Health and population activities.

It is significant to understand that, 1/4th population of the world's children live in SAARC countries and more than 3.5 million children under-5-years old died from poverty-related causes. Almost 2/3rd of the region's children were under nourished and fewer than half the children were likely to complete five years of primary education. The main obstacles to child survival and development in the region are malnutrition, poor sanitation and hygiene, poverty and illiteracy.

In order to address these problems regional countries have formulated plan of action and convene Summit's either yearly/every two years at different places in the region. The second SAARC Summit saw held at Bangalore (India) on 16th, 17th November, 1986 which called for concrete efforts create an environment favourable to the realization of the rights of the child. The Fifth SAARC Summit was held at Male (Maldevies) on 21-23 November 1990. The year 1990 had been recognised as the "SAARC year for girl child" and prioritise the problem and initiate policy intervention for vulnerable section of the child population in the region. The Sixth SAARC Summit was held at Colombo (Sri Lanka) on 21st December, 1991. Subject of children's right was high on the agenda in this Summit. This Summit adopted a Regional Plan of Action for Children with special focus on girl child and SAARC conference on 1992 focussed on strategies for implementation. The Seventh SAARC Summit was held again at Dhaka (Bangladesh) on 10-12 April 1993. This Summit stressed on its commitment to eradicate poverty from South Asia by social mobilization and human development and focussed on the right to work and primary education should receive the highest priority. The Eighth SAARC Summit was held at New Delhi

(Capital of India) on 2-4 May 1995. This Summit approved the establishment of a three-tier mechanism for dealing with poverty issues. The first tier would comprise of the Secretaries to the Government's concerned with poverty eradication and social development in SAARC countries. The second tier comprises of finance and planning Secretaries and third tier would comprise of finance and planning ministers. The Eleventh SAARC Summit was held at Katmandu (Nepal) on 4-6 January 2002 during new millennium year. The eleventh session in Kathmandu had brought into two conventions. SAARC convention on preventing and combating trafficking in women and children for prostitution, 2002 and SAARC convention on Regional Arrangements for the promotion of child welfare in South Asia, 2002. It also made efforts of poverty alleviation in the region and drawn a practical road map for alleviating poverty in the region.

4.5. World Health Organization (WHO)

In 1945, The United Nations Conference on International Organisation meeting was held in San Francisco. It unanimously approved a proposal by Brazil and China to set-up an autonomous International Health Organisation within the United Nations System. The constitution of the World Health Organisation (WHO) was adopted by the International Health Conference, convened by the United Nations Economic and Social Council (ECOSOC) in New York in 1946. In July 1948, this organisation was brought into relationship with the UN and finally on 1st September 1948, it started functioning as a permanent organisation.[43]

One of the basic objectives of WHO as per Art. 1(1) is to promote maternal and child health welfare and to foster the ability to live harmoniously in a changing environment. WHO concerns with health needs and health care. It defined health "as a state of complete physical, mental and social well-being not merely the absence of disease and infirmity". WHO as serious concern over the drug testing and its effect on infants and children. It focussed on dis-advantages and effects on bottle feeding and advantages of breast milk feeding to make polio-free nations, for the promotion and potential health of children. WHO reported on World Health Day (7th April 1995) that, 146 countries have had no cases of Polio.

5. CONCLUSION

It is very difficult to draw conclusion with reference to International Instruments regulating child labour. The main contribution of the Convention on the rights of the child has been codification of children rights into one International document and recognising aspirations which mankind has for its children.

Conventions and Declarations make promises and set high aspirations. But the state parties face practical difficulties in implementation due to socio-economic and cultural and political systems. There are no implementing provisions either in the conventions or declarations. There is no responsibility or accountability upon the state parties for their acts and omissions.[44]

The UN Declaration of the Human Right to Development, 1986 emphasises on people centered development, focussing on the interests of poor and less advantaged. The people must be active participants in developmental activities. So steps are taken for the welfare of child labourers and gradual abolition of child labour. The 1999 Worst Forms of Child Labour Convention represents an important strategic shift in the child labour movement, for it recognises the important prioritizing efforts.[45]

The Convention requires ratifying states to design and implement programmes of action to eliminate the worst forms of child labour as a priority and to establish or designate appropriate mechanisms for monitoring implementation of the Convention in consultation with employers and workers organisation. It also says that the ratifying states should provide support for the removal of children from the worst forms of child labour, and their rehabilitation; ensure access to free basic education or vocational training for all children removed from the worst forms of child labour; identify children at special risk; to take into account the special situation of girls.[46]

The UN General Assembly special session on child was held in New York, in May 2002 and brought out a Final Outcome Document entitled "A World Fit for Children" on 10th May 2002 and Nations will always, abide by the principle of "First call for children" for their survival, protection and development giving the highest priority.

A comprehensive strategy has to be designed to address the basic causes that create and perpetuate child labour. An Action Plan that identifies a set of specific interventions that will have an impact on the basic causes of child labour and create alternatives that improve the quality of life of child workers and their communities will have to be formulated.

NOTES AND REFERENCES

1. Article 32, The United Nation Convention on the Rights of the Child.
2. Mamata Rao, *Law Relating To Women And Children,2nd* edn., New Delhi: Eastern Book Company, 2008, p. 414; also see Andrew Kaka Badse; *Children in England,*. Published in The Administration for Child Welfare, 1979.

3. *Ibid.*, also *see* Srinivas Gupta, "*Human Rights of the Child*", (1994) 7 CILQ.
4. UNICEF The State of the World's Children, 2000 (UNICEF, New York), 2000, p. 14.
5. D. Venkateshwar Rao, *Child Rights—A Perspective on International and National Law,* New Delhi: Manak Publications, 2004, pp. 8-9.
6. *Ibid.*, pp. 40-41.
7. P.K. Padhi, "Child Labour: Yesterday, Today and Tomorrow" (2004), Journal Section Lab. I.C., pp. 179-80.
8. Adopted and proclaimed by General Assembly Resolution 217A (III) of 10th Dec. 1948.
9. Preamble to the Universal Declaration of Human Rights, 1948.
10. UKTS 6, 1977 Cmnd., 6702 Adopted and open for signature, ratification and accessation by General Assembly Resolution 2200 A(XXII) of 16th Dec. 1966. Entry into force, 3rd Jan. 1976 in accordance with Article 27.
11. UKTS 6, 1977 Cmnd., 6702 Adopted and open for signature, ratification and accession by General Assembly Resolution 2200 A(XXI) of 16th Dec. 1966. Entry into force, 23rd Mar. 1976 in accordance with Article 49.
12. Dr. (Mrs) Ashraf U. Kazi and Francis Tasneem, "Existence Of Child Labour In The Twenty-first Century And Human Rights: International Perspectives And Legal Implications", Vol. 2, No. 2 (2007), *The Bangalore Law Journal,* p. 15, *see* also Dabscheck B., Human Rights and International Relations (1998), 4(2), *Australian Journal of Human Rights*, pp. 61-70
13. Dr. U. Chandra, *Human Rights,* 6th edn., Allahabad: Allahabad Law Agency Publication, 2006, p. 248.
14. Dr. Savita Bhakry, "*Children in India and their Rights*", New Delhi: National Human Rights Commission, 2006, pp. 29-30.
15. S. Pandiaraj, "Elimination of Child Labour in India towards a glorious illusion" ?, Vol. 46 (2004), New Delhi: *Indian Journal of International Law,* p. 84.
16. *Supra* note 13, pp. 253-54.
17. Article 44.2, Convention on the Rights of the Child.
18. Article 44.1, Convention on the Rights of the Child.
19. *Supra* note 5, pp. 101-02.
20. *Ibid.*, p. 102.
21. Adopted by the General Assembly of the United Nations in its General Assembly Summit in 1990—India State party agreed to at the World Summit for Children on 30th Sep. 1990, declaration reads 1, we have gathered at the world summit for children to undertake a joint commitment to make an urgent universal appeal to give every child a better future.
22. *Supra* note 2, pp 407-08.
23. Subsequently it has also been reaffirmed in the (i) World Conference on Education for All, at Jomtien, in March 1990, (ii) World Summit on the Children in the autumn of 1990; and (iii) SAARC countries Conference on children in 1991-92.
24. Dr. Durga Das Basu, *Human Rights in Constitutional Law,* 2nd edn., Agra: Wadhwa and Company Law Publishers, 2005, p. 982.
25. Fact Finding Report of Second World Children Congress Delhi, 2005.
26. *Supra* note 12.
27. Dr. G.M. Kothari, *A Study of Industrial Law,* 3rd edn., Bombay: N.M. Tripathi Pvt. Ltd, Bombay, 1978, p. 26.
28. *The Hindu,* 11th June 2009.

29. Convention concerning the prohibition and immediate action for the elimination of the worst forms of child labour (ILO) No. 182 adopted 17th June 1999 (herein after ILO 1999 Convention, 1999 recommendations.)
30. ILO 1999 Convention, "Considering the need to adopt new instruments for the prohibition and elimination of the worst forms of child labour, as the main priority for National and international action, including International Co-operation and assistance.
31. Helen R. Sekhar, *Child Labour—Situation and Strategies for Elimination*", Noida: V.V.Giri National Labour Institute, 2007, pp. 81-82.
32. The Minimum Age Convention 1973 (No. 138) was adopted by ILO, setting out the minimum age standards for employment which came into force from 19.06.1976. This aimed at achieving total abolition of child labour, this Convention replace the previous Conventions on minimum age of employment of children.
33. H. Kamlakar Halambi, Sanjeev Kumar, "*Hand Book for the Orientation of Employer's Organization Members and Office Bearers on the Elimination of Child Labour*", International Labour Organisation, New Delhi: ILO–IPEC Karnataka Child Labour Project (Funded by Govt. of Italy), p. 62.
34. David M. Smolin, "Strategic choices in the International Campaign against Child Labour", Vol. 22 (2000), *Human Rights Quarterly*, p. 949.
35. *Supra* note 33, p. 135.
36. *Supra* note 31, p. 101.
37. *Supra* note 33, p. 63.
38. *Supra* note 5, p. 56.
39. Helen R. Sekhar, *Towards Combating Child Labour*, 2nd edn., Noida: V.V. Giri National Labour Institute, 2005, p. 19.
40. *Supra* note 5, p. 57.
41. *The Hindu*, 22nd July 2006, "*India Dangerous for Children*".
42. UNICEF, State of World's Children Report, 2009, also *see* Vinod Bhanu, "*Centre for Legislative Research and Advocacy*", New Delhi.
43. *Supra* note 5, pp. 54-55.
44. *Supra* note 5, pp. 220-21.
45. *Supra* note 34, p. 987.
46. Asha Bajpai, *Child Rights in India, Law, Policy and Practice*, New Delhi: Oxford University Press, 2003, p. 197.

7

Child Labour in United States of America, UK, Russia, China, South Africa, South Asia and other Countries: A Comparative Analysis

I. INTRODUCTION

The problem of child labour is a global phenomenon and is not restricted to the poor, developing countries of the world, though it may manifest itself in varying forms and intensities among countries from different socio-economic milieu. It is also an extremely complex problem since; it is interlinked in cause and consequence to the social, economic, cultural and political systems which favour a few at the cost of others. In addition, the grossly exploitative and abusive conditions in which wide majority of children are made to work are an indication of their overall victimization by oppressive hierarchies on the basis of age, caste, class, gender and religion. Due to various reasons the children of all the countries including India are obliged to suffer neglect and destitute. The history of child labour is bound up with the status of the child, his rights and privileges in different societies.

In the developed industrial countries, the problems of child labour and deprived children are ignored. There are hundreds of children working to maintain their families and themselves. The major employment sector in which child workers are employed is prostitution. Today in the developed world child prostitution is very much in demand.

Besides, the children from the poor black homes, porturicans and other social minorities in the United States of America are working in factories and small establishments.[1]

However, the problem of child workers is not as acute as in the developing countries of the Third World.[2] In most of the developing countries, development efforts have been lopsided. As a result, the gaps between rural and urban areas, between one region and another, and between one section of people and another section have considerably widened. This has resulted in a massive spread of poverty in many countries in rural areas. In urban areas, following western capitalist model of development, huge infrastructural facilities have been made available which has resulted in the over care of the urban sector and neglect of the rural sector. This too in a situation when majority of the population is still living in rural areas and livelihood of a large segment of the rural population depends on agriculture and allied activities.[3]

The agrarian structures of all the developing countries are again characterised by land related inequalities. Many efforts have been made by many governments in the Third World to redistribute land to landless and semi-landless households through various land reform measures. But the problems of poverty and exploitations are so tenacious and chronic that landlessness and destitution could not be stopped. This structural problem is the single most important cause of the emergence of a large number of working children in rural and urban areas. The destitute people generally migrate to cities and towns during acute unemployment and economic distress. It is again the children of the unfortunate migrants who constitute the largest segment of the urban working children.[4]

It would be appropriate to study the problems and prospects of child labour in different countries of the world to understand the situation and analyse.

2. CHILD LABOUR IN UNITED STATES

Before the United States became an independent, sovereign nation, children worked alongside other family members and were considered an integral part of the work force. Children were socialised to contribute to the maintenance of the family through apprenticeships. This arrangement exemplified the child's relationship to both work and family in pre-industrial society. In the pre-colonial and post-colonial U.S., children worked both on family forms and in cottage industries. Children in the agricultural and industrial sectors worked for long hours and in conditions that were detrimental to their physical and mental health. For parents and children, education was a secondary importance to supplementing the family income.[5]

The idea that people are responsible for their poverty and misery is rooted in the English poor laws. Many of the early settlers from Europe, including the Puritans, brought religious beliefs establishing a strong work ethic. They believed that social and economic degradation could be prevented by hard work and prudent saving. These beliefs provided the impetus to justify child employment, instilling in parents and employers that it was their role to prepare the children for adult life by teaching them positive work habits.[6]

Early in the history of the United States, children who were destitute and neglected were placed in private homes as domestic workers, in other instances, by court rulings, they were bound as apprentices. Boys were apprenticed until the age of eighteen or twenty one, and girls until they were eighteen years old or in marriage, work was considered training that provided children with skills in certain trades and occupations. Many children, however, received little or no training and their education was ignored. They carried out menial tasks and were underfed and inadequately clothed.[7]

Some children born to parents in slavery were sold into servitude. Prior to civil war, most African-American children who were enslaved worked on farms and plantations; approximately 5 percent worked in mines and factories. During the anti-slavery period, children's apprenticeships bore striking similarities to forced bondage. Apprenticeships continued through the nineteenth century, especially in the Southern States. Whites in the Southern States used apprenticeships as a way to further enslave young African-Americans and secure a cheap source of labour.

In the United States child labour was considered a cheap and manageable workforce. The cities provided a wide array of employment opportunities for children. Girls and boys were engaged in similar jobs, although more boys were engaged in street type occupations. More girls on the other hand worked at home helping their mothers in house-hold tasks such as cooking, cleaning, laundry, ironing, mending, sewing, and caring for younger siblings. Some girls worked in textile mills and factories as spinners and weavers. They sent their wages home or saved their pay for education, job training, or a marriage dowry.

In the early twentieth century, when most crop planting and harvesting was performed by hand, more children were engaged in farm work than any other occupation. A belief at that time was that farm work was good for children's health. Some children moved from farm to farm with their families, carrying out the same backbreaking tasks as their parents. Entire migrant labour families, most of whom were African-American and other ethnic minorities, worked in the fields; this included children as young as three and four years old. Some families spent the entire year following the crops, staying at locations for just a couple of weeks. Migrant farm workers and their families were denied access to health and welfare services and, in certain areas, their children were allowed to attend the local schools. Even if the children were allowed to attend school, work always came first. Many families who lived in the city would get involved in agricultural work during the spring and summer months. [8]

In the United States the term child labour is commonly used to denote employment that is harmful to a child's physical, cognitive, emotional, social and moral development. In the United States, work that is detrimental to children's well-being is called *oppressive child labour* in the Fair Labour Standards Act (FLSA) of 1938. This is the main legal instrument ensuring the safety and protection of child workers. The use of the term child labour in the United States means work carried out by teenagers.[9] Moreover, Labour in occupations deemed hazardous for children under sixteen was then considered by the children's Bureau to be oppressive. Of the 8,50,000 children under sixteen years of age in employment, only 6% of them were in jobs that protected them according to this FLSA Law.[10]

There is a general consensus that oppressive child labour is not present in contemporary U.S. society, recent studies and media stories provide evidence that it does exist. It is predominantly prevalent in the agricultural sector, with few federal and state laws for protection. Children in the non-agricultural sector are subject to health and safety hazards as well as illegal employment. Although the prevailing opinion is that children work because of their desire to acquire material items, researchers have found that children work in order to supplement their families' income; some even work at two jobs. A recent study reported additional reasons for children working: (a) for fun; (b) to occupy time; (c) to keep out of trouble; and (d) to help people in need.[11]

Estimates from a 1997 longitudinal study indicate that 50% of youth of twelve years of age are engaged in some employment activity. Estimates increase to 57% at age fourteen, and at age fifteen it is 64%. Other studies reported that 2.9 million adolescents in the fifteen through seventeen-year-old age group were employed during the school months and 4.0 million during the summer months of 1996-98. The number of adolescents in farm work in the United States is not known. The United Farm Workers' Union estimates that 800,000 children are employed on family owned farms and as hired workers.[12]

It is difficult to track child labour with any accuracy. In the U.S., the Bureau of Labour Statistics (BLS) collects data on persons who are fifteen years and older, but these estimates are not used in official government figures. In addition, United States child labour laws allow children under fifteen years of age to work within family owned farms and businesses as well as in other selected jobs, including as news carriers. The Current Population Survey (CPS) excludes this data from its estimates. As a result, child labour statistics represent conservative underestimates.[13]

About 8 lakh to 1.5million children of age group fifteen, work in agriculture industry of United States in horrible conditions. They do hard physical labour and work for twelve hours a day, due to which they get permanent deformities and heat illness. They get exposed to pesticides and sometimes they are injured seriously. Their life span comes down to forty nine years. Majority of these children are school dropouts. Law made for children who work in agricultural fields are poorly enforced in United States. In the *Department of Labour* v. *Elderkin*,[14] a ten year old boy was working near a dangerous machine. He met with an accident. The court held the farm owner guilty, for employing children in dangerous occupation and hazardous work.[15]

2.1. Critical Analysis of Child Labour Policy of United States of America

The member nations of International Labour Organisation signed International Child Labour Treaty on 16th June 1999 in Geneva and the United States Senate also ratified Child Labour Treaty and it came into force on 19th November 2000. Though there is Child Labour Treaty, children still work in dangerous industries in United States. Children work in horrible conditions due to which they sometime get injured and even die. United States fails to protect its children from hazardous works. The New Deal programs focus on regulation which consists of child labour standards, maximum working hours, fair wages, etc. However, racism and discrimination has led to many restrictions on New Deal Legislation.[16]

The 1966 Amendment of Fair Labour on Standards Act, 1938 (FLSA) prevented children from working on farms consisting of hazardous occupation and the 1947 amendment prevented children below 12 years from working on any farm. Children between 12 and 16 years of age were permitted to work on the farm, only if their parents were working on the same farm.[17] Human Rights Watch Report says that 16 years old children work 14 hours a day, 6 days per week from April to November while harvesting in farms. For this work of eighty-four hours per week, children are not given overtime wages and this is allowed under the exemptions of FLSA. Though there is labour law and legislation since 60 years, child labourers of agricultural industry are not protected from hazardous working conditions, low wages and long working hours. The Report further says that, children used knives, climb ladders and work near heavy machinery. According to the survey done by the department of labour in foreign countries, children work for long hours without rest. They are exposed to toxic chemicals which cause lung, skin, respiratory diseases, permanent physical handicaps and cancer.[18]

There are many exemptions under United States Labour Law which permits child labour. Due to these exemptions if the child is employed by his parents, the child is allowed to earn less than minimum wages and child can work for a number of hours without any limitation provided: the work is not during school hours. Under Article 4(1) of the Child Labour Treaty, each signatory state can have its own interpretations of the word 'hazardous work'. Under Article 3(1) of Child Labour Treaty, Children should not do hazardous work and it also prohibits work in farms which are not family farms. Due to the exemption of family farm, any employer could stand in the place of parent and employ children.[19] Thus, the law in U.S.A. is full of drawbacks and extends no resistance to child labour.

3. CHILD LABOUR IN ENGLAND

Child labour was prevailing in England beginning from 14th century. The first Statute of 1388 laid down that any boy or girl; which used to labour at the plough or cart or other labour or service of husbandry till they be of the age of 12 years, that from thenceforth they shall abide of the same labour.[20]

For the protection of the child from exploitation, various measures were undertaken and legislations enacted. The increase in population in England compelled the parents to send their children to do some profitable work. In 1536, the Government of England, enacted a legislation for the employment of poor children in agriculture or other crafts between the ages 5 to 14 years.[21]

Subsequently, Government of England enacted the statute of Apprentices, 1563; the Act of 1601; the Act of 1697; the Health and Morals of Apprentices Act, 1802; The Factories Act, 1833; The Mines Regulation Act, 1842; The Factories Act, 1844; the Factories Act of 1860 and 1870; Factories Act, Extension Act and Workshops Regulation Acts, 1867; the Factories Act, 1874; The Act of 1876; The Factory and Workshops Act, 1878; The Factory and Workshop Act, 1871; The Factory and Workshops Act, 1901; Coal Mines Regulation Act; The Children and Young Persons Act, 1933; The Factories Act, 1937; The Education Act of 1944; and The Factories Act, 1961. These enactments indicate that Government of England was serious about prohibiting the employment of children.

Today in England, the children are engaged in part time activities. The Emrys Davies Report, 1972 came as a shock.[22] The report found that three quarters of all children between 13 and 15 had some sort of part time employment. Dr. Davis divided these jobs into two categories,[23] labelled 'A' and 'B' Category. 'A' contained those which were subject to various bylaws, they included manual work, delivery rounds, jobs in shops and on farms. Category 'B' covered domestic work, child care and voluntary service and other jobs not subject to any control. The Davis Report was a major factor in promoting new legislation. The Employment of Children Act, 1973 gave the Government new powers to restrict the employment of persons under the upper limit of school leaving age. The intention of the former was to enable the Government to give better protection to children doing part-time work. But after this restriction the child prostitution has increased dramatically in England due to the financial need. On February 12, 1978, the *Sunday Times* reported that Scotland Yard had thirty-six names of 18 years old girls who had been cautioned or arrested for prostitution of whom ten were under 16. It is, therefore, suggested that some outlet for growing feelings of independence and a desire or need to earn many, should be recognised. Otherwise youngsters may more readily turn to crime or prostitution.

4. CHILD LABOUR IN RUSSIA

The concept of child labour does not exist in Russia, a socialist country. Friedrich Engel has rightly pointed out: "On the first day immediately following the seizure of political power, the working class must take more decisive measures for curbing female and child labour (the bill) for the ten hours or even eight hours working days.[24]

Further, speaking of the reasons for the appearance of child labour under capitalism, Karl Marx, emphasized:[25]

> "In so far as machinery dispenses with muscular power, it becomes a means of employing labour of slight muscular strength, and those whose bodily development is incomplete, but whose limbs are all the more supple. The labour of women and children was, therefore, the first thing sought for the capitalists who used machinery."

The Soviet State had taken various steps to protect its women and children. Some specific protections are provided to women and children by legislation. The employment of women and young persons under 18 in hazardous work is prohibited by Article 129 of the Code of Labour

Laws. Such types of work were listed by the National Code of Labour of Russia in 1932. Later on, these lists were changed due to the improvement in sanitary conditions of labour and removal of hazards in certain employments. A standard of maximum weight that can be lifted was made according to the Article 129 of the Code of Labour Laws. Night and overtime work by children is prohibited.

In addition, there are certain specific rules to protect children. These are:[26]

(i) The employment of children below 16 is prohibited, but children below 15 years can be taken for educational work with the permission of a Trade Union;

(ii) The young person under 18 can be employed after a medical check-up. Later on he is required for medical examination not more than once a year;

(iii) Maximum permitted working hours for young persons between 16 and 18 years are 6 hours a day and from children for 15 to 16 years of age are 4 hours a day; and

(iv) The young persons under 18 can enjoy usually holidays of one month duration, but not less than 24 working days. As a general rule summer holidays are also provided to children.

5. CHILD LABOUR IN CHINA

Child labour is prevailing in China in different forms and different age groups. The history of child labour in China parallels the development of the public education system. The history of development is examined under four phases.[27]

5.1. Child Labour before the Opium War (1840-1942)

Before the Opium War, China was a traditional agricultural country. The family was the basic unit of productivity. Everybody, including children, played a role in productivity. Girls were involved in domestic work and boys were involved in farm work. Children also worked in family businesses such as tea shops, wood shops and drugstores. The involvement of children in agricultural productivity was an inseparable part of survival for the family and society. Education before opium wars was a luxury for only the wealthy families and those in the official classes of privilege. Children were sold to the wealthy persons and thereby exploited. Children once sold, they became slaves to wealthy families. The parents used to sign a contract and received a one time payment. Usually, the child would receive only housing and food, and were forbidden to leave until the contract ended. The bonded children were sold to Qing Lou-brothels that forced children into prostitution. Thus, there were no laws to either protect the children or eliminate the exploitative practices before the opium war.[28]

5.2. Child Labour after the Opium War (1843-1949)

During this period children continued to help the vast agricultural productivity, and the practice of tong yang xi and sale of female children persisted. With the foreign influence significant social changes impacted the life of children in China. The western education system influenced the curriculum and the structure of education. The concept of unified public education system, which enabled the children, from working families to attend school, was introduced. One of the most significant changes was extension of public education to girls, who were not allowed to go to school until 1907. During this period Child Labour Commission in Shanghai and the International Child Labour Standards developed at that time. Many laws which were passed not enforced due to many barriers like poverty, lack of birth records, lack of national educational organization, etc., and laws in reality existed only on paper.[29]

5.3. Child Labour Elimination in Communist China (1949-78)

During this period the Chinese Communist Party instituted economic reforms and expanded mass public education. Through its socialist moment and strict social control, child labour was eliminated. The practice of selling girls for prostitution, apprenticeships, and tong yang xi were regarded as forms of class exploitation and oppression were eradicated in this new social system. When people applied for employment, their age, family background, education and criminal record were checked. It was impossible for a young child to get employment.[30]

5.4. Child Labour after 1978

The Great Cultural Revolution ended in 1976. Economic reform began and China opened its doors to the world in 1978. Child labour again reappeared in this economic development. Within the free market economy factory owners and managers favour the labour of children because they are paid less than adults. In addition, they are frequently more docile workers and unaware of their rights. Some local government officials ignore child labour in factories as long as the business taxes are paid. Businesses and small factories owned by sub-contractors after do not have business licenses, and enforcement is typically weak in this uniformal sector. In order to escape notice, some reverse their work hours. Another technique used by some factories in remote areas is to move frequently. Conditions in these businesses are extremely hazardous.[31]

5.5. Recent Position of Child Labour in China

Children work in construction, electronics, the apparel industry and other industrial and commercial enterprises. Exploitation of children is rampant in the special economic zones set-up by the Government. Thus, child labour is yet to be eliminated in China. Many children under the age of 16 are still being hired to work long hours for low wages. So Government of China has committed to evolve education policy extending to the poor children, thereby child labour may be reduced.[32]

6. CHILD LABOUR IN SOUTH AFRICA

Child Labour is best understood in the context of societal values and cultural norms. South Africa has developed legislation for addressing the issues of child labour. The term child labour in South African government documents refers to the inappropriate or exploitative work activities of children.[33] In 1998, child labour in South Africa was defined as "Work by children under 18 which is exploitative, hazardous or otherwise inappropriate for their age, detrimental to their schooling, or social, physical, mental, spiritual or moral development".[34] The above definition includes household chores and activities in the household of the child's caregiver that are in appropriate for the child's age. Children can be found working as part of the daily routine of family life performing school maintenance, and working as farm labourers or in service jobs. Many of the jobs that children perform are neither harmful nor exploitative; other works in a myriad of exploitative or hazardous activities, thousands of children, however, work in ways that risk their health and safety, rob them of their childhood, and thwart normal physical and mental development. Children work in a number of industries that expose them to harsh environments, unsafe chemicals and equipment, and long working hours.[35]

The Mail and Guardian, one of the leading news papers in South Africa,[36] estimated that more than 13 million of South Africa's children work. Department of Labour in 1996 estimates that over 4 lakh children from the age of 10 through 14 are engaged in child labour. In June 1993, UNICEF and the National Children's Rights Committee (NCRC) reported that about 7,81,000, black South African and coloured children from the ages of 5 through 14 years were used in child labour, most of whom were believed to be employed in the informal and agricultural sectors. The number of white and Indian children for labour was reported to be negligible.[37]

In South Africa, child work is also a form of socialization and acculturation. Child work in and of itself is not necessarily harmful or exploitative, but if minors are required to work in hazardous conditions or excessive hours, then work becomes exploitative and can harm the physical and emotional development of the child.[38]

Understanding child labour in South Africa involves distinguishing between economic and non-economic work activities (ILO, 2000A).[39] Economic work activities involve work with or without pay that directly benefits the family. Any child under 18 who works to help in a family business or assist in family farming or fishing is considered engaging in economic work activities. Non-economic work activities for children consists of house keeping and other chores in the home of a care giver who is not a parent, and school maintenance such as cleaning class rooms and toilets, which are performed regularly on a non-voluntary basis. These unpaid activities, which are performed for others, are considered non-economic because there is no direct benefit to the parents. Schools in South Africa are not fully supported by Government funds, and families must pay a fee for their children to attend school. For many schools in South Africa, particularly schools attended by black Africans, School fees alone do not provide enough revenue to hire workers to do the routine cleaning and maintenance. Therefore, these tasks may be performed by school children. While there are no international standards concerning the number of hours a child can work each week in school maintenance, the ILO considers more than five hours a week performing school maintenance tasks excessive.[40]

The practice of child labour cause serious repercussions. Children, who engage in child labour are less likely to receive an education, may have their physical and social development compromised, or could experience working conditions that threaten their very lives. The African National Congress then ruling party in South Africa made its commitment to provide protection to its citizens, particularly to women and children, from abuse and violence. In 1997 Basic Conditions of Employment Act was introduced which established a minimum age for employment and the conditions under which a youth can be employed.[41]

The elimination of child labour is a complex issue. So the South African Government recognises that a comprehensive approach is needed to combat child labour.

7. CHILD LABOUR IN COUNTRIES OF SOUTH ASIA

7.1. Bangladesh

Bangladesh is a very young country that has faced problems similar to India's. As in most dominantly agricultural countries, children have historically worked alongside their parents and extended family members on farms, in fishing, and in trades. There is also a long history of children working as domestic servants and in light manufacturing. In its broadest terms, child labour has been an adopted practice. It has long been a response to severe poverty.

UNICEF 1991 reports that in 1989 there were 33.7 million children in Bangladesh in the age group of 5-16. More than half of them did not attend school, it can be inferred that children worked either for wage or for survival. In Bangladesh, four out of every ten children never attend school. More than half of those who do never get beyond second grade and more than three quarters do not complete primary level.[42]

According to Bangladesh Bureau of Statistics Labour Force Survey (1990), there are 5.7 million 10 to 14 years old children working in Bangladesh.[43] Another estimate puts the number at 15 million. Nearly all the child labourers in export industries is found in the garment industry. According to Bangladesh Ministry of Labour, "Children are found working in garments, bakeries and confectionaries, hotels and restaurants, transport, beedi factories, small engineering workshops, fish processing and other informal and unregulated sectors." Further, children drive rickshaws, carry goods for shoppers at markets, roll cigarettes, work in shrimp processing and are exposed to hazardous conditions in the leather industry.

Bangladesh Constitution provides safeguards to the children under Articles 23 and 24 which prohibit the employment of children in factories, mines or in any hazardous work. There are number of statutes which provide protection and stipulate the minimum ages at which children can legally work in certain sectors: (1) Mines Act states that, children below 15 years cannot be employed in mines and the minimum age of employment stated is 15 years with medical certificates of fitness; (2) For children under the age of 15, the Employment of Children's Act, 1938 prohibits work in Railways and Ports; (3) In commercial sides, the Shops and Establishments Act, 1965 prohibits the employment of children younger than 12; (4) The Factories Act, 1965 define child as a person who has not completed 16 years of age and it prohibits employment of children below 14 years in any factory and there is a penalty for violation of this Act under Article 14(1), the fine is upto 1000 Taka; and (5) The Children's Act, 1974 define child as a person below the age of 16 years and it prohibits the employment of children under the age of 15 years.[44]

With regard to inspection there is scarce resources as such enforcement of child labour became difficult. Factories Act, various Health and Safety codes are prescribed but are regularly violated. Consequently numerous lives have been lost to fires because doors have been locked and workers could not escape. The Bangladesh Constitution prohibits forced or bonded child labour, locking doors and requiring women to work overtime to meet a production dead line continued to shape conditions in the garment section. For people of eighteen years and over, prostitution is legal only with Government certification. However, ignored by law enforcement, and those who employ child prostitutes are rarely prosecuted and police and local authorities can be easily bribed.[45]

It is significant to mention that Bangladesh is a signatory to various International Human Rights Conventions namely, International Labour Organization Convention No. 59, concerning minimum age for Admission to Employment in industry, including U.N. Convention on the Rights of the Child and International Labour Organisation Convention 182 against the worst forms of child labour. There are eight laws related to child labour on the books, however these have not yet been implemented and no child labour cases have been filed.[46] Bangladesh too has not ratified International Labour Organisation Convention No. 138 concerning minimum age for admission to employment.

7.2. Thailand

There is an increased child labour practice in Thailand. Bangkok's Human Resource Institute recorded that at least 5 million Thai children, some as young as 7 years of age, work in 1993. Child labour does exist in export industries including garments, gems, leather bags, shrimps and sea-food processing. In 2001, the International Labour Organization estimated that 11.5% of children in the age group of 10-14 years in Thailand were working. Children work in agriculture construction manufacturing industrial services and fishing sector.[47]

In order to protect the rights of the children and prohibit child labour, Section 35 of the Thailand Constitution states that, "Forced labour shall not be imposed except by virtue of the law specifically enacted for the purpose of averting imminent public calamity or by virtue of the law which provides for its imposition during the time when the country is in a state of armed conflict or war, or when a state of emergency or martial law is declared."

Section 68 of Directive Principles of the State Policy provides that, the State should support and promote citizens development, especially children and youth, so that they may be physically, mentally, intellectually, morally and ethically sound.

There is a Labour Protection Act, 1998 in Thailand which sets the minimum age of employment at 15 years. Law permits children between the ages 15 and 18 to work only between the hours of 4 pm and 10 pm with the permission of Government authority. Children under 18 may not be employed in hazardous work, which is defined by the law to include any work involving hazardous chemicals, harmful temperatures or noise levels, exposure to toxic micro-organisms, the operation of heavy equipments, and work underground or under water. The inspecting officers have the right to remove child workers from business and place them in Government custody. Maximum penalty for the violation of child labour law under Labour Protection Act is one of imprisonment and fine of Rs. 200,000 or both.

Thailand is a party to the United Nations Convention on the Rights of the Child and it has not ratified International Labour Organisation Convention No. 59 concerning minimum age for admission to employment in industry, and International Labour Organization Convention No.138 concerning minimum age for admission to employment.[48]

7.3. Philippines

Child labour is recognised as a serious problem in Philippines in the year 1991. This country is known for wood and clothing industries which are based on small enterprises, child labour, both male and female, is extensively used. About 72% of the children are employed in wood industry and about 82% clothing manufacture.[49] The Philippines Department of Labour and Employment estimated that there were 7,77,000 Filipino workers in the age group of 10-14, and 1.4 million between 15 and 17 years. These figures exclude the large number of working children below the age of 10. In 1994, Department of Labour and Employment reportedly acknowledged that, altogether at least 5 million children work in commercial and industrial sectors in the Philippines. These figures coincide with UNICEF and International Labour Organisation estimates of 5 to 5.7 million working children in 1993.[50]

The Filipino Garment industry commonly uses child labour in the manufacture of products exported to United States. Child labour allegedly found in wood and rattan furniture making and in gold mining, but further research is required. In addition, there are reports of child labour in food processing (including sardine canning), fire works/ pyrotechnics, footwear, plastic bags, and so called 'muroami fishing'. There is no statistics on the number of child workers in Filipino export industry.[51]

Constitution of Philippines 1987 values the dignity of every human being and guarantees full respect for human rights. It recognises to protect children from all forms of neglect, abuse, cruelty, exploitation, and other conditions prejudicial to their development. Article II, Section 13 of the 1987 Constitution states that, "The State recognises the vital role of the youth in nation-building and shall promote and protect their physical, moral, spiritual, intellectual and social well-being. It shall inculcate in the youth patriotism and nationalism, and encourage their involvement in public and civic affairs".[52]

There is a Child Protection Act, 1992 which provides special protection to children against child abuse, exploitation and discriminations. Section 12 prohibits the employment of children under 15 years of age but they can be employed subject to fulfilment of certain requirements.[53] (1) Employer must obtain permission from the government for the employment of child; (2) He shall secure the protection, health, safety and morals of the child; (3) To pay suitable remuneration and fix proper working time; and (4) To provide programme for training and skill acquisition of child. There is a section 13 of Child Protection Act which intended to provide non-formal education for working children and section 14 prohibit employment of children in certain advertisements for example alcoholic beverages, intoxicating drinks, tobacco, and its by-products and violence.[54]

Any person, who violates the Child Protection Act, shall be liable for imprisonment of three months which may extend to 3 years and fine 1000 pesos which may extend to 10,000 pesos or with both. The Bureau of Women and Young Workers is charged with enforcing the child labour laws. But with a few number of labour inspectors, the monitories of child labour laws remains an enormous challenge.

Philippines is a party to United Nations Convention on the Rights of the Child and International Labour Organization Convention No. 59 concerning minimum age for admission to employment in industry and it is not ratified International Labour Organisation Convention No. 138 concerning minimum age for admission to employment.

7.4. Nepal

In Nepal Child Labour has assumed serious propositions. It is estimated that three million working children are in Nepal. Most working children are in agriculture and in the export-oriented Carpet Industry. Children are also working in garment industry, "Thanka" Painting, and in handicraft. In Kathmandu, there are more than 40,000 children working as carpet boys, brick and factory workers, restaurant boys and rag pickers.[55]

The Constitution of Nepal, 1990, seeks to protect the interests of children by conferring on them, certain fundamental rights, and imposing for their benefit certain 'directive principles' and policies of the State. The State shall make necessary arrangements to safeguard the rights and interests of children, ensure that they are not exploited, and make gradual arrangements for free education.[56]

The Constitution of the Kingdom of Nepal (1991) forbids the employment of children in a factory, mine or dangerous or hazardous workplace under the age of 14 years. Children's Rights and Welfare Act, 1992 define child as a person who has reached the agé of 16 and states that a child who has not attained the age of 14 shall not be employed in any work as a labourer. The Act was enacted to protect the rights and interests of the Nepalese children to ensure their physical, mental and intellectual development.

The Labour Act, 1992, and Labour Rules, 1993 contains special provisions for the prohibition of employment of children below 14 years and prohibits admission to hazardous work for minors (aged between 14 and 18 years). The Government of Nepal has enacted the Child Labour (Prohibition and Regulation) Act, 1999 in response to its ratification of the International Labour Organisation; Minimum Age Convention No. 138 has made important amendments in the Labour Act, 1992. The Child Labour Act, enlists specific occupations as hazardous work and prohibits the use of children below 16 years of age in such activities.[57]

Nepal Government had also enacted Self-Governance Act, 1997 for making provisions for decentralized action for children and against child labour. Nepal is signed various international Conventions like International Labour Organisation Worst form of Child Labour Convention (No. 182); International Labour Organisation Minimum Age Convention (No. 138); International Labour Organisation Forced Labour Convention (No. 29); United Nations Convention on the Rights of the Child. (CRC).

7.5. Pakistan

Child labour is rampant in Pakistan. According to one estimate, among 40 million children aged 5-14 years in Pakistan and 3.3 million, i.e. 8.3% were economically active in 1996.[58] Most Pakistani children work in agricultural sector. So, child labour is rural oriented, and a large number of children also work in urban centres, weaving carpets, manufacturing, surgical instruments and producing goods for export. There are allegation of children working in other industries including leather, foot wear and mining, millions of children who are under a system of bonded labour to work in brick kilns, carpet industries, agriculture, fisheries, stone brick, crushing, shoe making, power looms, etc. Bonded Labour Liberation Front estimates that 8 million children are bonded in Pakistan. Half a million are allegedly, bonded in carpet industry alone. Some of these reportedly come from Afghanistan, Bangladesh and Burma. Child slavery and carpet industry are flourishing in Pakistan. S. Hafeez opines that[59] most of the children all over Pakistan work in the carpet industry. Weaving carpets is a family occupation transmitted from generation to generation. In the informal carpet industry, family children are easily absorbed at home and formal, where the industrialist has his own loom installed at his factory. So, here "Carpets are the countries 5th largest foreign currency earner".

There are various Constitutional provisions which prevent exploitation and protect the interest of children under Article 11(1) which forbids slavery; Article 11(2) prohibits all forms of forced labour and traffick in human beings; and Article 11(3) prohibits employment of children below the age of 14 years in any factory or mine or any other hazardous employment. There are various legislations which prohibit the employment of children below specified age limit, i.e. 14 years. The Employment of Children Act, 1991 is the latest statute in the area of child employment and was enacted in response to enforcing Conventions on child labour. This Act prohibits the employment of children below 14 years of age in certain occupations and processes. The Pakistan Law Commission in its meeting held on 29th May 1999 resolve to enhance the present age limit for child work from 14 years to 15 years to protect him or her against any possible harm to their physical or mental/ psychological growth. There is also the Bonded Labour (Abolition) Act, 1992 which abolishes and makes illegal bonded labour in Pakistan and cancels all obligations of bonded labourers to their employers and declared that, there is obligation on the part of the bonded labour to repay any bonded debt and same is cancelled and no suit could be brought for the recovery of such debt. Any person who violates this law is imprisoned from 2 years to 5 years or fine of Rs. 50,000 or with both. Pakistan is a party to International Labour Organization Convention No. 59, concerning minimum age of employment in industry and United Nations Convention on the Rights of the Child. Pakistan has not ratified International Labour Organisation Convention No. 138 concerning minimum age of employment.

7.6. Sri Lanka

In the year 1999 The Srilankan Department of Census and Statistics estimated in 1999 that 14.9% of children in the age group of 5-14 years in Sri Lanka were working. Most of the working children are in agricultural sector.[60] Children are also working in informal sector like manufacturing, hotels and domestic services. Children who were migrated from rural areas to urban households work as domestic servants under bonded system to repay the debt borrowed by their parents. Government estimates that more than 2000 children are engaged in child prostitution. Child soldiering is also prevailing in the country between January 2002 and November 2004, UNICEF documented 4600 cases of child recruitment by the LTTE (Liberation Tigers of Tamil Ealam), but only 1208 children were released from its forces.[61] Constitution of Sri Lanka 1978 provide various safeguards under Article 27(13) that, State pledges to "promote with special care the interest of children and youth so as to ensure their full development, physical, mental, religious and social and to protect them from exploitation and discrimination".

In addition the Draft Constitution (August 2000) Article 22 provides special Rights for Children, guaranteeing a child to be protected from abuse; to have access to free education between the ages of 5 and 14, and not to be employed in any hazardous activity. It also defines conclusively a child is a person under the age of 14 years. Among the various legislations the Employment of Women, Young Persons and Children's Act, 1956 is concerned with child labour which prohibits work by children that may be injurious, work by children during school hours and work by children under 14 years in general and under 18 years in industrial settings at night. Further, children below 14 years are prohibited to work in any family industrial operations. The minimum age of employment of children was raised from 12 to 14 years in December, 1999 by an amendment to the Employment of Women Young Persons and Children's Act, 1956. Again in 2003, this Act was amended to allow children below 14 years old to work only in part time family agriculture work or participate in technical training. National Child Protection Authority Law (1998) was established for effective implementation of National policy for the prevention of child abuse, etc. Provision for penalty is made whereas compensation is paid to victims, by employers violating the minimum age of employment laws. Penalties for trafficking children could be imposed with prosecution and imprisonment of 5-20 years and a fine. Sri Lanka has ratified various Conventions, namely, International labour Organisation worst forms of Child Labour Convention (No. 182); International Labour Organisation Minimum Age for Employment Convention (No. 138); International Labour Organisation Abolition of Forced Labour Convention (No. 105); and UN Convention on Rights of the Child (CRC).

7.7. Afghanistan

The International Labour Organization estimated that 23.8% of children aged 10 to 14 years in Afghanistan were working in 2002.[62] Child workers are reported to be numerous in rural areas. Particularly in animal herding, and collecting paper and fire wood. Children are also found working in urban informal sector engaged in activities such as shining shoes, begging, or rummaging of scrap metals in the streets. There are reports that children continue to join or forcibly recruited into armed insurgent groups.

Article 49 of the Constitution of Afghanistan States that; "Forced labour is forbidden. Active participation, in times of war, calamity and other situations threatening public life and welfare is one of the primary duties of every Afghan. Children shall not be subjected to forced labour".

The Labour Law 1999 under Article 15 provides that in special situation the child who has not completed the age of 14 could be appointed as a servant. If the child has completed the age of 13, the child can be admitted as a learner and work can be assigned. Independent jobs cannot be delivered to the child. Further the Labour Code prohibits children under the age of 15 from working more than 30 hours a week. Afghanistan has ratified many Conventions; important among them are UN Convention on the Rights of the Child and International Labour Organization Convention 182 Prohibition and Immediate Action for the Elimination of the Worst Forms of Child Labour, 1999.[63]

8. COMPARATIVE ANALYSIS

According to International Labour Organization, there are 250 million child labourers in the world of which 61 percent are in Asia, 32 percent in Africa and 7 percent in Latin America. In terms of number of child labourers Asia tops, whereas, in proportion of children, Africa tops where every third child is working. Although the international focus is on formal sector (export) industries, in reality only five percent of all child workers work there.[64]

Further, with reference to another analysis, statistics shows that, Child labour is most rampant in Asia with 44.6 million or 13% of its children doing commercial work followed by Africa at 23.6 million or 26.3% which is the highest rate and Latin America at 5.1 million that is 9.8%. In India, 14.4% children between 10 and 14 years of age are employed in child labour, in Bangladesh 30.1%, in China 11.6%, in Pakistan 17.7%, in Turkey 24%, in Cote D'lvorie 20.5%, in Egypt 11.2%, in Kenya 41.3%, in Nigeria 25.8%, in Senegal 31.4%, in Argentina 4.5%, in Brazil 16.1%, in Maxico 6.7%, in Italy 0.4% and in Portugal 1.8%. The above figures only give part of the picture. No reliable figures of the child workers below 10 years of age are available, though they comprise a significant amount.[65]

Child labour levels are high in many developing countries. The accurate measure of child labour is, however, difficult to obtain, as there is no clear-cut definition of child labour according to international law. Children are often excluded from the official statistics. The minimum age for a child's employment into work also varies across regions. Therefore, the estimate of child labour would vary depending on how we define work, how we define a child, and how we collect data.[66]

This represents the minimum age for work and the compulsory education age for different countries.

According to International Labour Organisation estimates of

2004, 317 million children were 'economically active' in the age group of five to 17 years, across the world, of whom 218 million hazardous work. For the narrower age group of five to 14 years olds, the corresponding figures are 191 million economically active children, 166 million child labourers, and 74 million children in hazardous work. The highest number of child workers in the age group of five to 14 years is found in Asia-Pacific (122.3 million) followed by sub-Saharan Africa (49.3 million) and Latin America and the Caribbean (5.7 million). While Asia has the highest number of child workers, sub-Saharan Africa has the highest proportion of working children. (ILO, 2006a).[67]

However, there is difference between an 'economically active child;' and 'child labour', as per the estimate produced by the ILO. For example, the ILO treats a child as 'economically active' if the child has worked one hour or more in the reference week.[68] The definition of child labour for those in the age group of five to 11 years is synonymous with the 'economically active'; for those in the age group of 12 to 14, child labour consists of those who have worked 14 hours or more, but less than 43 hours non-hazardous work per week for those who have one hour or more hazardous work per week. Children in the age group of 15-17 years are generally allowed to work. However, if they are engaged in hazardous work, they are considered as child labourers.

The United States and the United Kingdom shares a common history in the area of child labour. In the earlier days America accepted child labour for one thing, most people had little knowledge of what was going on the government did not record national statistics children. For another, children were treated better than in England. Although the general public accepted whipping rooms, believing that, punishment kept the devil out of the child, 'the beating were not as brutal as those in England. Furthermore, there were no American girls dragging loaded coal deep underground in coal mines. Another reason for accepting child labour was that many people believed working children kept parents from becoming dependent upon public charity. In addition, working children kept production cost down, and this made the nation competitive abroad.[69]

Finally, people believed that children benefited morally from their work. It was an established belief that 'idleness was a sin and industry a virtue'. From the earliest colonial days, the long standing belief that works was good for children. It built character and taught responsibility and thrift. While these may indeed result from work, in fact the employer benefited for more than the employee.[70]

Today child labour is defined as the illegal employment of children when the children are under the legal minimum age, when they work longer hours than allowed by law, when their compensation is unfair, illegal or non-existent, or when the working conditions endanger their health.[71]

The Child Labour Coalition, a group that includes such organisation as the American Academy of paediatrics, American Federation of Teachers, Consumer Federation of America, General Federation of Women's Clubs, National Education Association, Children's Defence Fund, and various labour unions wants Congress to enlarge the number of prohibited teenage occupation and work activities, reduce the number of hours of children work, and vigorously enforce the laws with higher fines.[72]

In United States of America majority of child workers are employed in agriculture and a high proportion of these are from immigrants families. The reasons which lead to child employment vary substantially with local condition and local cultures. These are divided into three broad categories:[73]

(i) Where a family simply cannot afford to keep a child at home, so he or she is put out to earn;
(ii) There are children whose families cannot afford to keep them at home and realize on whatever financial value they may have on the market; and
(iii) It falls within the system of bonded labour.

United States has signed International Child Labour Treaty, despite this children work in dangerous industries. There was a lack of enforcement machinery and there are many exemptions under U.S. labour law which permits child labour and due to these parents by taking undue advantage employ their children.

In England child labour was prevailing since 14th century and continued till today even after introduction of several domestic laws due to social economic situation in developing countries offers very poor living conditions for the majority of population.

The USSR Government has undertaken various drastic steps to combat child labour and challenges ahead in the process of elimination of child labour.

In China, there was a rampant child labour practice prevailing in the early period but after the beginning of economical reforms again child labour increased but the China Government has evolved education policy for elimination of child labour.

International Labour Organisation has estimated the highest rates of child labour in Africa. In South Africa child work was considered as a form of socialization and there was no universal age limit for employment of children. Children work in Schools maintenance.

Children are allowed to work non-hazardous and during normal hours. It has made a distinction between economic and non-economic work activities.

In Bangladesh (South Asia) child labour has been an accepted practice because of extreme poverty. More children work in garment industry and thereby children are exploited. Out of 33.7 million children in the age group of 5-16 more than half of them did not attend school and 8 million children not going to school. Though various legislations introduced they have not practically implemented. Though Bangladesh has signed various Conventions but it shows, there is a little response.

In Thailand, 11.5% of children in the age group of 10 to 14 years were working. Thailand law permits children between the ages 15 and 18 to work only between the hours of 4 pm and 10 pm with the permission of the Government authority. This shows Government is intended to protect children below 15 years from exploitation more so, children are allowed under the law to work after school hours. This is a progressive measure undertaken by the Government.

The historical record reveals an astonishing co-relation between the progress of education and decrease in the volume of child labour. The highest number of school enrolment coincides with the lowest number of school age children per teacher, and are found in the most developed countries.[74] The United States of America, the United Kingdom and New Zealand and are such countries where child labour is least apparent. However, the relationship between child labour and illiteracy may not be one of cause and effect. Some countries such as Mexico, Columbia and Thailand, Spain and Italy, have largely succeeded in eradicating illiteracy but remain confronted by the child labour problem. The child labour is also rooted in the traditions and attitudes of the regions where it is practiced.[75]

Philippines is known for wood and clothing industries, where in, child labour is extensively used. Government of Philippines enacted number of legislations for prohibition of child labour but due to understaffing and few numbers of inspectors, elimination of child labour remained as a problem.

In Nepal child labour is a serious problem. Most working children are in agriculture and carpet industry. Legislations in respect of eradicating child labour remained as a problem and required effective enforcement and creating public awareness.

Pakistan is known for carpet industry where in most of the children all over the Pakistan work in the carpet industry. Law Commission of Pakistan recommended to the Government to enhance present age of 14 years to 15 years. Bonded Labour (Abolition) Act which was in Pakistan is to some extent effectively implemented. The Bonded Labour Liberation Front of Pakistan estimates some 8 million children in Pakistan are in handed employment in April 1984. The bonded Labour liberation front of India discovered 32 children aged 6 to 14, all employed by the same loom owner.

In Sri Lanka, who ever violates Child Labour Laws National Child Protection Authority Law shall be prosecuted and compensation is paid to victims by employers.

In Afghanistan forced Labour is forbidden and the Labour Code prohibits children under the age of 15 from working more than 30 hours a week. Thus, the problem of child labour is a global phenomenon, which is found in both developed and developing nations.

Thus, the problem of child labour is a global phenomenon, which is found in both developed and developing nations.

Notes and References

1. M.H. Rehman, Kanta Rehman, *Child Labour and Child Rights: A Compendium*, New Delhi: Manak Publications, 2002, p. 22.
2. *Ibid.*, p. 24.
3. *Ibid.*, p. 25.
4. *Ibid.*, p. 25.
5. Cathryane, L. Schmitz, Elizabeth Kimjin Traver and Desi Larson, "*Child Labour: A Global View*", p. 188.
6. Hawes, 1991; Hobbs, Mc. Kechine and Lavalette, 1999; Zinn, 1995, "*Child Labour: A World History Companion*" cited in Cathryne, L. Schmitz, "*Child Labour; A Global View*", p. 188.
7. *Ibid.*, pp. 188-89.
8. Freedman in Cathryne, L. Schmitz, "*Child Labour: A Global View*", p. 190.
9. *Supra* note 5, pp. 186-87.
10. *Ibid.*, p. 190.
11. Pieris, 2003 in Cathryne, L. Schmitz, "*Child Labour: A Global View*", p. 187.
12. *Ibid.*, also see Human Rights Watch, 2000.
13. *Ibid.*, p. 187.
14. *Department of Labour* v. *Elder Kin*, 2000 WL 960261, 2 (DOL, Adm, Rev.) Bd. 2000.
15. Corlett, C., Impact of the 2000 Child Labour Treaty on United States Child Labourers (2002) 19, *Arizona Journal of International and Comparative Law*, 713-33.
16. *Ibid.*
17. Lorenz, C., "The Search for Constitutional Protection of Labour Standards" (2000) 23 *Seattle. V.L. Rev.*, p. 569.
18. *Supra* note 15.
19. *Ibid.*
20. Ivy Pinchbeck and Margaret Heweitt, Children in English Society (1969), Vol. I, also see, F. Challies and D. Elliman, *Child Workers Today* (1979), p. 20.
21. J.C. Kulshreshta, *Child Labour in India* (1978), p. 20.
22. Embrys Davis, *Work out of School*, London: Councils and Education Press, 1972, also see Aloc Fyfe, *Child Labour* (1989), p. 34.
23. *Ibid.*

24. Karl Marx and Friedrich Engles, Soch, 2nd ed., Vol. 23, p. 406.
25. Great Soviet Encyclopedia, 1975, Vol. 8, p. 20.
26. *Supra* note 21, pp. 47-48.
27. *Supra* note 5, p. 43.
28. *Ibid.*, pp. 43-44.
29. *Ibid.*, p. 45.
30. *Ibid.*, p. 46.
31. *Ibid.*, p. 47.
32. *Ibid.*
33. *Ibid.*, p. 152.
34. ILO, 2000b, p. 1.
35. *Supra* note 5, p. 145.
36. *Ibid.*, p. 146.
37. *Ibid.*, p. 147.
38. *Ibid.*, p. 150.
39. *Ibid.*
40. *Ibid.*
41. *Ibid.*, p. 152.
42. *Supra* note 1, p. 25.
43. Helen R. Sekhar, *Child Labour Legislation in Select Countries of South Asia*, Noida: V.V. Giri National Institute of Labour.
44. *Ibid.*
45. *Supra* note 5, p. 18.
46. *Ibid.*, p. 19.
47. *Supra* note 43.
48. *Ibid.*
49. Obsterhout, Henk Van, "Child *Labour in the Philippines: The Muro-Ami-Deep-Sea Fishing Operations*", 1988, see also M.H. Rehman, *Child Labour and Child Rights*, New Delhi: Manak Publications, 2002, p. 30.
50. *Supra* note 43.
51. *Ibid.*
52. *Ibid.*
53. *Ibid.*
54. *Ibid.*
55. *Supra* note 1, p. 40.
56. *Supra* note 43. p.
57. *Ibid.*
58. *Ibid.*
59. H. Hafeez, "*Child Labour in Pakistan*" (1978).
60. *Supra* note 43.
61. *Ibid.*
62. *Ibid*
63. *Ibid.*
64. Subhash Sharma, "Trends, Causes and Consequences of Child Labour in India", Vol. LV, No. 2, April-June (2009) *The Indian Journal of Public Administration*, p. 222 and also see ILO, "*Strategies for Eliminating Child Labour. International Conference on Child Labour*, Oslo, Oct. 1997.

65. Dr. G.B. Patil, *Child Labour: A Stigma on Humanity*, 1st edn., Bangalore: KILPAR Law Studies Series, 2009, pp. 9-10
66. Rasheda Khanam and Mohammed Rehman, "Child Labour in Developing Countries: The Role of Education, Poverty and Birth Order", Vol. 10, July-Dec. (2008) *Journal of Social and Economic Development*, p. 176.
67. *Ibid.*, pp. 176-77.
68. *Ibid.*, also see The ILO, Statement, The work performed must be in the Labour Market and hence excludes non-labour market production, such as housework. Therefore, the definition of child labour by ILO is appropriate for studies of the formal sector Labour Market.
69. C.K. Shukla and S. Ali, "*Encyclopedia of Child Labour Priorities for 21*st *Century*", Vol. I, p. 230.
70. *Ibid.*
71. *Ibid.*, p. 232.
72. *Ibid.*, p. 240.
73. My name is today, "Children in News", Vol. XII, Nos. 2 and 3, Butterflies programme with street and working children, New Delhi, pp. 223-24.
74. *Ibid.*
75. *Ibid*

8

Child Labour in India and the Judicial Response: A Critique

"Bestow blessings on those
Little, innocent lives
Bloomed on Earth,
Who have brought the message
of joy from heavenly garden".

—*Rabindranath Tagore*

1. INTRODUCTION

The Child has been the subject of special laws and legal provisions. Because of its tender years, weak physique, and inadequately developed mind and understanding, every child needs protection against moral and physical harm and exploitation by others. In the formative years of its life, the child needs special care service to realize its full potential for growth and development. There are about 300 Central and State Statutes concerning children. These have been enacted with an intention to protect and help children and achieve the goal of child labour welfare enshrined in our National charter.[1] Further these laws are applicable to children in various spheres of life, which are regulatory, protective and correctional in nature. Laws are seeking to protect and promote the rights of child. Under the law, children are entitled to special care, assistance and essential needs and they should be given the highest priority in the allocation of resources. In this chapter the main focus is on the analysis of post-independence laws.

1.1. Constitutional Provisions

Our Constitution-makers were wise and sagacious to provide, that children should receive distributive justice in free India. The rights against exploitation were mentioned in the draft proposed by Dr. B.R. Ambedkar, K.M. Munshi and K.T. Shah. While Dr. Ambedkar's draft simply provided that subjecting a person to forced labour or involuntary servitude would be an offence, K.M. Munshi's draft article suggested for abolition of all forms of slavery, child labour, traffic in human beings and compulsory labour.[2]

Constitution of India contains provisions for survival, development and protection of children; these are mainly included in Part III and Part IV of the Constitution, i.e., fundamental rights and directive principles of state policy. India follows pro-active policy towards tackling child labour problem. The concern for children in general and child labour in particular is reflected through the Articles of the Constitution of India. In Article 23, it prohibits traffic in human being and begar and other similar forms of forced labour. Under Article 24 it has laid down that "no child under the age of 14 years shall be employed to work in any factory or mine or engaged in any other hazardous employment". Article 39(e) and (f) requires the State and secure that the tender age of children are not abused and to ensure that they are not forced by economic necessity to enter avocations unsuited in their age or strength. Those children are given opportunities and facilities to develop in a healthy manner and conditions of freedom and dignity and that childhood and youth are protected against exploitation and against moral and material abandonment. Article 45 provides, for free and compulsory education for all children until they complete the age of 14 years. Article 51A(k) makes it a fundamental duty of the parent or Guardian to provide opportunities for education to the child or ward between the age of 6 and 14 years. Art. 21-A recognizes that the Right to Education as fundamental right and it mandates that, the state shall provide free and compulsory education to all children of age of six to fourteen years in such manner as the state may, by law, determine.[3]

Legislation to control and regulate child labour in India has existed for several decades. Legislations have sought to address two broad concerns; (1) Prescribing minimum age limit for employment of children and regulation of working hours for children; and (2) Ensuring the health and safety of the child labourers by prohibiting the employment of children in hazardous work. Several statutory provisions prohibiting child labour and protecting interests of children of tender age working as a child labour have been enacted before and after independence to fulfil the commitment to international community and to oblige the mandate provided under Constitution to eradicate the evil of child labour.

There are number of child labour legislations prohibiting the employment of children below 14 years and 15 years in certain specified employments. However, contrary to our international commitment and all proclamations in the country's Constitution, and despite all the legislative measures, child labour is a harsh reality. Due to lack of political will and in absence of realistic measures to tackle the problem, the percentage of child labour in the total labour force of the country kept on increasing over the years. In fact, the evil of child labour has not only survived but has become deep rooted and multi-dimensional.

2. INDIAN STATUTORY PROVISIONS

In order to implement the constitutional and international obligation towards eradication of child labour in different occupations, the following legislative enactments have been in force, and continue after the Child Labour (Prohibition and Regulation) Act, 1986.

It would be better to appraise various statutes and statutory provisions enacted in the existing labour laws to tackle the problem of child labour.

2.1. The Children (Pledging of Labour) Act, 1933

Historical Background

The Royal Commission on Labour was established in 1929 to inquire into various matters relating to labour in this country. The Report of the Commission was finalized in 1931. The Commission had examined the conditions of the child labour in different industries and had found that children had been obliged to work for any number of hours per day as required by their masters. Further it found that, children were subjected to corporal punishment. The Commission had felt great concern at the pledging of children by parents to employers and return for small sums of money; and this system was found to be worst and exploitative of children. So the Commission recommended that any bond pledging a child should be regarded as void. The recommendations of the Commission was discussed in the Legislative Assembly and the Children (Pledging of Labour) Act, 1933 came to be passed, which may be said to be the first statutory enactment dealing with child labour. The main object of this Act was to eradicate the evils arising from the pledging of labour of young children by their parents to employers in lieu of loans for advances. The statement of objects and reasons provides[4]: "The Royal Commission of Labour found evidence in such widely separated areas as Amritsar, Ahmedabad and Madras of the practice of pledging child labour, that is, the taking of advances by parents or guardians on agreements, written or oral, pledging the labour of their children. In some cases, the children so pledged were subjected to particularly unsatisfactory working conditions. The Commission considering that the state would be justified in adopting strong measures to eradicate the evil, and the Bill seeks to do so by imposing penalties on parents by agreements pledging the labour of children and on person knowingly employing children whose labour has been pledged. Previously, the Act extended to whole of India except Jammu and Kashmir but after 1st September 1971, it has also been extended to Jammu and Kashmir.[5] The Act declares that an agreement, oral or written, express or implied to pledge the labour of child below 15 years of age by the child's parents, guardians as void and makes the contracting parties, liable for penalties.[6] Under this Act, 'Child' means a person who has not completed the age of 15 years.[7] This Act was passed with an intention to protect child from exploitation in various hazardous occupations but it remained a dead letter. No judicial efforts were made to protect the child from exploitation.

2.2. The Employment of Children Act, 1938

The Employment of Children Act, 1938 which had been in force till repealed and replaced by Child Labour (Prohibition and Regulation) Act, 1986. The main object of the Act was to prevent exploitation of child labour in workshops and other specified occupations and to regulate the employment of children in certain industrial employments. The Act was passed to implement the Convention adopted by the 23rd Session of International Labour Organization (1937), which inserted a special Article on India. Children under the age of 13 years shall not be employed or work in the transport of passengers, or goods or mails by rail, or in the handling of goods at docks, quays of wharves, but excluding transport by hand. Children under the age of 15 years shall not be employed to work in occupations to which this Article applies which are scheduled as dangerous or unhealthy by the competent authority.

The Statement of objects and reasons of the repealed Act stated;[8] "The twenty-third session of the International Labour Conference adopted a Convention in which a special Article for India was inserted fixing the minimum age at which children may be employed or may work in the transport of passengers, goods or mails by rail, or in the handling of goods at docks wharves or quays at 13 years. This Bill provides for prohibiting the employment of children under 15 in occupations connected with the transport of goods passengers or mails on railways and for raising the minimum age fixed by section 6 (1A) of the Indian Ports Act, 1908, to 14, the age recommended by the Royal Commission of Labour. A simple procedure enabling employers to safeguard themselves against transgression of the Act by furnishing themselves with or requiring candidates for employment to possess, certificate of age is provided in the Bill." The key points of this Act are;

(a) Prohibited the employment of children under 15 years in occupations connected with transport of goods, passengers, mail or railways;[9] (b) Raised the minimum age for handling goods on docks from 12 to 14 years; (c) Provided for the requirement of a certification of age; (d) In pursuance of the International Labour Conference at its 31st session held in 1948 adopted a Convention (No. 90) concerning night work of young persons employed in industry. Accordingly in 1951, a provision was added for prohibition of the employment of the children between 15 and 17 years at night in railways and ports and also provided for requirement of maintaining register for children under 17 years; and (e) In 1978, a provision was added for prohibition of employment of a child below 15 years in occupations in railway premises such as under picking or cleaning of ash pit or building operations, in catering establishment and in any other work, which is carried on in close proximity to or between the railway lines. The penalty for the breach of the Act, punishable with simple imprisonment extending to one month or fine upto Rs. 500 or both.[10] One of the draw backs of the Act is that it has not provided any provision in regard to the health, safety, medical examination and welfare of children. This Act was amended as many as 5 times during the year 1939, 1948, 1949, 1951 and 1978 only to ameliorate better working conditions to children.

2.3. Factories Act, 1948

The Factories Act, 1948 prohibits employment of a child below 14 years in any factory. This Act, extends to the whole of India except the state of Jammu and Kashmir.[11] Section 67 of the Act, enacts an absolute prohibition of employment of a child in any factory. It means no child below the age of 14 years can be asked to work or if he himself wants to work can be permitted to work in any factory. The provision is intended to safeguard the needy children who may like to work at the cost of their health and life. The Act distinguishes between 'child', 'adolescent' and 'adult.'[12] 'Child' is a person who has not completed the age of 15 years[13]; an 'adolescent' is a person who has completed age of 18 years[14] and an 'adult' is a person who has completed the age of 18 years.[15] The Act defines a 'young person' as one who is either a child or an adolescent'[16] A child below the age of fourteen is not allowed to work in a factory.[17] A child above the age of fifteen and below the age of eighteen cannot be employed to work for more than four and half hours and cannot be employed during the night.[18]

In *M.C. Mehta* v. *State of Tamil Nadu*,[19] it was held that children can be employed in the process of packing, but the packing should be done in an area away from the place of manufacture to avoid exposure to accident. The minimum wages for child labour should be fixed. The tender hands of the young workers are more suited to sorting out the manufactured product and processing it for the purpose of packing.

In *Walker T. Ltd.* v. *Martindale*,[20] the court held that, prohibition is absolute and not restricted to employment in one of the manufacturing process. Thus a child employed as a sweeper to clean up the floor of a factory is also in contravention of provisions of Factory Act, even though he is not employed in any of the manufacturing process. Sec. 68, provides that non-adult workers have to carry tokens. The children who are of 14 years but those are below 18 years can be allowed to work in any factory if the child concerned has been given certificate of fitness by a certifying surgeon and the said certificate is in the custody of the manager of the factory and the child so employed carries a token with him while he is at work in which a reference of such certificate has been made. Section 69 deals with the manner in which the fitness certificate is issued and the procedure to be followed by a certifying surgeon in case the certificate is to be issued, renewed or revoked. Under this Act, there is a provision for a weekly day of rest, every child worker who has worked for a period of 240 days or more in a factory during a calendar year is entitled during the subsequent year for leave with wages at the rate of one day for every 15 days of work as against every 20 days in the case of a child worker.[21]

2.4. The Minimum Wages Act, 1948

The Act extends to the whole of India except the State of Jammu and Kashmir.[22] The Minimum Wages Act was enacted for the improvement of the economic conditions of the working people in industries in our country. It provides for fixing minimum rates of wages in certain employment to which provisions of this Act applies. It intended to prevent exploitation of labour and for the purpose it authorizes the appropriate government to take steps to prescribe minimum rates of wages in the scheduled industries. The Act was enacted with the objectives of fixing, reviewing, revising and enforcing the minimum rates of wages relating to scheduled employments to the notified under the law by the appropriate government, i.e. Central/State. The intention of the Act is to fix minimum rates of wages in which the labour force is vulnerable to exploitation, i.e. is not well organized and has no effective bargaining power. It provides for an institutional mechanism and procedure for fixation, review, revision and enforcement of minimum rates of wages. 'Minimum Wage' has not been defined in the Act. In essence, the minimum wage represents the basic subsistence wage below which no employer can go, although nothing prevents him from paying above this statutorily notified wage. According to the Judgment of the Supreme Court, an industry or industrial establishment does not have the right to exist if it cannot guarantee payment of the minimum wage. However, the following five norms recommended by the Indian Labour Conference in its 15th session held at Nainital in 1957 are kept in view by the appropriate government for fixation and revision of minimum wages: (1) Three consumption units for one earner; (2) Minimum food requirement of 2700 colories per average Indian adult; (3) Clothing requirements of 72 yards per annum per family; (4) Rent corresponding to the minimum area provided for under the governments Industrial Housing scheme; and (5) Fuel, lighting and other miscellaneous items of expenditure to constitute 20 percent of the total minimum wage.

The Supreme Court of India in its Judgment in the case of *Reftakes Brett and Co.* v. *others,*[23] held that the children's education; medical requirement; minimum recreation; provision for old age; and marriage, should be added to the norms and criteria already recommended by Indian Labour Conference.

The Act defines a child as a person below 15 years. It provides for minimum wages for children and apprentices. It also has provision regarding hours of work and physical fitness. Under this Act, adult means a person who has completed the age of 18 years[24] and adolescent means a person who has completed the age of 14 years but less than 18 years.[25]

There are however two provisions in the law that have a direct relevance to child labour, which appears that the Act did not have any objective of elimination of child labour. Sub-section 3 of section 3(A) read as follows. In fixing or revising minimum rates of wages under this section:

(a) Different minimum rates of wages may be fixed for:

(i) different scheduled employments;

(ii) different classes of work in the same scheduled employment;

(iii) adults, adolescents, children, and apprentices; Rule 24 says, Number of working hours which shall constitute a working day;

(1) The number of hours which shall constitute a normal working day shall be (a) in the case of the adult, nine hours; (b) in the case of a child, four and half hours; and

(2) The working day of an adult worker shall be so arranged that inclusive of the intervals of rest, if any, shall not spread over more than twelve hours on one day.

There are two anomalies arising out of the above provision. One is that, in rural areas and in the unorganized and informal sectors of employments it is extremely difficult to fix the hours of work and also to enforce the hours so fixed. Even though children are barred from working for over four and a half hours a day, in actual practice they work for over eight hours and sometimes even more than ten and twelve hours. A recent study conducted by UNICEF of children employed in brick kilns in Thane district of Maharashtra confirms this. Even when children actually work for more than the stipulated hours of work they are not paid overtime. The provision of 'spread over', as in rule 24(2) is invariably, honoured in the breach. Such unduly long hours of work are not in the interest of children and are likely to cause irreparable damage to their health, psyche, and overall development.[26]

The second anomaly arises from a bare reading of Sec. 11. Section 11, deals with payment of wages. Ordinarily under Sec. 11(1) such wages shall be paid in cash, Sec. 11(2) however, permits payment of wages either wholly or partly in kind where it has been the custom to pay wages in kind after satisfying itself that it is necessary in the circumstances of the case to do so.[27]

2.5. The Plantation of Labour Act, 1951

This Act extends to whole of India except the State of Jammu and Kashmir.[28] It applies to plantations in Tea, Coffee, Rubber or Cinchona, etc. in which 30 or more persons are employed. It prohibited the employment of children less than twelve years in plantation.[29] The child worker (A person who has completed 15 years) can be allowed to work if employed only between 6 am and 7 pm. The total maximum working hours in a week for a child and an adolescent prescribed under the Act, are 40 hours. A child who has completed his twelth year and adolescent will not be allowed to work in any plantation unless he is certified to be fit by a duly appointed certifying surgeon and such a child or adolescent is required to carry with him while he is at work a token giving a reference of such certificate. The certificate granted under section 27 of this Act, remains valid for a period of one year. The Act, prescribed a few welfare measures in the nature of suitable rooms for the use of children below the age of 6 years and education for the children of workers employed in plantation.

There is also a provision for penalty for using false certificate of fitness under the Act. The Plantation Labour Act, 1951 has now been amended by Sec. 24 of Child Labour (Prohibition and Regulation) Act, 1986 to bring the age of the child in line with the definition under the said Act. Now under the amended Sec. 2(a) and (c) child means a person who has not completed his fourteenth year of age. Section 24 has been omitted and in section 26, in the opening portion, the words "who has completed this twelth year" have been omitted

2.6. The Mines Act, 1952

This Act extends to the whole of India.[30] This Act defines child as a person who has not completed his 15 years.[31] The Act not only prohibits the employment of children in mines, but also prohibits the presence of children in any part of a mine which is below ground or in any open cast working in which any mining operation is being carried on.[32] Even an adolescent is not allowed to work in any part of a mine which is below ground, unless he has completed his 16th year and has a medical certificate of fitness for work.[33] A certificate is valid only for twelve months.[34] Under the Act, adolescent is allowed to be employed in any mine except between 6 am and 6 pm. The provision with respect to employment of children under Mines Act, 1952 are more stringent than those under the Factories Act, 1948. It prohibits the employment of person below 18 years to work in any mine.

The Act, stipulated two conditions for underground work in a mine, (i) requirement to have completed 16 years of age, and (ii) requirement to obtain a certificate of physical fitness from a surgeon. Apprentices and other trainees, not below 16 years of age, may be allowed to work, under proper supervision, in a mine by the manager, provided that in case of trainees other than apprentices, prior approval of the Chief Inspector or an Inspector is required to be obtained before they are allowed to work.

The Central Government is the administrative authority under the Mines Act and it administers the Act and through inspectors having usual powers. Under section 48 of the Act, provisions of maintaining register of all those persons employed in the mine, has been made showing— (a) The age and sex of the employee; (b) The nature of the employment (whether above ground or below ground, and if above ground whether is open cast working or otherwise) and the date of commencement thereof; (c) In the case of an adolescent, reference to certificate of fitness granted under section 40.

The Act also contains the provisions related to the powers of inspectors and maintenance of records. Section 87 of this Act, further lays down "No suit, prosecution or other legal proceeding whatever shall lie, against any person for anything which is in good faith done or intended to be done under this Act."

There are penal provisions to ensure observance of the provisions of the Act. If a person below 18 years of age is employed in a mine in contravention of section 40, the owner, agent or manager of such mine shall be punishable with fine upto Rs. 500. However, it is obvious that, the relevant penal provisions are not adequate.

2.7. The Merchant Shipping Act, 1958

The Act, prohibits the employment of children in any capacity, who are below 14 years of age.[35] on sea-going ships, except (a) in a scholarship or training ship; or (b) In a ship in which all persons employed are members of one family; (c) In a home-made ship of less than two hundred ton gross; or (d) Where such person is to be employed on nominal wages and will be in the charge of his father or other adult or a male relative. Similarly, employment of young persons under 18 years of age as trimmers and strikers is also made conditional in any ship to the extent of production of medical fitness certificate from a competent authority. Further the Act empowers the government to make necessary rules regarding employment of young person as and when the occasion demand. The Act also makes provision for modest penalty of a fine of Rs. 50 for violating these provisions.

2.8. The Motor Transport Workers Act, 1961

This Act applies to whole of India.[36] Minimum age required for employment in every transport undertaking employing five or more workers[37] is 15 years.[38] The State Governments are authorized to apply all or any of the provisions of the Act to any motor transport undertakings employing less than 5 workers.[39] Now as amended by section 26 of the Child Labour (Prohibition and Regulation) Act, 1986, by which word 'fifteenth' in clauses (a) and (c) of section 2 has been substituted by word 'Fourteenth'. Thus, the Act prohibits employment of children below 14 years. The adolescents are prohibited to work unless a certificate of fitness is granted[40] which is valid only for one year.[41] An adolescent can work only for 6 hours including a rest interval of half an hour and between 10 am and 6 pm only.

2.9. The Apprentices Act, 1961

There is no comprehensive law dealing with matters relating to training of apprentices and their service conditions before this Act was passed. The only statutory provisions regarding apprentices were found in the model standing orders framed under the Industrial Employment (Standing Orders) Act, 1946. The Government of India appointed an expert committee to examine this matter and to recommend for undertaking a separate legislation regulating the training of apprentices in the industries. Consequently, the parliament enacted Apprentices Act, 1961.

This Act extends to the whole of India.[42] Under this Act, no person shall be eligible for being engaged as an apprentice, or to undergo apprenticeship training unless he is atleast 14 years of age.[43] The main objective of the Act is to regulate and control the training of apprentices and supplement the availability of trained technical personnel for the industrial concerns. It provides for practical training to the graduate and diploma engineers. Any person who is not less than 14 years of age and satisfies the prescribed standards of education and physical fitness can undergo apprenticeship training in the designated trade under an employer. The Act applies to only designated trade notified by the Central Government after consultation with the Central Apprenticeship Council.

The Act deals with matters such as qualifications for being engaged as an apprentice, contract of apprenticeship, period of apprenticeship, termination of apprenticeship contract, number of apprenticeships for a designated trade, practical and basic training, payment of apprentices, health safety and welfare of apprentices, hours of work, overtime, leave and holidays, conduct and discipline obligations of employers and apprentices, offer and acceptance of employment, etc.

The Act enjoins upon the employer to pay compensation to apprentices in accordance with the provisions of Workmen's Compensation Act, 1923, if personal injury is caused to them by accident arising out of and in the course of their training between 10 p.m. and 6 a.m. except with the approval of the Apprenticeship Advisor. Thus, the Act, adopts a flexible approach and leaves most of the matters to be decided by the executive and other authorities. Violation of the provisions of this Act on the part of the employer is punishable for a term which may extend to six months or with fine or with both.

Thereafter the Apprentice Act, 1961 was amended by Apprentices (Amendment) Act, 1973 to protect the Rights of Apprentice trainees. The Act prohibited undergoing apprenticeship training of a person under 14. Apart from legislative protection provided to the children, the various State Governments enacted shops and commercial establishments Acts, suitable for their respective states. In these Acts, minimum age of employment was quite different. To mention few, the age of employment is 12 years in Assam, Bihar, Gujarat, Madhya Pradesh, Maharashtra, Karnataka, Orissa, Rajasthan, West Bengal and Delhi. It is 14 years in Andhra Pradesh, Kerala, Tamilnadu, Punjab, Uttar Pradesh and Pondicherry.

2.10. Beedi and Cigar Workers (Conditions of Employment) Act, 1966

This Act extends to the whole of India.[44] This is a special legislation for regulating conditions of work of Beedi and Cigar workers. Although the Factories Act, applies to such workers but the employers intentionally split the concerns into small units to escape the provisions of the Factories Act. Further, a special feature of this industry is that the manufacturers of Beedis get the work done through contract labour and also in private dwelling houses which again leads to avoidance the provisions of the Factories Act. This Act tries to meet such difficulties.

Section 24 of the Act enacted for the welfare of labour and for regulating and enforcing better conditions of labour, amongst those who are engaged in the manufacture of Beedis and Cigars, prohibits employment of children in industrial premises, where any process connected with the manufacture of Beedis and Cigars takes place. "Child" for the purpose of this Act, means a person who has not completed fourteen years of age.[45] The employment of young persons between 14 and 18 years is prohibited between 7 pm and 6 am.[46] Provisions for canteen[47], first aid,[48] ventilation[49], and cleanliness[50] are made under the Act. The administration of the Act rests with the State who appoint Chief Inspector or Inspector for the purpose. The Act provides for penalties for breach, which may be imprisonment upto three months or a fine upto Rs. 500 or both.[51]

The Supreme Court in the case of *M/s P.M. Patel and Sons* v. *Union of India*,[52] has held that the terms of the definition of employee are very wide. They include not only persons employed directly by the employer but also employed through a contractor. Moreover, they include persons employed in connection with the work of the factory engaged in the task of rolling Beedis. Therefore, the home workers rolling Beedis are employees under this Act.

2.11. Contract Labour (Regulations and Abolition) Act, 1970

The Act also extends to the whole of India.[53] The Act applies to establishment and contractors employing 20 or more workers.[54] It is not applied to establishment in which work only of an intermittent or casual nature is performed.[55] There are no specific provisions under the Act pertaining to employment of children.

2.12. Shops and Commercial Establishment Act, 1969

Different states have enacted their own laws regulating employment of children in shops and establishments, restaurants and hotels and places of amusements and notified urban areas, etc., to which the Factories Act, 1948 does not apply. Time to time these Acts had been amended to meet the need of situation. These provisions regulate the daily and weekly hours of work, rest intervals, payment of wages, overtime pay, holidays with pay, annual leave, employment of children and young persons, etc. These Acts prohibits the employment of child in shops and establishments and he cannot be employed even as the family member of the employer. Generally speaking, a child is a person who has not completed the age of 12 years. However, the age requirement varies from 12 to 15 years in states. The minimum age for employment in shops and commercial establishments is 12 years in Bihar, Gujarat, Jammu and Kashmir, Madhya Pradesh, Karnataka, Orissa, Rajasthan, Tripura, U.P. West Bengal, Goa, Daman and Diu and Manipur, and 14 years in Andhra Pradesh, Assam, Harayana, Himachal Pradesh, Kerala Tamil Nadu, Punjab, Delhi, Chandigarh, Pondichery and Meghalaya. The minimum age of employment is 15 years in Maharashtra. Now after the insertion of Act. 21A no child under the age of 14 years can be employed in a work, in this light, an Act which permits employment of children under the age of 14 years becomes unconstitutional. There is no separate shops and commercial establishments Act in Andaman and Nicobar, Arunachal Pradesh, Dadra and Nagar Haveli, Lakshdweep, Nagaland and Sikkim.[56] The working hours for children are generally from 6 am to 7 pm. The maximum hours of work for children are usually 5 per day for young person or 30 per week for adolescents (Young Persons) they may be higher, i.e. 7 per day and 42 per week in Andhra Pradesh, Bihar, Tamil Nadu, Tripura, West Bengal, Pondichery; 6 hours per day in Jammu and Kashmir, Maharashtra, Uttar Pradesh, Karnataka, Madhya Pradesh, Orissa, Punjab, and three hours per day in Rajasthan.

All the states prohibit the employment of children and young persons in shops and commercial establishments during night.

2.13. Radiation Protection Rules, 1971

Children below 18 years of age are not to be employed at places where radiation takes place.

2.14. The Child Labour (Prohibition and Regulation) Act, 1986

Plethora of legislations were enacted since 1881 for progressively extending legal protection to the working children. Provisions relating to child labour under various legislations have concentrated mainly on aspects such as minimizing working hours, increasing minimum age and prohibition of employment of children in occupation and processes detrimental to the health and welfare of children of tender age.[57] The Children (Pledging of Labour) Act, 1933 followed by the Employment of Children Act, 1938 was the first statutory enactment dealing with child labour, was repealed by the Child Labour Act, 1986. The Child Labour (Prohibition and Regulation) Act is an outcome of various recommendations made by a series of Commissions.[58] This legislation was enacted to reform the legal measure, as the policy of both Prohibition and Regulation.

All the recommendations made by various Committees created a National consensus in favour of bringing a uniform comprehensive legislation to prohibit employment of children in certain other employments. To achieve this goal, the Child Labour (Prohibition and Regulation) Bill was introduced and passed in both houses of parliament in August 1986 with a view to prohibiting employment of children in certain types of jobs and regulating the conditions of employment of children in certain others.

2.14.1. The Statement of Objects and Reasons in the Bill Reads

There are a number of Acts which prohibit employment of children below 14 years and 15 years in certain specified employments. However, there is no procedure laid down in any law for deciding in which employments, occupations or processes the employment of children should be banned. There is also no law to regulate the working conditions of children in most of the employments where they are not prohibited from working and are working under exploitative conditions.

The Bill seeks to achieve the following objects:

(1) Ban the employment of children, i.e. those who have not completed their fourteenth year in specified occupations and processes;
(2) Lay down a procedure to decide modifications to the schedule of banned occupations or processes;
(3) Regulate the conditions of work of children engaged in forms of employment in which they are permitted to work;
(4) Prescribe enhanced penalties for employment of children in violation of the provisions of this Act and other Acts that forbid the employment of children; and
(5) Establish uniformity in the definition of child in laws concerning them.

The introduction of the Bill generated a lively debate in the Indian Parliament in which members cutting across party affiliation debated and provided rare insights into this age-old social issue. In course of the debate the members in particular took exception to the following:

The proviso in clause 3, Part 2 of the Bill which says, "provided that nothing in this section shall apply to any workshop wherein any process is carried on by the occupier with the aid of his family or to any school established by or receiving assistance or recognition from Government".

The members had also expressed apprehensions and reservations regarding the following:

(i) Past experience shows that labour laws are never implemented. The Child Labour (Prohibition and Regulation) Act will become yet another exercise in futility;

(ii) Hazardous work does not become safe merely because it is performed at home;

(iii) Any scheme of exemption provided in a law is bound to be misinterpreted and misused;

(iv) The intention of government should not be to regularize child labour merely because it exists; and

(v) A one sided and half-hearted approach of banning child labour in few establishments and regulating it in few others without adopting a holistic or integrated approach, without solving the problem of poverty and economic deprivation, without enforcing the Minimum Wages Act, without resolving the problem of universal enrolment and retention of all children of school-going age in the formal school system will serve little purpose.[59]

The apprehension and reservations expressed by the members were genuine and continue to be valid to this day.

2.14.2. The Main Features of the Present Act are:[60]

(i) It prohibits employment of children in most employments as detailed in the Schedule as Processes and Occupations. Most of them are hazardous in nature but the term hazardous has not been defined;

(ii) It intends to regulate employment of children in all establishments except those prohibited ones;

(iii) It provides for a Child Labour Technical Advisory Committee to advise the Central Government in matters of further prohibition, regulation, etc.;

(iv) Regulatory provisions made fixing the number of hours, period of work, prohibition of overtime, double employment, provision of weekly holidays, etc.;

(v) Requirement of the employer to give notice to Inspectors, maintenance of register, display of notice; provision for health and safety are also in Part III;

(vi) It provides for minimum penalty of imprisonment for 3 months and maximum one year and minimum fine of Rs. 10,000 and maximum fine of Rs. 20,000. Almost all the violations of the regulatory and mandatory provisions are declared as offence under the Act;

(vii) Any person can file a complaint but only a Metropolitan Magistrate can take cognizance of any offence; and finally;

(viii) The provisions made under the present Act is declared to be in addition to the provisions and protections of children already existing in other enactments.

2.14.3. Significant Provisions of the Child Labour (Prohibition and Regulation) Act, 1986

The Act is divided into four parts and contains 26 sections with one Schedule consisting of Part-A for Occupations and Part-B for Processes. The preamble to the Act, states that it is "An Act to prohibit the employment of children in certain employments and to regulate the conditions of work of the children in certain other employment. The Act prohibits the employment of any person who has not completed his fourteenth year of age[61] in occupations and process set forth in Part-A[62] and Part-B[63] of the Schedule of the Act. The prohibition under Part II, section 3 is not absolute as it does not apply to any workshop wherein any process is carried on by the occupier with the aid of his family or to any school established by, or receiving assistance or recognition from Government. Section 5 of the Child Labour (Prohibition and Regulation) Act provides for the constitution of a Child Labour Technical Advisory Committee to advise the Central Government for the purpose of addition to the schedule of the Act.

The Act thus classifies all establishments in two categories:

(i) The Act in which employment of child labour is prohibited; and

(ii) Those in which the working conditions of child labour shall be regulated.

If we analyze the preamble of the Child Labour (Prohibition and Regulation) Act, 1986 the intention of the parliament is not at all to prohibit the child labour altogether, rather they are permitted to work in a regulatory manner. Had it been the intention of the parliament to abolish the system of child labour then the nomenclature of the legislation would be the Child Labour Abolition Act in the form of Bonded Labour Abolition Act.

According to the Act child means a person who has not completed his fourteenth year of age[64] and the establishment for the purpose of this Act includes a shop, commercial establishment, workshop, farm, residential hotel, restaturant, eating house, theatre or other place of public amusement or entertainment.[65] The expression "Occupier" in relation to the establishment or a workshop, means the persons who has the ultimate control over the affairs of the establishment or workshop[66] and "Workshop" means any premises (including the precincts thereof) wherein any industrial process is carried on, but does not include any premises to which the provisions of section 67 of the Factories Act, 1948 (63 of 1948) for the time being, apply.[67] The word workshop is controversial and problematic found under section 3 because if the prohibited work is done in an informal place other than workshop it will not attract legal prohibition. Thus, Child Labour (Prohibition and Regulation) Act corresponds the Employment of Children Act, 1938 and lacunae in the present enactment continued so.

Part-III of the Act runs from section 6 to 13 deal with regulation of conditions of work of children. This part prescribes the norms for working hours and period of work, weekly holidays, guidelines to deal the disputes as to age, imposed legal responsibility to maintain the register on the occupation and health and safety of the working children. The policy of regulation of child labour in circumstances other than those where it is prohibited is a major component of the Act. However, regulatory provisions granting permission for child labour involves compromise with the interest of children and has far reaching effect on their career.

The Act, in its Part III regulates the conditions of work of children in establishments in which none of the occupations or processes referred to in section 3 is carried on.[68] It provides that no child shall be required or permitted to work between 7 pm and 8 am and to work overtime. The period of work shall not exceed three hours and no child shall work for more than three hours before he has had an interval for rest for at least one hour. The total working hours including interval for rest and the time spent in waiting for work shall not be spread over more than 6 hours per day. It is also provided that no child shall be required or permitted to work in any establishment on any day on which he has already been working in another establishment.[69]

The Act prescribes that every occupier in relation to an establishment in which a child was employed or permitted to work is required to give a written notice to the inspector containing certain particulars within whose local limits the establishment is situated within a period of 30 days from the date of the commencement of the establishment.[70]

According to section 10, in the event of any dispute regarding the age of a child, between the inspector and the occupier, the question should be decided on the basis of a certificate of age provided by the prescribed medical authority to whom such an issue has to be referred for decision. The Act under section 12 requires that, every occupier who employs children shall maintain a register to be available for inspection by an inspector at all times during working hours or when work is being carried on in any such establishment showing:

(a) The name and date of birth of every child so employed or permitted to work; (b) hours and periods of work of any such child and the intervals of rest to which he is entitled; (c) the nature of work of any such child; and (d) such other particulars as may be prescribed.

The Act further prescribes that every railway administration, every port authority and every occupier shall display a notice containing abstracts of section 3 and 14 in the local language and in the English language in a conspicuous place.[71] The Act also empowers the appropriate Government to make rules for the health and safety of the children employed or permitted to work in any establishment or class of establishments.

Part-IV of Child Labour (Prohibition and Regulation) Act deals with procedure for prosecution of offences and penalties under the Act. It provides a procedure relating to the offences. A positive feature of the Act under Sec. 16 is that: (a) Any person, police officer or inspector may file a complaint of the commission of an offence under this Act in any court of competent jurisdiction; (b) Every certificate as to the age of a child which has been granted by a prescribed medical authority shall, for the purposes of this Act be conclusive evidence as to the age of the child to whom it relates; and (c) No court inferior to that of a Metropolitan Magistrate or a Magistrate of the First Class shall try any offence under this Act.

2.14.4. Penalties under the Child Labour Act

The penalties under this Act are relatively more stringent than the earlier Acts and violating the provisions relating to child labour in certain other Acts results in a penalty under this Act.[72]

The penalties[73] under this Act are as follows:

(i) Whoever employs any child or permits any child to work in an hazardous employment shall be punishable with imprisonment for a term which shall not be less than three months but which may extend to one year, or with fine which shall not be less than ten thousand rupees but which may extend to twenty thousand rupees, or with both;[74]

(ii) For a repeated offence, the punishment is imprisonment for a term which shall not be less than six months but which may extend to two years;[75] and

(iii) For failing to give notice to the inspector as required by section 9, or failing to maintain a register as required by section 11, or making any false entry in the register, or failing to display an abstract of section 3, or of failing to comply with any other provisions of this Act or rules, the punishment is imprisonment which may extend to one month, or with fine which may extend to ten thousand rupees or with both.[76]

It is to be noted that the Act provides for both fine as well as imprisonment. But in practice, in those few instances where the employer is prosecuted, he is generally fined.

2.14.5. *Critical Analysis of Child Labour (Prohibition and Regulation) Act, 1986*

There are certain shortcomings in the Act. The Child Labour Act was passed with the object of achieving two contradicting goals, *viz*, prohibition and regulation of child labour which is not in conformity with Article 24 of Constitution and the Act is in favour of regulation rather than abolition of Child Labour.[77] There is another major lacuna in the Act, i.e. the absence of any measures for rehabilitation of the child. The proviso annexed to section 3 is abused by employing children in respect of families and work experience acquired by children. This proviso helps employers to pose as family members of the children working in their premises and thus continued to exploit the children, this is how the employer escapes from prosecution. Hence, burden of proof is to be fixed on the occupier to prove that the child is a member of his or her family.[78] Further the age of the child has been differently defined in different laws. There is no a criterion or scientific parameters for defining the age of the child. Thus, laws leads to confusion and uncertainty.

The definition of children given under Child Labour (Prohibition and Regulation) Act, 1986 is in contradiction with United Nations Convention on the Rights of the Child, 1989 and Juvenile Justice (Care and Protection of Children) Act, 2000. Article 24 of the Constitution indirectly permits the child labour because Article 24 reads;

> "No child below the age of fourteen years shall be employed to work in any factory or mine or engaged in any other hazardous employment". By reading above Article 24 it is observed that Constitution of India does not create an absolute bar to the employment of children below the age of 14 years. Their employment is prohibited only in factory or mine or in any other hazardous employment. Child below the age of fourteen years shall be employed to work in all establishments other than factory or mine or hazardous employment. Various laws and policies relating to child labour and child rights appear to work in isolation. There is no nexus between each other. The right to education did not have direct bearing upon the child labour law. Policy perspectives relating to children and childhood are confused. The Right of Children to Free and Compulsory Education Act, 2009[79] intended to provide free and compulsory education all the children of the age 6-14 years. But under Child

Labour (Prohibition and Regulation) Act, 1986 laying down that children below fourteen years can work in non-hazardous occupations and processes is a mockery in providing justice to the children. The Chairperson of National Commission for Protection of Child Rights said, "The child labour policy itself is flawed and existing child labour law was violating the fundamental right to education. Thus, there is a need to amend the Act to make it in consonance with the Right to Education.[80] The definition of child labour needs to include children working in the farm-lands. The National Policy on Children, 1974 is now outdated. It should be more children-oriented and Rights-based in order to be effective. The laws and policies now have to confirm to the international standards laid down in the U.N. Convention on the Rights of the Child.

2.14.6. An Analysis of the 2006 Amendment to the Child Labour (Prohibition and Regulation) Act

The Child Labour (Prohibition and Regulation) Act, 1986 does not ban child labour per se, and leaves the millions of child labourers in the domestic and unorganized sectors, outside its purview. According to extremely conservative Governmental estimates, about 1,85,595 children are estimated to be engaged in domestic work and roadside eateries,[81] which have been refuted by the statistics compiled by NGOs, which estimate the number at around 20 million.[82] On August 01, 2006, the Government imposed a ban on employment of children as domestic servants or servants in dhabas (road side eateries), restaurants, hotels, motels, teashops, resorts, spas or in other recreational centers.[83] The ban has been imposed under the Child Labour (Prohibition and Regulation) Act, 1986 on the recommendation of the Technical Advisory Committee on Child Labour headed by the Director General, ICMR, and has become effective from 10th October, 2006.[84] The Ministry of Labour has recently issued a notification to this effect giving three-months mandatory notice. Employing children in these categories would make the offender liable to prosecution, and may result in imprisonment upto two years and/or fine shall not be less than Rs. 10,000 but may extend to Rs. 20,000.[85]

The Technical Advisory Committee while recommending a ban on employing children in these occupations had said that although these occupations are not capable of being classified as *per se* hazardous, there is a high risk that children may be subjected to physical violence, psychological traumas, and at times, even sexual abuse. Such incidents being committed in the close confines of the households or dhabas or restaurants, often go unnoticed and unreported. Being kept out of the regulation mechanism inbuilt in the original 1986 Act, children employed in these sectors are made to work for long hours and are made to undertake various hazardous activities severely affecting their health and psyche. The Committee has said that the children employed in road-side eateries and highway dhabas were the most vulnerable lot and were easy prey to sex and drug abuse as they come in contact with all kinds of unscrupulous people. This recent measure initiated by the Central Government takes care of a major criticism against the 1986 Act, and is expected to go a long way in ameliorating the condition of helpless working children.

2.14.7. Abolition of Child Labour Bill, 2006—An Analysis

Despite prohibition imposed by the Constitution on employment of children below fourteen years of age in any hazardous employment, millions of children are forced by their parents to work in different establishments, which have not already been classified within the prohibited sectors, including employment as domestic help. Hence, the Abolition of Child Labour Bill, 2006 has been placed before the Parliament which envisages a stricter regime, and includes sectors such as domestic work, agricultural operations, construction activities, transport industry, etc.[86] The greatest merit of the new Bill is that, apart from putting prohibitions on child labour, it also seeks to provide for their rehabilitation. Section 6 of the Bill has mandated that even if an employer employs a child, he should send him to school, failing which he will be punished with imprisonment for a term which my extend to three months and a fine of Rupees Ten Thousand. This provision while discouraging child labour, indirectly points at a policy of rehabilitation of child labour, the proposed Act, lays down a separate penalty for companies employing child labour. In case a company employs a child for remuneration without sending him to school, the person in charge of the company at that point of time, shall be held liable to be punished with imprisonment which may extend to six months, or with fine which may vary between Rs. 1 lakh and Rs. 5 lakhs. Moreover, the licence of the company shall be liable to be cancelled, and the company shall also be required to meet the educational and such other requirements of the child as may be necessary for his development and education upto graduation level. Section 7 says that if any child is found to be self-employed and he has no parents or guardians to support him, he shall be immediately sent to a hostel for students by the Central Government and all expenditure on this account shall be met by the Central Government. Thus, the Bill of 2006 has a definite policy towards rehabilitation of child labour, and is hence a welcome piece of legislation.

From the above discussion, it is clear that the Government has taken cognizance of child labour as a major social problem in India, and is taking a number of steps to eradicate it. Although nothing can be predicted about the potential success of this legislative intent, it must be admitted that the efforts are steps in the right direction. Unfortunately this bill is not yet passed.

3. JUDICIAL DECISIONS AND CHILD LABOUR

The response of the judiciary with regard to Child Labour in India is highly commendable. It has in real sense brought a revolution in the field of child labour in India. It has always endeavored to expand and develop the scope of law so as to respond to the hope and aspirations of the framers of the Constitution as well as the people of India. Time and again, it has pronounced glorious judgments for eliminating the problem of child labour in India. With regard to child labour in India, Justice Subba Rao, the former Chief Justice of India, rightly remarked; "Social justice must begin with the child. Unless a tender plant is properly nourished, it has little chance of growing into strong and useful tree. So, first priority in the scale of justice should be given to the welfare of children.[87] Supreme Court has played an important Role to control the problem of child labour and has shown its concern for child labour by bringing occupations or processes under the courts order by the direct application of constitutional provisions. Human Rights jurisprudence in India has a constitutional status and sweep; Article 21 of the Constitution can be termed as 'Magna Carta' of human rights. This Article guarantees right to life and liberty to every human being. Right to life and liberty is a cherished and prized right under the Constitution.

Supreme Court replaced the liberal concept of Article 21 taken in *Maneka Gandhi* v. *Union of India,*[88] and *Francis Coralie Mullin* v. *Union Territory of Delhi,*[89] held that Article 21 included protection of health and strength of workers, men, women and tender age of children against abuse. According to the court, the opportunities and facilities for children to develop in a healthy manner and in conditions of freedom and dignity and educational facilities are included in Article-1.

In *Peoples' Union for Democratic Rights* v. *Union of India,*[90] commonly known as *'Asiad Workers Case'*, it was brought to the notice of the Supreme Court that children below 14 years of age employed in the construction work. It was held that construction work is clearly a hazardous occupation and it is absolutely essential that the employment of children under the age of 14 years must be prohibited in every type of construction work. Referring to Article 24, Justice P.N. Bhagavathi and Justice Bahrul have held that "apart from the requirement of International Labour Organization Convention No. 59, we have Article 24 of the Constitution which even if not followed up by the appropriate legislation, must operate "*proprio vigore*" and construction work plainly and indubitably a hazardous employment, it is clear that by a reason of constitutional prohibition no child below 14 years can be allowed to be engaged in construction work". And specifically in Employment of Children Act, 1938, no child below 14 years can be employed in construction work.[91] The Supreme Court observed that "There can be no doubt that notwithstanding the absence of specification of construction industry in the schedule to the Employment of Children Act, 1938, no child below the age of 14 years can be employed in construction work and the Union as also every State Government must ensure that the constitutional mandate is not violated in any part of the country". The Judgment was eye an opener about the lacunae of the law and the need to reform in order to be comprehensive. In accordance with this judgment, the construction work has been added item No.7 as prohibited, occupation in Part 'A' of Schedule to the Child Labour Act of 1986.

In *Labourers, Salal Hydro Project* v. *State of Jammu and Kashmir*,[92] Bhagavati, J. with R.S. Pathak and Amarendra Nath Sen, JJ., delivered another valuable decision to protect the interest of large number of child labourers working in the construction of Salal Hydro Project, a hazardous work. The court was constrained to remark that the problem of child labour is a difficult problem and it is purely an account of economic reasons that parents often want their children to be employed in order to be able to make both ends meet. The court said that this is an economic problem and it cannot be solved merely by legislation. So long as there is poverty and destitution in the country, it will be difficult to eradicate child labour.[93]

The Court conceded that having regard to the prevailing socio-economic conditions, it is not possible to prohibit child labour altogether and in fact, any such move may not be socially or economically acceptable to large masses of people. That is why Article 24 limits the prohibition against employment of child labour only to factories, mines or other hazardous employments. The Central Government was directed to persuade the workmen to send their children to a nearby school and arrange not only for the school fees to be paid but also provide free of charge, books and other facilities such as transportation, etc. The Court also suggested to the Central Government that "whenever it undertakes a construction project which is likely to last for some time it should provide that children of construction workers who are living at or near the project site should be given facilities for schooling and this may be done either by the Central Government itself or if the Central Government entrusts the project work or any part thereof to a contractor, necessary provision to this effect may be made in the contract with the contractor".[94]

With regard to child labour in Beedi Industry, in *Rajangam, Secretary, Dist. Beedi Workers Union* v. *State of Tamil Nadu and others,* [95]with *K.C. Chandra Segaram* v. *State of Tamil Nadu and others,*[96] various allegations were made regarding failure to implement the provisions of the labour laws, manipulation of records regarding employees, non-payment of appropriate dues for work taken, etc. including the child labour and specifically the non-implementation of the Beedi and Cigar Workers (Conditions of Employment) Act, 1966. To protect child labour, the Apex Court suggested that "tobacco manufacturing has indeed health hazards. Child labour in this trade should therefore, be prohibited as far as possible and employment of child labour should be stopped either immediately or in a phased manner to be decided by the State Governments........the provisions of the Child Labour Act, 1986 should be strictly implemented."[97] The Court further admitted that the exploitation of labour is rampant in the beedi trade and suggested that 'in view of the health hazard involved in the manufacturing process, every worker including children, if employed, should be insured for a minimum amount of Rs. 50,000 and the premium should be paid by the employer'.[98]

In M.C. *Mehta* v. *State of Tamil Nadu and others,*[99] Supreme Court allowed children to work in a prohibited occupation like fireworks. Ranganath Mishra and M.H. Kania, JJ. opined that "the provisions of Article 45 of Constitution in the Directive Principles of State policy still remained a far cry and through according to this provision", all children upto the age of fourteen years are supposed to be in the school, but economic necessity forces grown-up children to seek employment. Children can, therefore, be employed in the process of packing of fireworks but packing should be done in an area away from the place of manufacture to avoid exposure to accident.[100] It is a matter of surprise that the Supreme Court in this case allowed the children to be employed in match factories of Sivakashi in Madras and said that, the children must be provided basic diet during working period. This judgment is not in accordance with the constitutional spirit.

Further Supreme Court in *M.C. Mehta* v. *State of Tamil Nadu and others,*[101] popularly known as *'Child Labour Abolition case'* has held that the children below the age of 14 years cannot be employed in any hazardous industry, mines or other work. It would be appropriate to quote brief facts that, when news about an accident in one of the Shivakashi crackers factories was published in the media, wherein several children reported dead, the Supreme Court took "*Suo motu*" cognizance of it. The Court gave certain directions regarding the payment of compensation. An Advocate's Committee was also constituted to visit the area and report on the various aspects of the matter.[102]

A three Judge Bench of the Supreme Court comprising Justice Kuldip Singh, Justice B.L. Hansaria, and Justice S.B. Majumdar delivered a land mark Judgement on 10 December 1996 in writ petition (Civil) No. 465/1986. This Judgement is of considerable importance and is a progressive advancement in public interest litigation and child jurisprudence. The decision has attempted to tackle the problem of child labour.

M.C. Mehta, a environmentalist, lawyer, filed a writ under Article 32 of the Constitution of India, as the fundamental right of children against exploitation (Article 24) was being grossly violated in the match and fireworks industries in Sivakashi where children were employed. The Court then noted that the manufacturing process of matches and fireworks is hazardous, giving rise to accidents including fatal cases. Therefore, keeping in view the provisions contained in Article 39(f) and 45 of the Constitution, it gave directions as to how the quality of life of children employed in the factories could be improved. The Judges further observed that 'it is a stark reality that in our country like many others, children are exploited a lot.'[103] Court had remarked that "child labour is a big problem and has remained intractable even after 50 years of country having become independent, despite various legislative enactments prohibiting employment of a child in a number of occupations and avocations."[104] The Court said employment of the child below 14 years was unconstitutional in diction and if it had to be seen that all these children had a fundamental right for education, it seemed that the least the Court ought to do was to see the fulfilment of the legislative intent behind the Child Labour (Prohibition and Regulation) Act, 1986.[105]

It was observed that every employer should be asked to pay a compensation for every child employed in contravention of the provisions of the Act, a sum of Rs. 20,000; while the state shall pay Rs. 5,000 if it failed to provide alternative employment to the adult member of the child's family. Both the amounts shall go to the Corpus Welfare Fund, the income from which would be used for the education of laid off children and their welfare.[106]

The judges made it clear that the liability of the employer to contribute Rs. 20,000 for each child to the Corpus Welfare Fund would not cease even if he would desire to discharge the child currently employed. Since the income generated from the Corpus would not be enough to dissuade the parents to seek employment of the child, the state owes a duty to come forward and discharge its obligation by providing a job for one adult member of each of the child's family in lieu of its job. However, the judges made it clear that they were not issuing any direction to the state to provide the jobs to the adult members presently. Instead they were leaving the matter to be sorted out by the government.

Factory inspectors were directed to see that the working hours of the child in non-hazardous industries were not more than four to six hours a day and that the child receives education for at least two hours a day and the entire cost of education is borne by the employer.[107]

In the above said M.C. Mehta case,[108] with regard to Sec. 14 of the Child Labour (Prohibition and Regulation) Act, 1986 to apprise the developing restitutive jurisprudence, the Supreme Court observed "Taking guidance there from, we are of the view that the offending employer must be asked to pay compensation for every child employed in contravention of the provisions of the Act a sum of Rs. 20,000 and the inspectors, whose appointment is visualized by section 17 to secure compliance with provisions of the Act, should do this job. The inspectors appointed under section 17 would see that for each child employed in violation of the provisions of the Act, the concerned employer pays Rs. 20,000 which sum could be deposited in a fund to be known as "Child Labour Rehabilitation-*cum*-Welfare Fund". The liability of the employer would not cease even if he would desire to disengage the child presently employed". Karnataka High Court in *Hayat Khan* v. *Deputy Labour Commissioner,Regional Office, Belgaum and others* [109] observed, offending employer must be asked to pay compensation of Rs. 20,000 for every child employed in contravention of the Child Labour Act.

In *Sheela Barse* v. *Union of India*,[110] it was held that child is a national asset, and it is the duty of the state to look after the child with a view to assuring full development of its personality. Judicial institutions have played a significant role not only for resolving disputes but also has always endeavoured to expand and develop the law so as to respond to the hopes and aspirations of the people who are looking to the judiciary to give life and content to law.

With a view to safeguard the interest of bonded child labourer Supreme Court delivered a judgment with important observation in a leading case in *Bandhua Mukti Morcha* v. *Union of India and others*.[111] On behalf of the Court, Justice Bhagwati remarked that "it is a problem which needs urgent attention of the Government of India and the State Governments and when the Directive Principles of State Policy have obligated the Central and State Government to take steps and adopt measures for the purpose of ensuring social justice to the have-nots and the handicapped. It is not right on the part of the concerned governments to shut their eyes to the inhuman exploitation to which the bonded labourers are subjected......" It is therefore, essential that which ever be the State Government it should, where there is bonded labour, admit the existence of such bonded labour, and make all possible efforts to eradicate it. By doing so, it will not only be performing a humanitarian function, but also discharging a constitutional obligation and strengthening the foundations of participatory democracy in the country.[112]

Further, in the case of *Neeraja Choudhary* v. *State of M.P*,[113] the Court said that 'it is not enough merely to identify and release bonded labourers, but it is equally, perhaps more important that, after identification and release, they must be rehabilitated, because without rehabilitation, they would be driven by poverty, helplessness and despair into serfdom once again.[114] Not only, that, "the Bonded Labour System (Abolition) Act, 1976 has been enacted pursuant to the Directive Principles of State Policy with a view to ensuring basic human dignity to the bonded labourers and any failure of action on the part of the State Government in implementing the provisions of this legislation would be the clearest violation of Article 21, apart from Article 23 of the Constitution"[115] and, therefore, the Apex Court directed the State Government to provide rehabilitative assistance to these freed bonded labourers within one month from the date of giving the decision. Because "freedom from bondage without effective rehabilitation after such freedom will indeed be of no consequence and in the absence of proper arrangement for such rehabilitation being made, the entire purpose of the Act, will be frustrated".[116]

The observation made by the Supreme Court in another judgment in *Bandhua Mukti Morcha* v. *Union of India and others (II)*,[117] a public interest litigation was filed alleging employment of children aged below 14 in the Carpet Industry in the State of Uttar Pradesh. Reports of a Commissioner/Committee appointed by the Supreme Court confirmed forced employment of a large number of children, mostly belonging to SCs and STs and brought from Bihar, in carpet weaving centers in the State. It was held by the Court that the State is obliged to render socio-economic justice to the child and provide facilitates and opportunities for proper development of his personality.

It was observed by the Court that, "The child of today cannot develop to be a responsible and productive member of tomorrow's society unless an environment which is conducive to his social and physical health is assured to him. Neglecting children means loss to society as a whole. If children are deprived of their childhood-socially, economically, physically and mentally—the nation gets deprived of the potential human resources for social progress, economic empowerment and peace and order, social stability and good citizenry. The founding fathers of the Constitution, therefore, have emphasized the importance of the role of the child and the needs for its best development and projected the rights in the Directive Principles including the children as beneficiaries. Their deprivation has a deleterious effect on the efficacy of democracy and the rule of law."

The Supreme Court of India in *Rosy Jacob* v. *Jacob A. Chakramakkal*,[118] observed that "The children are not mere chattels; nor are they mere play things for their parents. Absolute rights of parents over the destinies and the lives of their children has in the modern changed social conditions, yielded to the considerations of their welfare as human beings so that they may grow up in a normal balanced manner to be useful members of the society..."

With regard to the payment of wages to the child worker, the Child Labour Act is silent. Notifying under the Minimum Wages Act, 1948, some states have required payment to child workers, 60% of the wages payable to adults.[119] Consequently, this policy encourages prospective employer to employ child labour than an adult. The Karnataka High Court analyzing this policy in *A Srirama Babu* v. *Chief Secretary, Government of Karnataka*,[120] has observed. "This needs a re-look and an abolition of such difference would certainly go a long way in increasing employment potential for grown up and dissuade the employer from employing child labour". So it is essential that the state should step into retard the trend to employ child labour.

In *M.C. Mehta and Bandhua Mukti Morcha cases*, Supreme Court, of course, delivered land mark judgments but while observing both the judgments it appears that full scale of abolition of child labour of all types was not aimed. The court was conscious about practicality. Supreme Court observed in *Bandhua Mukti Morcha*:

> "Total banishment of employment may drive the children into destitution and other mischievous environment, making them vagrant, hard criminals and social risks, etc. Therefore, while exploitation of the child must be progressively banned, other simultaneous alternatives to the child should be evolved including providing education, health care, nutrient food, shelter and other means of livelihood with self-respect and dignity of person. Immediate ban of child labour would be both unrealistic and counterproductive. Ban of employment of children must begin from most hazardous and intolerable activities like slavery, bonded labour, trafficking, prostitution, pornography and dangerous forms of labour and the like".[121]

The idea of total prohibition of child labour was not endorsed by the conference of State Labour Ministers also in 1997 on the ground that this objective had to be realized progressively and could not be effected overnight. They agreed about the urgency of providing free, compulsory and universal primary education.[122]

The High Court of Karnataka in *A. Srirama Babu case*,[123] looked to the issue of eradication of child labour in sericulture industry, especially weaving of silk sarees, where children in the age group of five to eight were engaged in huge numbers. While the schedule to Child Labour Act is silent about this industry, the court enunciated the criterion of hazardous work. To be hazardous, the work should be either inherently injurious to the children or the conditions of work are harmful to their health. The Court held that all employments which cripple the health of a child and which disable him from being a healthy member of the society should be treated as a hazardous industry. It directed the Commissioner of Labour to issue notices to the deviant establishments for appropriate action. One shocking disclosure made by the Court is with regard to improper use by the State Administration of funds released by the Central Government.[124]

3.1. Judicial Response to Child Labour and Right to Education

Education develops the human personality. A right to education is indispensable in the interpretation of a development as a human rights.[125] This right to development is also considered basic human right.[126] Education of children is an important right of a child. Education is critical for economic and social development.[127] It is crucial for building human capabilities and for opening opportunities. The social benefits of education spread in many directions. Education leads to better health care, smaller family norms, greater community and political participation, less income inequality and a greater reduction of absolute poverty.[128] The abolition of child labour must be preceded by the introduction of compulsory education, since compulsory education and child labour laws are interlinked. Article 24 of the Constitution bars employment of child below the age of 14 years.[129] Article 45 is supplementary to Article 24 for if the child is not to be employed below the age of 14 years he must be kept occupied in some educational institutions. Now Article 45 is amended.

3.1.1. Importance of Education

In *J.P. Unnikrishnan* v. *State of Andhra Pradesh*,[130] Supreme Court while dealing with education as a fundamental right has emphasized the importance of education by stating that; "The fundamental purpose of education is the same at all times and in all places; it is to transfigure the human personality into a pattern of perfection through a synthetic process of the development of the body, the enrichment of the mind, the sublimation of the emotion and the illumination of the spirit.

Education is a preparation for a living and for life, here and hereafter". Further an old Sanskrit adage states; "That is education which leads to liberation", liberation from ignorance, which shrouds the mind, liberation from superstition, which paralyses effort, liberation from prejudices which blind the Vision of the Truth. Education is enlightenment. It is the one that lends dignity to a man as was held in *University of Delhi* v. *Ramnath,*[131] The Supreme Court held that "Education seeks to build up the personality of the pupil by assisting his physical, intellectual, moral and emotional development".

In *P.A. Inamdar* v. *State of Maharashtra,*[132] Supreme Court observed that; Education is "Continued growth of personality, steady development of character, and the qualitative improvement of life. A trained mind has the capacity to draw spiritual nourishment from every experience, be it defeat or victory, sorrow or joy. Education is training the mind and not stuffing the brain".

Swamy Vivekananda has quoted "We want that education by which character is formed, strength of mind is increased, the intellect is expanded, and by which one can stand on one's own feet". "The end and aim of all education, all training should be man-making. The end and aim of the training is to make the man grow. The training by which the current and expression of will are brought under control and become fruitful is called education.[133] Planning Commission of India stated that[134] education is an important input both for the growth of the society as well as for the individual. Properly planned educational input can contribute to increase in the Gross National Products, cultural richness, built positive attitude towards technology and increase efficiency and effectiveness of the governance. Education opens new horizons for an individual, provides new aspirations and develops new values. It strengthens competencies and develops commitment. Education generates in an individual a critical outlook on social and political realities and sharpness the ability to self-examination, self-monitoring and self-criticism".

"The term 'Knowledge Society', 'Information Society' and 'Learning Society' have now become familiar expressions in the educational parlance, communicating emerging global trends with far-reaching implications for growth and development of any society. These are not to be seen as mere cliché or fade but words that are pregnant with unimaginable potentialities. Information revolution, information technologies and knowledge industries, constitute important dimensions of an information society and contribute effectively to the growth of a knowledge society".

"Alwin Toffler (1980) has advanced the idea that power at the dawn of civilization resided in the 'muscle'. Power then got associated with money and in 20th century it shifted its focus to 'mind'. Thus, the shift from physical power to wealth power to mind power is an evolution in the shifting foundations of economy. This shift supports the observation of Francis Bacon who said 'knowledge itself is power'; stressing the same point and upholding the supremacy of mind power, in his characteristics expression, Winston Churchill said, "The Empire of the future shall be empire of the mind". Thus, he corroborated Bacon and professed the emergence of the knowledge society".

It could be seen that several international documents have recognized the right to education as a human right.[135] The process of moulding the right to education as a fundamental right was triggered-off by *Mohini Jain's case*[136] and subsequently strengthened by *Unni Krishnan's case*[137] which ruled that right to education is a fundamental right that flows from the Right to life in Article 21 of the Constitution. Every child/citizen has a right to free education upto the age of 14 years thereafter the right would be subject to the limits of the economic capacity of the state. This decision was upheld and confirmed by the 11 Judge constitutional bench of the Supreme Court in *TMA Pai Foundation* v. *Union of India*.[138] In the year 2002, the Indian Constitution through its 86th Amendment Act, has made "Right to Education a Fundamental Right".[139] The State is obliged to duty bound to provide free and compulsory education to all children of age 6-14 years in such manner as the state may by law determine. It was also provided that, it is the fundamental duty of a parent or guardian to provide opportunities for education to his child between the age of 6 to 14 years.[140] In pursuance of this development in the field of education recognizing it as fundamental right, the Parliament has enacted the Right of Children to Free and Compulsory Education Act, 2009[141] which provides for free and compulsory education to all the children of the age of 6 to 14 years. Chief components of the enactment were:

(i) Adding Article 21-A in Part III (Fundamental Right);
(ii) Modifying Article 45; and
(iii) Adding a new clause (k) under Article 51-A (Fundamental Duties) making the parent or guardian responsible for providing opportunities for education to their children between 6 and 14 years.

4. CONCLUSION

Inspite of several legislative measures by enactment of statutory provisions to curb employment of children in hazardous employment and those injurious to health, the exploitation of children by different profit-makers for their personal gains continued unabated in utter disregard of constitutional injunction and statutory prohibition.

From the analysis of the relevant statutory provisions of the Indian laws relating to child labour, it has become abundantly clear that the statutes vary as to the age limit of a child employed or permitted to work in various occupations. There is no law fixing minimum age for employment of children in agriculture. The Factories Act, 1948, fixes minimum age of 14 whereas the International Labour Organisation Convention prescribes minimum age for any employment to be 15. In the case of plantations, the age of employment has been fixed at 12 years but in the case of non-industrial employment the minimum age varies from 12 to 14 years. Thus, Indian Laws relating to child labour are deficient from the international standards as laid down by the International Labour Organisation but even then they can be considered satisfactory in view of the prevalent economic conditions of the country. There are plethora of statutes[142] to prevent the misuse of children in hazardous employment and to protect the general rights of the children. But sociological studies have revealed either the ineffective nature of these laws or their blatant violations.

Inspite of these legislative enactments and the pro-active role played by various agencies, child labour continues to be a major problem. A large number of children are exploited and deprived of what is due to them. Ironically total laxity prevails the enforcement of the provisions with not much evidence of conviction.

The complete Abolition of child labour and proper regulation thereof in accordance with the statutory provisions should be the cherished and prime objective of a civilized society. It is also pertinent to state that the Judiciary played a significant role in protection of child labours. Many path breaking judgments of the Supreme Court have done a great deal by expanding the human rights doctrine. It would not be out of place to mention the historic judgment of the Supreme Court on December 10, 1996 banning child labour in non-hazardous industries. The judgment specified the hazardous and the most dangerous occupations from where child labour should be eliminated. Penalty to the employer at Rs. 20,000 per child be paid and a corpus to be found through the amount so collected. This was to be spent on education and rehabilitation of the children. The court also ordered that the working hours of a child labour should not exceed 4-6 hours a day and not less than 2 hours a day should be set a side for the child's education. The responsibility for imparting this education is that of the employer. Judiciary in India played a very significant role in promoting child welfare. It has taken the lead to save the child from exploitation and improve their conditions. Judicial mandate clearly demonstrates that right to education is necessary for the proper flowering of the children and their personality.

Thus, the judiciary has always made concrete efforts to safeguard them against the exploitative tendencies of their employers, by regularizing their working hours, fixing their wages, laying down rules about their health and medical facilities. The judiciary has even directed the states that it is their duty to create an environment where the child workers can have opportunities to grow and develop in a healthy manner with full dignity in consensus of the mandate of our Constitution.

Notes and References

1. See Encyclopedia of Social Work in India, (1987), Vol. I. p. 69.
2. The framing of Indian Constitution—A study, Vol. V, p. 243.
3. Article 21A inserted by the Constitution (Eighty-sixth Amendment) Act, 2002, Sec. 2.
4. Gazette of India, 1932, Part V, p. 195.
5. The Children (Pledging of Labour) Act, 1933, Sec. 1(2).
6. *Ibid.*, Secs. 4 and 5 the penalty for breach of law is fine upto Rs. 50 for parents/ guardians and a fine upto Rs. 200 for a employer, Sec. 2.
7. *Supra* note 4.
8. Gazette of India, 1938, Part V, p. 284.
9. The Employment of Children Act, 1938, Sec. 3(3).
10. *Ibid.*, Sec. 4.
11. The Factories Act, 1948, Sec. 1(2).
12. *Ibid.*, Sec. 2.
13. *Ibid.*, Sec. 2(c).
14. *Ibid.*, Sec. 2(b).
15. *Ibid.*, Sec. 2(a).
16. *Ibid.*, Sec. 2(d).
17. *Ibid.*, Sec. 67.
18. *Ibid.*, Sec. 71(i), and 71(i)(a).
19. (1991) SCC, 283: 1991 SCC (L&S) 299.
20. (1916) 85 E.L.K.B. 1543.
21. Factories Act, 1948, Sec. 79.
22. Minimum Wages Act, 1948, Sec. 1(2).
23. Civil Appeal No. 4336 of 1991.
24. *Supra* note 21, Sec. 2(aa).
25. *Ibid.*, Sec. 2(a).
26. Bharat Singh, "*Crime Against Child Labour*", p. 256.
27. *Ibid.*
28. The Plantation of Labour Act, 1951, Sec. 1(2)
29. *Ibid.*, Sec. 24.
30. The Mines Act, 1952, Sec. 1(2).
31. *Ibid.*, Sec. 2(2).
32. *Ibid.*, Sec. 45(i).
33. *Ibid.*, Sec. 40(i).
34. *Ibid.*, Sec. 41(i).

35. Merchant Shipping Act, 1958, Sec. 109. The age of the child which was earlier 15 in Sec. 109 is now amended and brought down to 14 by Sec. 25 of the Child Labour Act, 1986.
36. Motor Transport Workers' Act, 1961, Section 14.
37. *Ibid.*, Section 1(4).
38. *Ibid.*, Section 21.
39. *Ibid.*, Section 1(4).
40. *Ibid.*, Section 22.
41. *Ibid.*, Section 23(2).
42. The Apprentices Act. 1961, Section 1(2).
43. *Ibid.*, Section 3.
44. Beedi & Cigar Workers (Conditions of Employment) Act, 1966, Section 1(2).
45. *Ibid.*, Section 2(b).
46. *Ibid.*, Section 25.
47. *Ibid.*, Section 16.
48. *Ibid.*, Section 15.
49. *Ibid.*, Section 9.
50. *Ibid.*, Section 8.
51. *Ibid.*, Section 32.
52. AIR 1987 SC 447.
53. Contract Labour (Regulation & Abolition) Act, 1970, Sec. 1(2).
54. *Ibid.*, Section 1(4).
55. *Ibid.*, Section 1(5).
56. Child Labour in India, Document 4, Vol. XXX (3), (1979), Delhi: *The Indian Journal of Public Administration*, p. 933, *cited* in D. Venkateshwar Rao, *Child Rights*, Delhi: Manak Publications, 2004, p. 143.
57. Awards Digest: *Journal of Labour Legislation*, Vol. XX, Nos. 7 to 12, cited in Asha Bajapai, *Child Rights in India*., New Delhi: Oxford University Press, 2006, p. 163.
58. The National Commission on Labour, 1969; The Gurupadswamy Committee on Labour, 1976 and Sanat Mehta Committee, 1984.
59. *Supra* note 26, cited in legal aspects, pp. 243-44.
60. Jose Verghese, *Law on Employment of Children*, New Delhi: Capital Foundation Society, pp. 16-17.
61. Child Labour Act, 1986; Sec. 3, "*No child shall be employed or permitted to work in any of the occupations setforth in Part A of the Schedule or in any workshop wherein, any of the processes set forth in Part B of the schedule is carried on*".
62. There are 15 occupations setforth in Part-A of the schedule under section 3. Further employment of child as servants or workers and employment of children in Dhabas (roadside eateries), restaurants, hotels, Motels, Tea-Shops, Resorts, Spas or other recreational centers are notified on 10th July, 2006 and added by SO, 1942 (E) dated: 10.10.2006.
63. There are 57 processes setforth in Part-B of the Schedule.
64. Child Labour (Prohibition and Regulation) Act, 1986, Sec. 2(ii).
65. *Ibid.*, Section 2(iv).
66. *Ibid.*, Section 2 (vi).
67. *Ibid.*, Section 2(x).
68. *Ibid.*, Section 6.
69. *Ibid.*, Section 7.
70. *Ibid.*, Section 9.
71. *Ibid.*, Section 12.
72. *Ibid.*, Section 15, Modified applications of certain laws in relation to penalties.

73. *Ibid.*, Section 14.
74. *Ibid.*, Section 14(1).
75. *Ibid.*, Section 14(2).
76. *Ibid.*, Section 14(3).
77. P.P. Jayanti, "Child Labour—A Socio-Legal Study", *KUJLS* 143 to 158 (1988).
78. *Supra* note 63, Section 3 proviso: provided that nothing in the section shall apply to any workshop wherein any process is carried on by the occupier with the aid of his family or to any school established by or receiving assistance or recognition from Government.
79. The Right of Children to Free and Compulsory Education Act, 2009 (35 of 2009) received the Assent of the President on 26.8.2009 and came into force w.e.f. 1.4.2010, Sec. 2(c).
80. Kavita Chowdhary, "Rights Body Seeks Amendments to Ineffective Child Labour Act", *Mail Today*, 13, August 2008 cited in my name is Today- Children in News "*Butterflies*", Vol. XVI, New Delhi, 2009, p. 221.
81. *Source*: Government of India, Census 2001.
82. *The Hindu*, "Ban on Domestic Child Labour came into Effect", October 11, 2006.
83. Press Information Bureau, Government of India, MLD/L.53 (Cpi-iw) 1.8.2006.
84. The Provision of Constitution of the Technical Advisory Committee has been laid down in Section 5 of the Child Labour (Prohibition and Regulation) Act, 1986.
85. *Supra* note 64, Sec. 14.
86. See The Abolition of the Child Labour Bill, 2006, Section 4.
87. See, Subha Rao, J., *Social Justice and Law*, Delhi: National Publishing House, 1974, p. 4.
88. AIR 1978 SC 597; 1978 (I SCC 248).
89. (1981) I SCC, p. 608.
90. AIR 1982 SC 1473: (1982) 3.SCC 235; 1982 SCC (L & S) 275.
91. AIR 1982 SCC 1481.
92. (1983) 2 SCC 181; AIR 1984 SC 177.
93. *Ibid.*, p. 191.
94. Sudesh Kumar Sharma, "Child Labour: Problems and Prospects" (1999), *Cochin University Law Review*, p. 268.
95. AIR 1993 SC 404; 1993 Lab IC 4.
96. *Ibid.*
97. *Ibid.* at 405.
98. *Ibid.*
99. AIR 1997 SCC 283.
100. *Ibid.*
101. *Ibid.*
102. The Committee consisting of Shri R.K. Jain, a Senior Advocate, Indira Jaisingh, another senior advocate, and Shri K.C. Dua Advocate, submitted its Report on 11 November, 1991.
103. *Supra* note 100, p. 701.
104. *Ibid.*
105. *Ibid.* at 709.
106. *Ibid.* at 710.
107. *Ibid.* at 711
108. *M.C Mehta* v. *State of Tamil Nadu and Others* (Child Labour Abolition Case), 6 SCC 756; 1997 SCC (L & R) 49; AIR 1997 SC 699.
109. 2008-i-LLJ January 2008, *Labour Law Journal*, 2008, January, p. 284 (W.A. No. 3812/ 2005) (L-WC) dated: June 22, 2007.

110. (1993) 4 SCC 204.
111. AIR 1984 SC 802.
112. *Ibid.*
113. AIR 1984 SC 1099
114. *Ibid.*, See also *P. Shiva Swamy* v. *State of A.P.*; 1988 Lab IC 1680.
115. *Ibid.*
116. *Ibid.*
117. (1997) 10 SCC 549.
118. (1973) I SCC 840; at Para 15; AIR 1973 SC 2090.
119. P. Iswara Bhat, *Law and Social Transformation*, 1st edn., Lucknow: Eastern Book Company, 2009, p. 619.
120. ILR 1997 Kar. 2269.
121. (1997) 10 SCC 549.
122. *Supra* note 118, p. 623.
123. *A Sriram Babu* v. *Chief Secretary, Govt of Karnataka*, ILR (1997) Kar. 2269.
124. *Supra* note 118.
125. *Leyla Sahin* v. *Turkey*, decided by the European Court of Human Rights on 10th Nov. 2005.
126. Election Commission of India, St. Mary's School, 2007, AIR SCW 7761.
127. Earl Warren, C.J. in *Brown* v. *Board of Education* (1953).
128. 165th Report of the Law Commission of India on Free and Compulsory Education for Children 1998, p. 3.
129. Article 24 of Constitution: *"No child below the age of fourteen years shall be employed to work in any factory or mine or engaged in any other hazardous employment".*
130. AIR 1993 SC 2178, 1993 AIR SCW 863 (1993); I SCC 645, JT 1993(I) SC 474.
131. AIR 1963 SC 1873 at p. 1874.
132. AIR 2005 SC 3226 (2005); 6 SCC 537; 2005(5)SC 544; AIR 2005SC at p. 3254 also *see* External Values for a changing society, Vol. III, Education for Human Excellence, Bharatiya Vidya Bhavan, *Bombay*, p. 19.
133. *Ibid.*, p. 20.
134. India-Vision 2020 Published by Planning Commission of India at p. 250.
135. Various International authorities provides for Right to Education; Art. 26 Universal Declaration of Human Rights; Article 18, International Covenant on Civil and Political Rights; Act 2, Protocol No. 1, European Convention on Human Rights; Articles 12, 30, 31 of the American Declaration on the Rights and Duties of man, 1960, Article 16 of African Charter on Human and People's Rights, 1981; Articles 5 and 7, International Convention on Elimination of all forms of Racial Discrimination on Articles 10, 14, & 16, Convention on the Elimination of all forms of Discrimination against Women: Articles 4 & 22, Convention relating to the status of Refugee, Articles 23, 24, 28, 29, 32 & 40, Convention on the Rights of the Child, 1989.
136. *Mohini Jain* v. *State of Karnataka*, AIR 1992, SC 1858.
137. *J.P. Unnikrishnan* v. *State of A.P.*, AIR 1993, SC 2178.
138. AIR 1996, SC 2652.
139. Article 21-A of the Constitution.
140. Amendment of Article 51-A of the Constitution by inserting clause (K) by the Constitution (86th Amendment) Act, 2002, Sec. 4.
141. (Central Act, No. 35 of 2009) received the Assent of the President on 26th August 2009, came into force w.e.f. 1.4.2010.
142. The Children Act, 1960, Juvenile Justice Act, 1986, the Child Labour (Prohibition and Regulation) Act. 1986, etc.

9

Role of Non-Governmental Organisations in Rehabilitation of Child Labour: An Analysis

"Life doesn't count for much unless you're willing to do your small part to leave our children—all of our children—a better world. Even if it's difficult. Even if the work seems great. Even if we don't get very far in our lifetime".

—Barack Obama, President of the United States

1. ROLE OF NGOS IN REHABILITATION OF CHILD LABOUR

NGOs, some time called as a fifth unofficial organ of the Government, may play a very vital and significant role in the task of elimination of child labour. NGOs may initiate certain measures of creating awareness among the employers and parents regarding the evils of child labour. The existing penal provisions of child labour laws may be highlighted among the erring employers. NGOs may add to the efforts of the Government in elimination of child labour. The enforcement staff must seek the involvement of NGOs at all stages. Thus NGOs must be encouraged to become partners in elimination of child labour along with Government.[1]

The intervention of NGOs are in the areas of counseling awareness, creating social mobilization, encouraging community participation, rescuing children from work, providing vocational training, enrolling children in schools and ensuring their retention by minimizing dropouts, monitoring the functioning of schools, bringing children from informal rehabilitation schooling system into the formal mainstreaming schooling system, preparing educational kits and facilitating interaction between the various stakeholders, like Government Officials, Teachers, Employers, etc.[2]

NGOs have been working to find a solution to the problem of child labour. Many NGOs have grown in size and capabilities conducting research and training while developing effective and innovative programmes to shift children from work to school. The work of NGOs in the field of primary education, microfinancing and alternative income generation programmes have also made an important contribution in the effort to eradicate child labour in both urban and rural India. NGOs make significant improvement in their performance in promoting sustainable development and livelihood for the poor.[3]

The NGOs constitute important social capital for activating at the gross root level, the policy of preventing and eradicating the child labour practice and rehabilitating and main streaming the released child workers into the learning system.[4]

The importance of NGOs lies in the fact of their vital and effective role played by them in the social spectrum at the gross root level. The effectiveness of the NGOs is attributed to two major factors: (1) NGOs are relatively acceptable to the people due to their aversion towards government officials in some areas, (2) since NGOs work at grassroot level, they will have an intense knowledge and experience about day-to-day problem and cultural resistance for the change of concerned people. Apart from this, they also have the experience in running special schools with certain advantages over government agencies.

The NGO's are believed to be better motivators than the government machinery with respect to any problem concerning child labour and child abuse. The National Commission for the Protection of Child Rights while submitting the strategy paper for elimination of child labour to the Planning Commission for the Eleventh Five Year Plan suggested the revamping of the National Child Labour Programme, 1988, so that child labour can be identified and working children can be successfully rehabilitated and mainstreamed. In order to achieve this, NCPCR recommended that an army of social mobilisers be trained, who can conduct successful 'rescue' operations and enrol the children in Transitional Education Centers. The NCPCR envisaged these to be both residential and non-residential and as stepping stones towards full and successful rehabilitation and absorption of erstwhile working children into the formal education processes of the country.[5]

Karnataka had evolved its own legal mechanism to rescue and rehabilitate children and penalize their employers. As far as children employed in domestic work are concerned, the Labour Department, child line or NGOs have '*suo motu*' taken up cases under the Minimum Wages Act and Juvenile Justice Acts, ever since the Minimum Wages notification for domestic workers came into effect in April 2004. Violators were hauled up before child welfare committees, with the Labour Department mobilizing the relief packages for the wronged child.[6]

Thus, NGOs served as active and enthusiastic partners in the way of elimination of child labour through their various approaches. The NGOs may move ahead with one or more of the objectives:

(1) Society-centered objectives;
(2) Family-centered objectives;
(3) Child-oriented objectives; and
(4) Government-oriented objectives.

Today in India there are several NGOs working relentlessly for the prevention and elimination of child labour. Some of them are as follows:[7]

(1) Action Aid India

One area of focus of Action Aid India is education and 'left out' children (including street and working children). It reaches more than 5 million of the most poor and marginalized people, supporting them overcome their poverty and marginalization by accessing their right to food, shelter, work, education, healthcare, human security and a voice in the development decisions affecting their lives and livelihood.

(2) CARE India

CARE works hand-in-hand with vulnerable families, especially women and girls, to help them access their rights. Care India is associated with the issue of gender and sexuality and empowering communities to fight HIV/AIDS. One of the main areas of activity of CARE in India is girls' education. The NGO works in 11 Indian states.

(3) Child Relief and You (CRY)

CRY believes that permanent change in the lives of children is only possible when we tackle the root causes that continue to keep the children uneducated, hungry and vulnerable. All children are equal, with equal rights guaranteed to them in the Constitution of India. CRY targets underprivileged Indian children, including child workers. The NGO carries out child development initiatives all over India. It is based in Maharashtra.

(4) Global March against Child Labour

The Global March against Child Labour is a global movement against child labour. It is a movement to mobilize worldwide efforts to protect and promote the rights of all children, especially the right to receive a free, meaningful education and to be free from economic exploitation and from performing any work that is likely to be harmful to the child's physical, mental, spiritual, moral or social development. It has partners in over 150 countries and is based in New Delhi.

(5) CINI ASHA

The NGO seeks to improve the quality of life of socially disadvantaged children living in urban areas through education, health and social mobilization. The Primary beneficiaries of CINI ASHA programmes are street children, children living in slums, squatter colonies and children of sex workers.

(6) CREDA (Centre for Rural Education and Development Action)

CREDA is a non-government, grassroots organization working for rural development. Its activities focus on child development from a rights perspective; and women's empowerment through economic development, an income generation programme, health and environment awareness and integrated rural development. The NGO's works on the issue of child labour as a special focus of child-related activities. It has undertaken projects for the elimination and rehabilitation of child labour around Varanasi (Uttar Pradesh).

(7) Concerned for Working Children (CWC)

CWC is working towards total eradication of child labour in all sectors and seeks to empower children so that they can gain control over their lives and be self-reliant. The project targets children forced to work in unorganized and organized hazardous situations due to poverty, children from broken homes, neglected/forgotten children, orphans, etc. CWC is working at local, national and international levels through action, policy research, and lobbying and advocacy roles. CWC works in the field of child labour in Karnataka.

(8) Salaam Baalak Trust

This NGO works with street and working children in and around New Delhi railway station. It provides basic services to the children, including formal and non-formal education. Its vision is to restore the childhood, learning and the joy of professional life.

(9) Prayas

Prayas is an NGO working since 1988 for the welfare of street and neglected children, destitute and working children. It addresses issues related to lack of sensitivity and infrastructure for their rehabilitation, education and reintegration. Prayas covers Delhi, Bihar and the earthquake affected areas of Gujarat. It is working in the tribal population. Prayas is a ray of hope for the underprivileged of our society.

(10) Save the Children (UK) in India

Save the Children works for the elimination of the worst forms of child labour. Currently, the international NGO runs three projects with working children in Rajasthan, West Bengal and Jammu and Kashmir. Save the Children specifically focuses on health, education, poverty and exploitation, as well as the issue of equality and justice as its priorities for the disadvantaged section of the society.

(11) M. Venkatarangaiya Foundation (MVF)

One of the primary goals of the Foundation is to eliminate child labour by universalizing school education. The Foundation mainly works in Andhra Pradesh. MVF also focuses on bonded labour and education, and more recently child marriages and other problems faced by the girl child. Strengthening of middle and high schools, training of all stakeholders and development of strong non-MVF groups are its major initiatives. MV Foundation has achieved remarkable success in the short period of time. In Andhra Pradesh, entire village communities are saying a firm "no" to child labour and opting to put their children in school.

(12) World Vision India

World Vision works with poor children providing education, food and health care. It also conducts special initiative programmes, targeting in particular, the street children, bonded child labourers and child victims of sexual exploitation. World Vision is a Charistain humanitarian organization working to create lasting change in the lives of children, families and communities living in poverty and injustice.

(13) Prathan

It focuses on universalization of pre-school education as an important strategy for achieving universalization of primary education. If every child can avail some kind of early childhood education, the chances are high that the child will go on to regular school. Moreover, the pre-school exposure will enhance and strengthen the child's subsequent school performance, in terms of achievement and attendance. Its aim is to expose unreached children from low-income families to early childhood education.

(14) Butterflies

Butterflies provide alternative education, as well as basic services to street and working children in the New Delhi area. It also provides emergency services like childline, night shelter, night reach or resilience centre, etc. Health care, advocacy and research are other areas where the Butterflies works relentlessly. The organization is actively involved in fund raising, communication, alliance building and training.

Apart from the above, the NGOs like Bandhua Mukti Morcha, Centre for Concern for Child Labour, Bharat Siksha Sanstha, Campaign against Child Labour, Katha, Ankuran, etc., are rendering yeomen service to the cause of child labour.

In Karnataka, NGOs like CRY, CWC (Concern for Working Child), ROAD, CHIGURU, APSA, MAYA, CACL and DON BASCO, CIF (Child India Foundation), Child Line, etc., have been rendering valuable services to the community children.

1.1. Role of NGOs in Rehabilitation of Child Labour in Gulbarga City

There are 15 NGOs working/functioning under the National Child Labour Elimination Project in Gulbarga city for rehabilitation of child labour during 2005-06, 2006-07 and 2007-08. All these NGOs are day care centers.[8]

(1) Vishwa Seva Mission, Gulbarga, Buland Parveg Colony, Gulbarga.
(2) Gram Pragati Seva Society, Gulbarga, Biddapur Colony, Gulbarga.
(3) Nisarga Rural Development Society, Sanjeev Nagar near H.P.S., Gulbarga.
(4) Grama Kiran Seva Society, near St. Joseph School, Ramnagar, Gulbarga.
(5) Karnataka Multi-purpose Women's Society, Sonia Gandhi, Ashraya Colony, Maalgatti Road, Gulbarga.
(6) Al-Fatima Women's Organization, Mohammadi Masjid, near Mohammadi Chowk, M.S.K. Mill, Gulbarga.
(7) Devajinayak Education Society, Sunil Nagar, Filters bed area, Gulbarga.
(8) Hyderabad-Karnataka Rural Development Society, C/o Mallikarjun, G.D.A. Colony, Shahabazar, Gulbarga.

(9) World Mission Society, Krishna Nagar, Gulbarga (Naveen).
(10) Gautami Consumers' Welfare Society, near S.T.B.T. opposite Chetan Higher Primary School Jagata, Gulbarga.
(11) Sahara Social Human Awareness Society, Mahaboob Nagar, Gulbarga.
(12) Al-Farah Mahila Mandala, Rangeen Masjid, Momeenpura, Gulbarga.
(13) Integrated Women and Child Development Society, near K.G.I.D. Office Nehru Ganj, Gulbarga.
(14) Hyderabad Karnataka Centre, AIR Wadi, near Jagadamba Temple, Gulbarga.
(15) Margadarshi Society, Hamaalgalli, behind Old City Bus Stand, Station Bazar, Gulbarga.

Out of the above 15 NGOs, following 6 NGOs are closed from the year 2008-09.

1. Gram Pragati Seva Society, Gulbarga, Biddapur Colony, Gulbarga.
2. Karnataka Multi-purpose Women's Society, Sonia Gandhi Ashraya Colony, Malgatti Road, Gulbarga.
3. Hyderabad Karnataka Rural Development Society, C/o Mallikarjun, G.D.A. Colony, Shahabazar, Gulbarga.
4. World Mission Society, Krishna Nagar, Gulbarga (Naveen).
5. Gautami Consumers Welfare Society, near S.T.B.T. opposite Chetan Higher Primary School, Jagata, Gulbarga.
6. Hyderabad-Karnataka Centre, Ayarwadi, near Jagadamba Temple, Gulbarga.

Out of the 15 NGOs functioned as day care centers during 2005-06 to 2007-08, following 9 NGOs were converted into residential centers from the year 2008-09, 2009-10 and 2010-11. They are:

1. Vishwa Seva Mission, Gulbarga, Buland Parvej Colony, Gulbarga.
2. Nisarga Rural Development Society, Sanjeev Nagar near H.P.S., Gulbarga.
3. Grama Kiran Seva Society, near St. Joseph School, Ramnagar, Gulbarga.
4. Al-Fatima Women's organization, Mohammadi Masjid, near Mohammadi Chowk, M.S.K. Mill, Gulbarga.
5. Devajinayak Education Society, Sunil Nagar, Filters bed area, Gulbarga.

6. Sahara Social Human Awareness Society, Mahaboob Nagar, Gulbarga.
7. Al-Farah Mahila Mandala, Rangeen Masjid, Momeenpura, Gulbarga.
8. Integrated Women and Child Development Society, Near K.G.I.D Office, Nehru Ganj, Gulbarga.
9. Margadarshi Society, Hamaalgalli, Behind Old City Bus Stand, Station Bazar, Gulbarga.

During 2010-11 all NGOs (Residential) were closed according to the directions of the then Deputy Commissioner, Gulbarga. Subsequently during 2011-2012 again 7 NGOs are working as day centres. They are as follows:[9]

1. Vishwa Seva Mission, Gulbarga
2. Al-Fatima Women's Organization, Gulbarga
3. World Vision Society, Gulbarga
4. SARDS
5. Vishwa Bharati
6. Marga Trust
7. Sahara.

50 children were admitted in all the 7 day centres, all children are school enrolled children. Each NGO (day centre) is given a budget of Rs. 21,200 per month for 50 children by the Government. For Nutrition Rs. 5 per day per child is given by the Government, i.e. 5×50×26 days = 6500. Two teachers can be appointed by the NGO by payment of salary of Rs. 1500 per month. One vocational teacher can also be appointed and there is a provision of payment of salary Rs. 1500 per month. One clerk can be appointed by payment of Salary Rs. 1400 per month. One helper/cook can be appointed and salary payable is Rs. 800 per month. Apart from this each NGO entitled to get building rent, electricity, water and other maintenance charges altogether at the rate of Rs. 1000 per month.

Education and Vocation and material for child, each NGO will be paid Rs. 850 per month. If all the children are attended more than 20 days, then all the 50 children are given stipend of Rs. 100 each. This clearly shows Government is motivating and encouraging for children for attendance of the school.

For Residential hostel Rs. 8 per child extra will be given to NGO in addition to Rs. 21,200.

The year-wise Rehabilitation of child labour chart is as shown on next page.[10]

2005-06	2006-07	2007-08	2008-09	2009-10	2010-11
466	1065	631	647	558	3347

NGO's cannot be the vehicle for totally eliminating child labour as they cannot affect the crucial factors responsible for children working, i.e., NGOs cannot ensure full employment, bring about a change in wages nor affect structural changes within a trade. At best, NGOs can initiate and support social mobilization and public education on the evils of child labour. Further, the NGOs cannot substitute the State. The basic function of NGOs is to empower community groups to raise their voices, initiate mobilization on social issues and make recommendations to the government policy-makers. For playing an effective and useful role, the NGOs need to educate themselves on the various laws/ legislations prevailing in the country especially those related to Child Rights and Human Rights. Whenever children are deliberately denied their fundamental rights to survival, growth and development, the NGOs must file cases and writ petitions and do investigative reports which can be verified, and publish them so that a public opinion is created. Indeed many of the Public Interest Litigation petitions emanated from them,[11] as evidenced by the above study of a selected number of cases. NGOs may either move the judiciary directly or alert the NHRC to move the Supreme Court after due investigation.[12] .

1.2. Profile of CHILDLINE in Rehabilitation of Children in General and Child Labour in Particular

CHILDLINE is a project supported by the Ministry of Women and Child Development (GOI) in partnership with State Governments, NGOs, International Organisations, the Corporate Sector, Concerned Individuals and Children.

CHILDLINE is a national, 24-hour; free emergency helpline and outreach service for children in need of care and protection. CHILDLINE number 1098 is a toll free number that is common in all the cities of India. Initially started in Mumbai in June 1996, CHILDLINE is currently operational in 122 cities.

CHILDLINE aims to reach out to the most marginalized children and provides interventions of shelter, medical, repatriation, rescue, death-related, sponsorships, emotional support and guidance.

CHILDLINE India foundation is the National Nodal Organization for CHILDLINE in India appointed by the Ministry of Women and Child Development for the purpose of Facilitation, training, monitoring, advocacy and initiating CHILDLINE in India.

CHILDLINE is the crucial link between children in need of care and protection and the available services. For children with different needs, who call in anytime, anywhere, and for anything, we act as a one-point contact which facilitates instant access to support, advice, active intervention or just a listening ear.

CHILDLINE across the nation have played very crucial role in rescuing child labourers. CHILDLINE Tirunelveli[13] rescues 3 young boys who where working in sweet bakery with the assistance of police department and department of labour and produced before Child Welfare Committee which directed children to temporary shelter home and after collecting details of their whereabouts, the children where repatriated with their parents and who were advised to enrol them in school. A criminal case was registered against the owner of the bakery under the Child Labour Act.

In other case[14] a child which was working in restaurant in Kolkata ran away from the place and began picking rags at the Sealdah station platform. CHILDLINE Kolkata found the boy working in a such a pitiable condition and produced before the CWC with his employer. CWC issued an order to send the boy to a temporary shelter home and an FIR was lodged against his employer under section 16(1) and 14 of Child Labour (Prohibition and Regulation Act), 1986 along with under section 23 of Juvenile Justice Care and Protection of Children Act, 2000.

A bonded child labour who worked for 10 years from Dawn to Dunk in order to pay back a loan of 3800 that his parents taken from their master was rescued from labourious job by CHILDLINE Kanchipuram.

CHILDLINE Gauwahati[15] had rescued 11 children who were working in hotels and restaurants with the assistance of Police department and Labour department on the eve of launching an anti-child labour campaign in November 2010. All children were produced before CWC and directed to put in residential bridge course school for rehabilitative training.

CHILDLINE Calicut[16] rescued 282 children in one year it shows its prompt response to act in emergency situations and it had rightly made meticulous intervention helped to save the lives of 282 children from measurable circumstances.

The Activities of CHILDLINE Across the Country[17]

Calls made to CHILDLINE April-December 2010 shown on next page.

Partner Organizations and their Roles[18]

The District CHILDLINE Nodel at Gulbarga comprises of 1 Nodal organization, 1 Collaborative organization and 4 sub-centres. However, at present 1 sub-centre is in place. The partners are Nodal –

Calls made to CHILDLINE April-December 2010

No. of Cities	30	18	17	22	87
Categories	*South*	*North*	*West*	*East*	*Total*
Medical Help	786	1,382	652	2,465	5,285
Shelter	2,899	732	654	1,554	5,839
Repatriation	3,189	1,713	306	1,632	6,840
Rescue	1,709	1,060	462	651	3,882
Death Related	10	23	5	40	78
Sponsorship	583	704	620	1,600	3,507
Missing	1,730	1,748	597	2,305	6,380
Emotional Support and Guidance	70,387	138,074	114,085	94,833	417,379
Silent/Confidence Building	83,418	39,913	64,600	56,675	244,606
Information/Referral to Services	103,766	31,920	36,296	69,413	241,395
Intervention Follow-up	44,708	17,712	9,601	26,574	98,595
Unable to locate Caller	1,608	470	104	1,373	3,555
Intervention Calls-I	314,793	235,451	227,982	259,115	1,037,341
Awareness Building Calls	30,620	20,023	6,002	29,428	80,073
Technical Connectivity Problems	113,524	178,257	154,587	86,551	532,919
Any other	4,413	3,006	1,644	6,199	15,262
Unclassified	63	71	80	253	467
Non-Intervention Calls-II	148,620	201,357	162,313	116,431	628,721
Total I & II	463,413	436,808	390,295	375,546	1,666,062

SSL Law College, Gulbarga, Collab-Don Bosco Pyar, Gulbarga (Gulbarga, Aland & Afzalpur taluks), Sub-Centre at Wadi-Margadarshi Society, Gulbarga (covering Chittapur, Chincholi and Sedam taluks). The roles of these organizations are as follows.

(i) Nodal Organisation (S.S.L Law College, Gulbarga)

Anchors the CHILDLINE activities at the city district level. A team of two, one person who functions as a city coordinator, who is supervised by a nodal Director (honorary post), who is head of the organization/department that has taken up responsibility, Coordination between the CHILDLINE Centers, the support organizations, the resource organizations/persons and the existing local networks.

Facilitating meetings with a CHILDLINE partner organizations once a month Liasioning between the district and state level mechanisms, where intervention of other agencies may be required Coordination and networking with various Government Departments on child protection issues. Creating awareness and advocacy Organizing meetings of the CHILDLINE Advisory Board (CAB) once every Quarter.

Orientation and sensitization of various Government Departments on child protection issues and coordination of the NICP training initiative.

Leading students to CHILDLINE as volunteers for creation of awareness Training of the CHILDLINE team, conducting sensitization training workshops with the systems Research and Documentation. Monthly reporting to CIF about the functioning of CHILDLINE in the city.

(ii) Collaborative Organization (Don Bosco Pyar, Gulbarga)

It houses and mans the CHILDLINE call centre on a 24 hour basis. Receive and respond to calls on the toll free number 1098 and will function 24 hours a day and convey the information to the relevant Sub-Centre.

Intervene in cases that require intervention. City mapping to identify high risk areas where vulnerable children are found. Intervention and case follow-up on a daily basis co-ordinate with resource organizations for services to be provided to children, for long term rehabilitation. Awareness and outreach in the community on a daily basis. Monthly open house with children who are users of the CHILDLINE service and to understand issues that concern them.

(iii) Sub-Centre (Margadarshi Society, Gulbarga)

Conduct outreach and awareness regarding the service. Intervene in cases referred to by the CHILDLINE Emergency Call Centre and by the volunteers selected at the local level. Maintain proper documentation of area covered during outreach and case interventions referred to the CHILDLINE Emergency Call Centre. Report to the CHLDLINE call centre regularly about the developments and follow-up actions. Networking with the systems within the community such as Anganwadi, ICDS, Panchayat Union, Police, Schools, Labour officials, etc. at the micro-level.

Memorandum of Understanding was signed on December 2008 with regard to disbursement of the funds from Chief Executive Officer, Zilla Panchayat, Gulbarga. H.K.E. Society's S.S.L. Law College was appointed as Nodal Organization in May 2009. Partnership agreement was signed between Child India Foundation and Implementation partners and formal appointment letters from CIF to Nodal Centre, Collab Centre, Sub-centre in December 2009.

March 2009 to September 2010 cases classification of Collab Center and Sub-center of Gulbarga.[19]

TYPE OF CASES: Collab Centre Cases

Sl.No.	*Type of cases*	*Numbers*
1.	Restoration cases	59
2.	Shelter cases	36
3.	Missing cases	04
4.	Death-related cases	01
5.	Medical help cases	08
6.	Emotional support and Guidance	24
7.	Sponsorship cases	01
	Total Cases	133

Sub-Centre Cases

Sl.No.	*Type of cases*	*Numbers*
1.	Restoration cases	55
2.	Shelter cases	45
3.	Missing cases	02
4.	Medical help cases	04
5.	Emotional support and Guidance	06
6.	Sponsorship cases	05
	Total Cases	117

Call Status from April 2010 to January 2011

Sl.No.	*Call types*	*Numbers*
1.	City Gulbarga	--
2.	Intervention	--
3.	Medical Help	11
4.	Shelter	55
5.	Restoration (within the country)	129
6.	Restoration (outside the country)	--
7.	Rescue from abuse	05
8.	Death-related	--
9.	Sponsorship	11
10.	Referred by another CHILDLINE	05
11.	Missing Children	--
12.	Child Lost	01
13.	Parents Asking Help	12
14.	Emotional Support & Guidance	46
15.	Unclassified	--

1. Partner Budget for CHILDLINE Gulbarga

A	*Budget for existing partners for 12 months*	*No. of Units*	*Non-recurring expenses*	*Total Non-recurring Budget*	*Recurring budget per month*	*Recurring expenses for 12 months*	*Total budget*
	Nodal	1	0	0	20000	24000	24000
	Collab	1	0	0	75500	906000	906000
	Sub-Centre	1	0	0	24000	288000	288000
	Grand Total						1434000
B	*Budget for CHILDLINE partners for 8 months*	*No. of Units*	*Non-recurring expenses*	*Total Non-recurring Budget*	*Recurring budget per month*	*Recurring expenses for 12 months*	*Total budget*
	Months				1	8	
	Sub Centres	3	44000	132000	24000	576000	708000
	Total partner budgets for 2010-11 (1A+1B)						2142000

2. CONCLUSION

Thus, the NGOs play a vital and significant role in the task of elimination of child labour. The role of NGOs in rescuing, rehabilitation and mainstreaming the child labourers is highly commendable. Childline across the nation have played very crucial role in protecting the rights of the children and rescuing child labourers.

Notes and References

1. Study material on successful prosecution of child labour cases, Department of Labour, Govt. of Karnataka, 2011, pp. 18-19.
2. Asha Bajpai, *Child Rights in India—Law, Policy and Practice*, 2nd edn., New Delhi: Oxford University Press, 2006, p. 185.
3. Dr. Nanjunda, D.C., *Child Labour and Human Rights—A Prospective*, Delhi: Kalpaz Publications, 2008, pp. 82-83.
4. P. Ishwara Bhat, *Law and Social Transformation*, New Delhi: Eastern Book Company, 2010, p. 625.
5. Centre for Legislative Research and Advocacy, "*Abolition of Child Labour*", New Delhi.
6. Ravi Sharma, "Frontline Magazine", Bangalore, Nov. 17, 2006, p. 25.
7. Helen R. Sekhar, *Child Labour: Situation and Strategies for Elimination*, Noida: V.V. Giri National Labour Institute, 2007, pp. 84-87.
8. Sources Collected from "*Elimination of Child Labour Project, Gulbarga*", 2005-06.
9. *Ibid.*, 2010-11.

10. *Supra* note 8.
11. *Centre for Enquiry into Health and Allied Themes (CEHAT) and others* v. *Union of India*, AIR 2001 SC; *Bandhua Mukti Morcha* v. *Union of India*, 1984 SC ; *Peoples Union for Democratic Rights* v. *Union of India*, AIR 1982 S.C; *Vishal Jeet* v. *Union of India*, AIR 1990 S.C.
12. D. Venkateshwar Rao, *Child Rights—A Perspective on International and National Law*, 1st edn., New Delhi: Manak Publications Pvt. Ltd., 2004, pp. 163-64.
13. Hello Childline, Issue 60, January 2011, CHILDLINE *India Foundation*, Mumbai, p. 4.
14. *Ibid.*, p. 6.
15. *Ibid.*, p. 7.
16. *Ibid.*, p. 11.
17. *Ibid.*, p. 45.
18. A Brief Note on CHILDLINE, Gulbarga, 1098, *Progress Report by CHILDLINE India Foundation*, March 2009 to March 2010, pp. 14-15.
19. Data collected from CHILDLINE Nodal Centre, S.S.L. Law College, Gulbarga.
20. *Ibid*, also see Reaching out to children in need of care and protection, CHILDLINE 1098, p. 14.
21. A brief note on CHILDLINE, Gulbarga, 1098 by Nodal Centre, SSL Law College, Gulbarga, p. 31.

10

An Empirical Study of Child Labour Status in Gulbarga City

"The day will come when nations will be judged not only by their military or economic strength, nor by the splendor of their capital cities public building but by the well-being of their people; by the provision that is made for those who are vulnerable and disadvantaged and by the protection that is afforded to the growing minds and bodies of their children".

—UNICEF, Annual Report

PART I

I. PROFILE OF GULBARGA CITY

Gulbarga is situated in the Hyderabad, Karnataka area. It is a historic city known for its cultural heritage. Once it was a capital of the famous dynasties of Bahamani kingdom. It was also ruled by famous dynasties like Rastrakutas and Chalukyas of Kalyan. Gulbarga is famous for its fort which was originally constructed by Raja Gulchand and developed by Bahamanies (Hasan Bahamani Gangu).

Gulbarga is the second largest of the 30 districts in Karnataka state, and stands third-population-wise. It is predominantly rural and agrarian with more than 80% of its population living in villages, drought and scarcity conditions often haunt the people of the district due to its geographic positioning. The district has low human development indicators and is also characterized by illiteracy, blind beliefs, poor health status, dominance of upper classes, oppression of groups like dalits—SC and STs, poor awareness of their rights, violation of child rights, primitive customs like child marriage, devadasi system, harassment of children and trafficking of human beings especially girl children. The low rain fall, problems of unorganized sector, instability of agriculture, old pattern of cultivation, indebtedness have all had their impact on lifestyle. The many economic and social hardships like migration of families in search of work to distant cities have had their impact on family and children converting them to become child labourers, street children, child beggars and rag pickers.

The population of Gulbarga, rural and urban, according to 2001 Census is 6,75,679. Rural population is 2,45,414 and urban population is 4,30,265. Male population is 3,48,665 and female population is 3,27,014. Area of Gulbarga is 1,734.53 sq. km. There are 6 Hoblies and 36 Gram Panchayats with one Municipal Corporation. 136 villages are inhabited and covered under Gulbarga city and 4 villages are inhabitated. There is 1 Member of Parliament–Loksabha and 2 MLAs (with North and South region) constituencies. Density of population is 390 persons per sq. mts. There are 2,79,168 persons are literates out of which 1,59,519 are male persons and 1,19,649 are female persons .There are 63,238 children are in the age group of 0-6 out of which 33,150 are boys and 30,088 are girls. The literacy rate is 76.1% out of which 83.8% are male persons and 67.8% are female persons. Sex ratio is 938.[1] According to Gulbarga District 2001[2] Census literacy rate of 7+ age group is 50%, dropout rate (primary) is 24.37%, out of school children (6-14) is 20.82%, infant mortality rate (IMR) is 67% and girls married below the age of 18 years is 48.90%

There are 3 Chemical Factories, 11 Engineering Factories and 58 other factories are located in Gulbarga. Thus, there are 72 factories and 3,450 employees are working in these factories. Apart from this there are number of Cement Factories like ACC at Shahabad, Vasavadatta Cement Factory at Sedam and Rajashree Cement Factory at Malkhed are located in the neighbourhood place of Gulbarga city. Further there are several stone quarries are spread over around the Gulbarga City and there are several private/public sugarcane factories have been set-up. Due to the location of these factories and industries, incidence of floating and migration population is very high.

With regard to education in Gulbarga city, there are 623 primary schools and 63,966 boys and 64,500 girls are studying in these schools. There are 239 High Schools and 16,094 boys and 16,564 girls students are studying in these schools. There are 718 Anganawadi Centres are working under the department of Women and Child Development, Gulbarga. There are 880 Self Help Groups (SHGs) are functioning under which 11,017 women are involved in these schemes. There are 50,896 Agricultural labourers are working in Gulbarga out of which 20,695 are male labourers and 30,201 are female agricultural labourers. There are 237 Fair Price Shops in Gulbarga and 10,804 persons are BPL ration card holders and 79,758 persons are APL ration card holders in Gulbarga city.

Gulbarga is situated in North Karnataka in the Hyderabad-Karnataka region and the city is continued as most backward region due to socio-economic reasons prevailing in the area since after state reorganization in 1956. Therefore, in the recent years a struggle and movement is launched by cross-section of the people and strong response is moved for the implementation of Article 371 in order to remove regional imbalances.

Employing large number of children as child labourers can be seen as a common phenomenon in Gulbarga city and its surroundings. The general backwardness of the region and poverty of the people have contributed to the prevalence of child labour practice. Children work mainly in hotels, garages, brick kilns and construction works. A sample of 41 children is chosen for the study from these work places. Data for the study is collected from child labourers, their employers, the parents and NGOs who are working in the field. The collected data has been analysed and interpreted in terms of the hypotheses of the study and is presented below.

PART II

ANALYSIS AND INTERPRETATION OF DATA

2. DATA OF CHILD LABOURERS

TABLE I

Distribution of Child Labour in Different Fields of Work

Field	*No. of Respondents*	*Percentage*
Garage	10	24.4
Hotel	13	31.7
Brick klin	13	31.7
Construction	05	12.2
Total	41	100.0

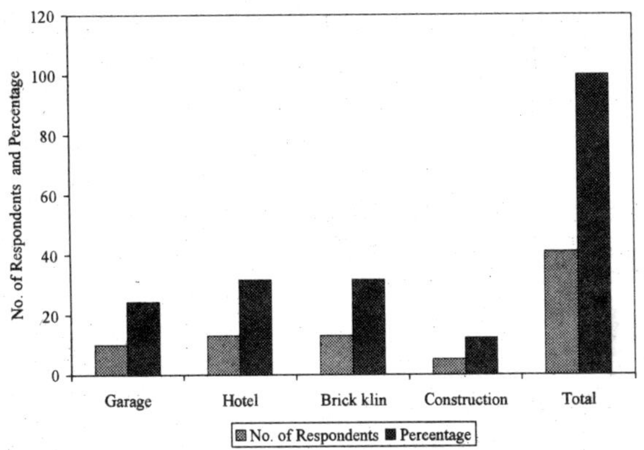

In the sample, 24.4% of respondents are taken from Garages, 31.7% are drawn from Hotel industry, 31.7% from Brick kilns and 12.2% are from Construction sector.

TABLE 2

Age-wise Distribution of Child Labour

Age (years)	*No. of Respondents*	*Percentage*
6-8	2	5.4
9-10	7	18.9
11-12	12	32.4
13-14	16	43.2
Total	37	100.0

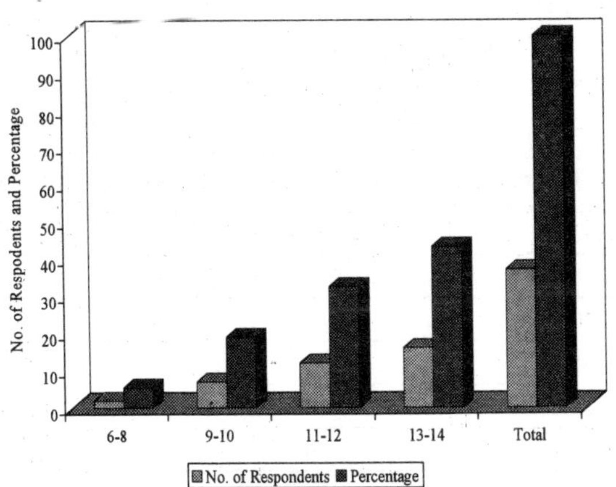

4.5% of the children are working in the age group of 6-8 years, 18.9% are in the age group of 9-10 years, 32.4% are in the age group of 11-12 years and 43.2% are in the age group of 13-14 years.

TABLE 3

Distribution of Child Labour on the Basis of Religion

Religion	No. of Respondents	Percentage
Hindu	27	67.5
Muslim	10	25.0
Christian	01	2.50
Others	02	5.0
Total	40	100.0

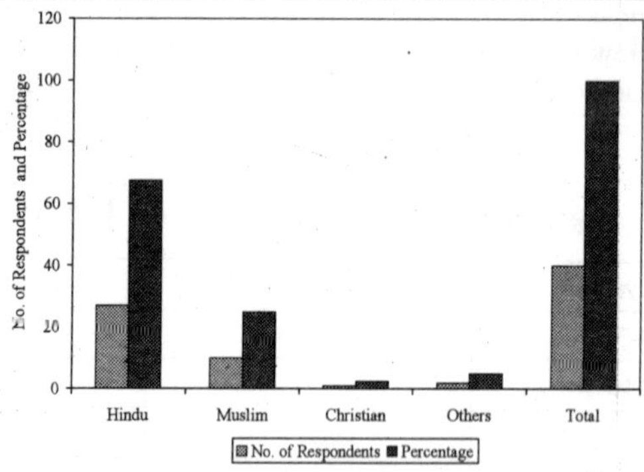

67.50% Respondents in the sample belong to Hindu religion, 25.00% Respondents belong to Muslim religion, 2.50% Respondents belong to Christian religion and 5.00% Respondents belong to Others. The analysis clearly shows that children belonging to Hindu religion are more working as child labourers.

TABLE 4

Caste-wise Distribution of Child Labour

Caste	No. of Respondents	Percentage
SC / ST	7	18.4
OBC	21	55.3
GM	6	15.8
Others	4	10.5
Total	38	100.0

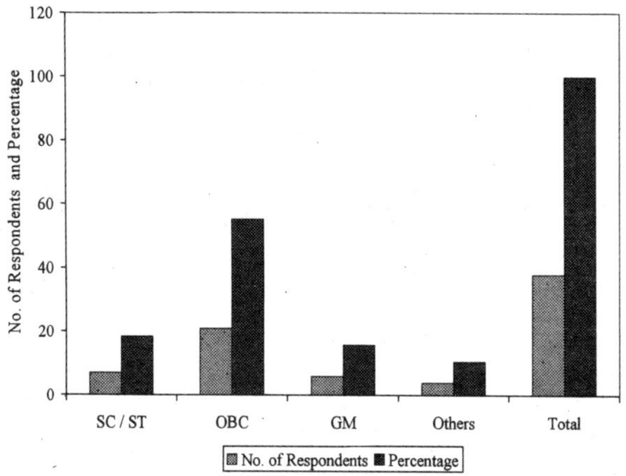

18.4% Respondents belong to SC/ST categories, 55.3% Respondents belong to OBC categories, 15.8% Respondents belong to G.M., 10.5% Respondents belong to others. The analysis shows that majority of child labourers belong to other backward communities consisting of under privileged sections of the society.

TABLE 5

Gender-wise Distribution of Child Labour

Gender	*No. of Respondents*	*Percentage*
Male	36	87.8
Female	5	12.2
Total	41	100.0

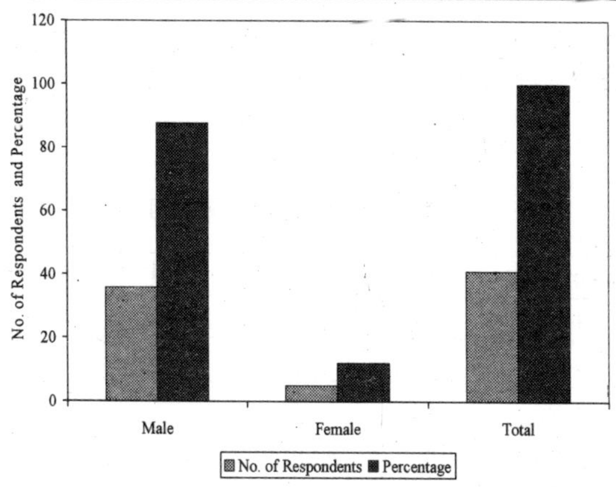

87.8% Respondents are male child labourers and 12.2% Respondents are female child labourers. The analysis shows that, more than 87% children working in different fields are male children, and 12.2% are female children.

TABLE 6

Mother Tongue of Child Labour

Mother Tongue	*No. of Respondents*	*Percentage*
Kannada	30	73.2
Hindi	10	24.4
Telugu	1	2.4
Total	41	100.0

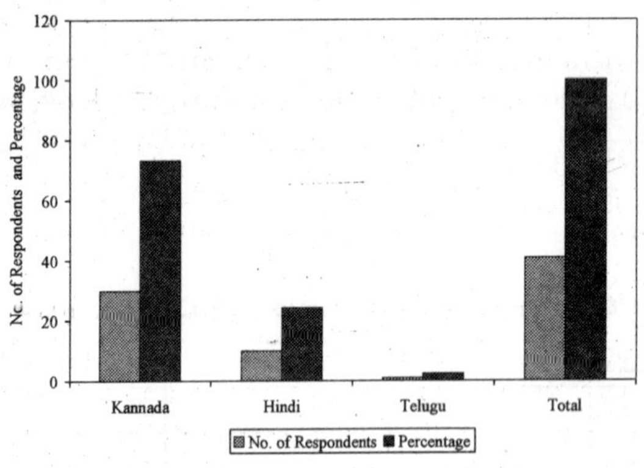

73.2% Respondents' mother-tongue is Kannada, 24.4% Respondents' mother-tongue is Hindi and 2.4% Respondents' mother-tongue is Telugu. Thus, the analysis indicates that more number of children speak Kannada.

TABLE 7

Members of the Family

Members	*No. of Respondents*	*Percentage*
1-5	12	29.3
6-7	23	56.1
8-10	6	14.6
Total	41	100.0

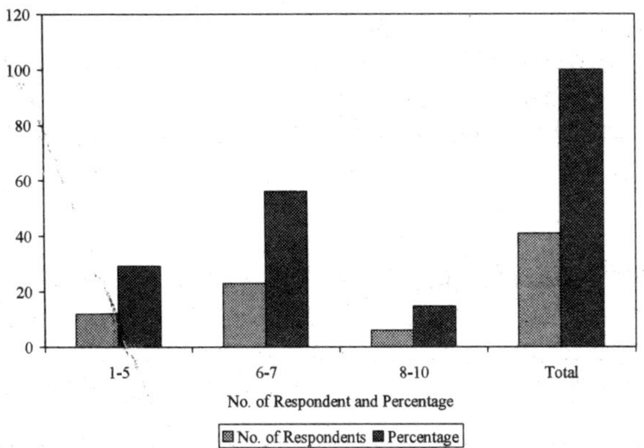

Out of 41 Respondent families, 29.3% families have 1-5 members, 56.1% have 6-7 members and 14.6% have 8-10 members. Thus, it is revealed that most of the children are from mid-sized families.

TABLE 8

Members Working in the Family of Child Labourer

Members working	*No. of Respondents*	*Percentage*
One	5	12.5
Two	9	22.5
Three	21	52.5
None	5	12.5
Total	40	100.0

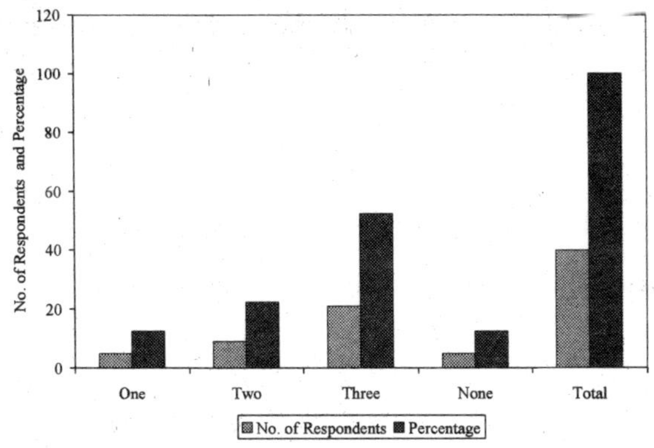

In 12.5% families one member is working, in 22.5% of families two members are working, in 52.5% families three members are working and in 12.5% of families no adult members are working. That means majority of child labourers are from families where other members are working.

TABLE 9

Distribution of Respondents on the Basis of Monthly Income of Family

Income of family	*No. of Respondents*	*Percentage*
No income	6	15.0
Less than 1000	6	15.0
1000 and Less than 2000	6	15.0
2000 and Less than 4000	22	55.0
Total	40	100.0

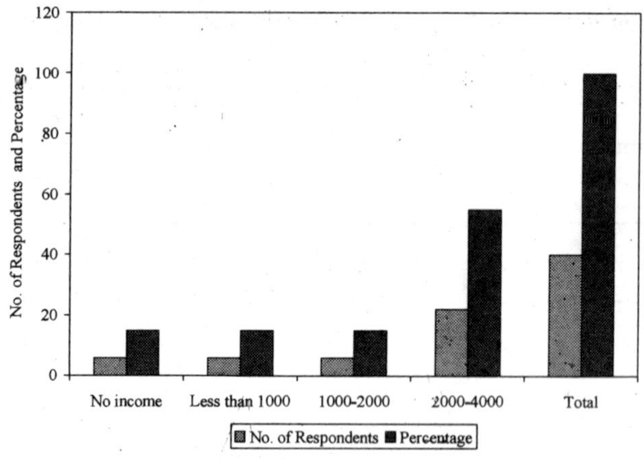

15% Respondwnts have no income in the family, 15% of families have less than Rs. 1000 income, 15% of families have income of Rs. 1000 to less than 2000 and 55% of families have income of Rs. 2000 to less than Rs. 4000. The analysis shows that inspite of income of 55% families is between Rs. 2000 to 4000, still children are forced to work as child labourers.

TABLE 10

Dropout of Child Labour from School

Dropout of Children	*No. of Respondents*	*Percentage*
Yes	26	63.4
No	15	36.6
Total	41	100.0

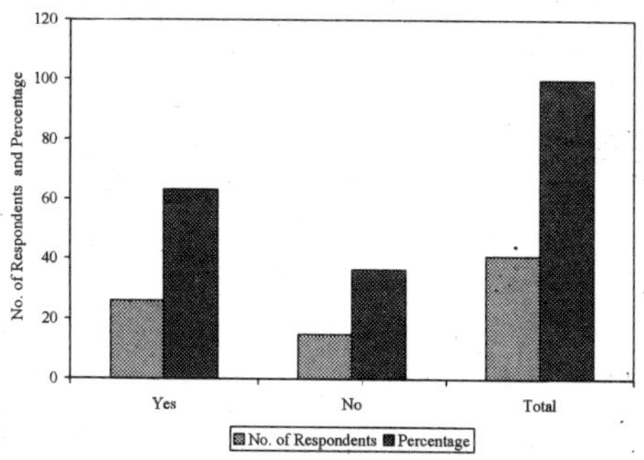

63.4% Respondwnts are dropouts from school, whereas 36.6% respondents never went to school.

TABLE 11

Distribution of Children on the Basis of their Interest in Education

Interest in Education	*No. of Respondents*	*Percentage*
Yes	07	17.5
No	33	82.5
Total	40	100.0

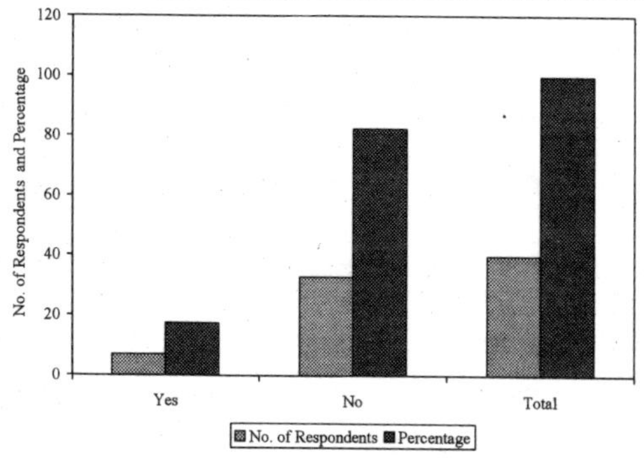

17.5% children have interest in education, whereas 82.5% children have no interest

TABLE 12

Distribution of Children on the Basis of Period of Working

Period of work	*No. of Respondents*	*Percentage*
0-Less than 1 year	16	39.0
1 year-Less than 2 years	15	36.6
2 years-Less than 3 years	6	14.6
3 years and above	4	9.8
Total	41	100.0

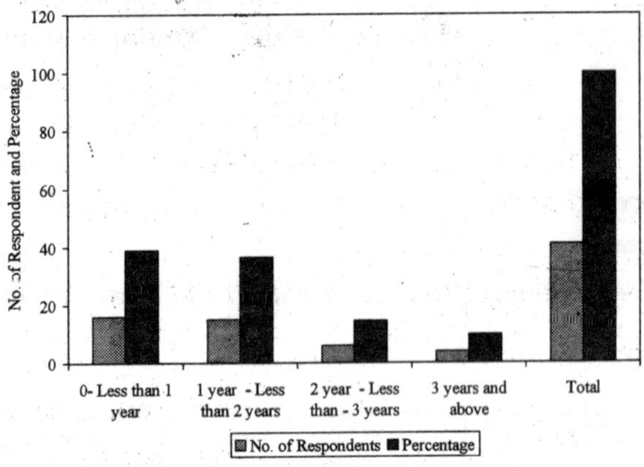

39% Respondwnts were working for less than one year, 36.6% respondents were working for more than one year and less than two years, 14.6% respondents were working for more than two years and less than three years and 9.8% respondents was working for more than three years and

TABLE 13

Distribution of Children on the Basis of Nature of Labour

Nature of Labour	*No. of Respondents*	*Percentage*
Hazardous	39	95.1
Non-Hazardous	02	4.9
Total	41	100.0

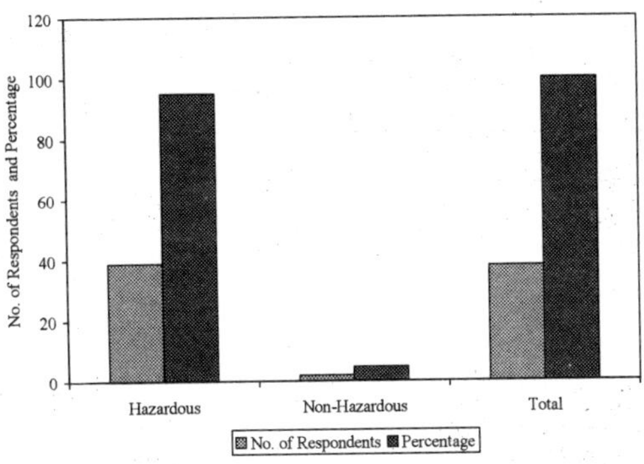

95.1% Respondwnts work in hazardous nature of employment, whereas 4.9% respondents work in non-hazardous nature of employment. This analysis clearly shows that, more than 95% children working in hazardous nature of employment.

TABLE 14 :

Age of the Child during Joining to the Work

Age of the Child	*No. of Respondents*	*Percentage*
8-10 years	17	41.5
11-12 years	12	29.3
13-14 years	12	29.3
Total	41	100.0

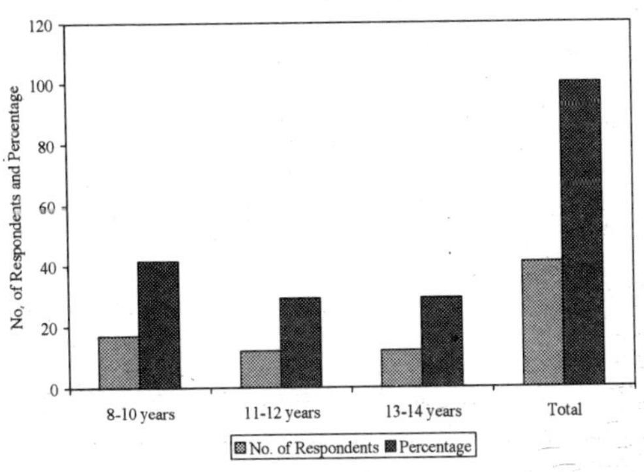

41.5% Respondwnts joined the work when they were in age group of 8-10 years, 29.3% respondents joined the work in age group of 11-12 years and 29.3% respondents joined the work in age group of 13-14 years.

TABLE 15

Working Hours in a Day

Working hours	No. of Respondents	Percentage
4-6 hrs	3	7.3
7-8 hrs	4	9.8
9-10 hrs	21	51.2
11-12 hrs	13	31.7
Total	41	100.0

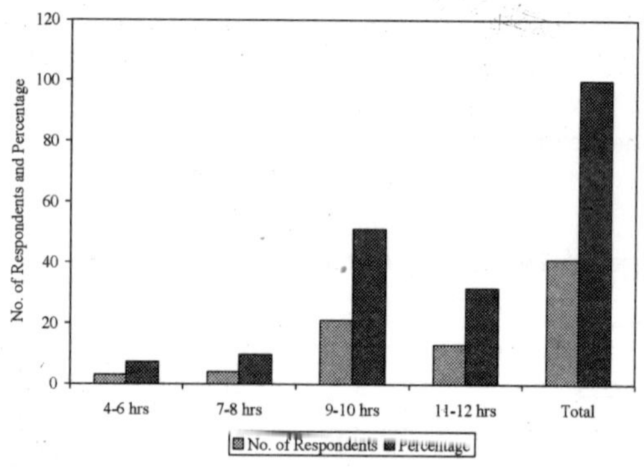

7.3% Respondwnts work 4-6 hours in a day, 9.8% respondents work 7-8 hours in a day, 51.2% respondents work 9-10 hours in a day and 31.7% respondents work 11-12 hours in a day. The analysis shows that majority of respondents work from 9-10 hours in a day. Consequently, working for long hours continuously affects the health, strength and body of children. This clearly indicates the exploitation of children to the maximum.

TABLE 16

Interval/Leisure Time between Working Hours

Interval / Leisure Time	No. of Respondents	Percentage
Yes	10	25.0
No	30	75.0
Total	40	100.0

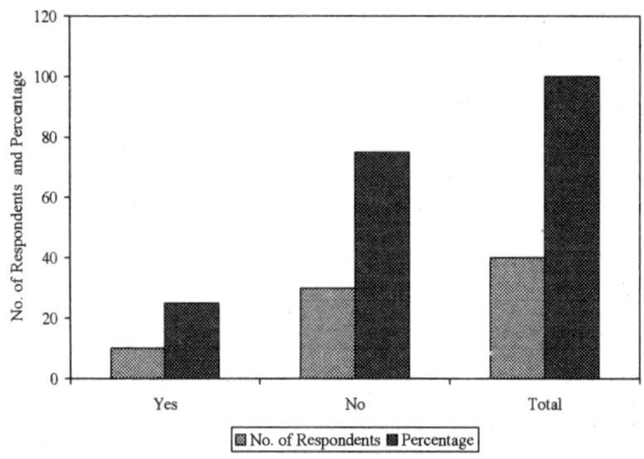

25% Respondwnts opined that they get interval/leisure time between working hours, whereas 75% respondents do not get interval/ leisure time between working hours. This table clearly shows that children were exploited by their employers and forced to work without leisure time.

TABLE 17

Reasons for Child Labour

Reasons	*No. of Respondents*	*Percentage*
Forced by parents	9	22.0
Poverty	18	43.9
Orphan/No Parents or single parent	8	19.5
Illiteracy and ignorance of parents	3	7.3
Inadequate income and large family size	3	7.3
Total	41	100.0

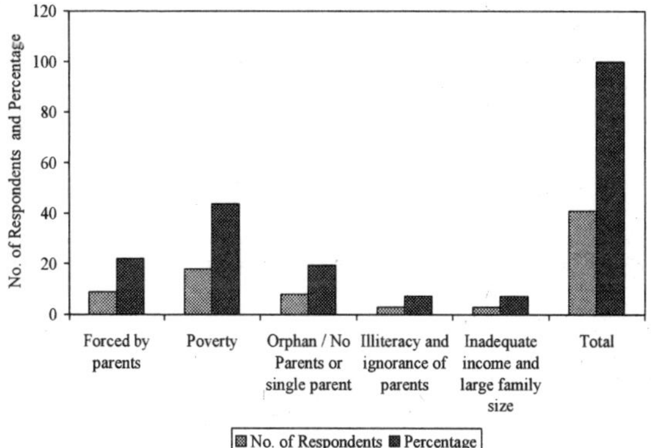

22% Respondwnts are working as child labourers, due to the pressure of their parents, 43.9% respondents are working due to poverty, and 19.5% children are working as their parents are not working, 7.3% children are working due to illiteracy and ignorance of parents and lastly 7.3% children are working due to inadequate income and large family size. Thus, the analysis reveals that, majority of children are working as child labourers due to poverty which is the root cause for this problem.

TABLE 18

Employer taking Care for Child Labourer during Illness

Care by employer	*No. of Respondents*	*Percentage*
Yes	17	41.5
No	24	58.5
Total	40	100.0

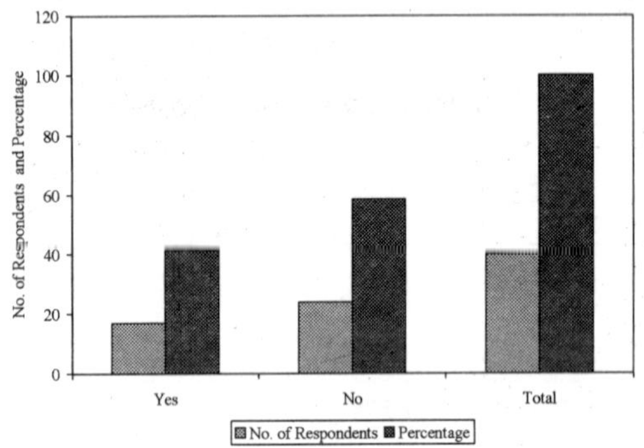

41.5% Respondwnts said employer take due care of them during illness, whereas 58.5% respondents said employer does not take care for them during illness. This is another instance of exploitation and inhuman treatment of child labourers by their employers.

TABLE 19

Wages Payable to the Child Labourer

Wages Payable	*No. of Respondents*	*Percentage*
Daily	9	24.3
Weekly	16	43.2
Monthly	12	32.4
Total	37	100.0

24.3% Respondwnts are paid wages on daily basis by their employer, 43.2% respondents are paid wages on weekly basis and 32.4% respondents are paid wages on monthly basis. The analysis shows that majority of children get their wages on week end.

TABLE 20

Receiver of Wages Earned by the Child Labourer

Receiver	*No. of Respondents*	*Percentage*
Parents	24	64.9
Guardian	5	13.5
Child	8	21.6
Total	37	100.0

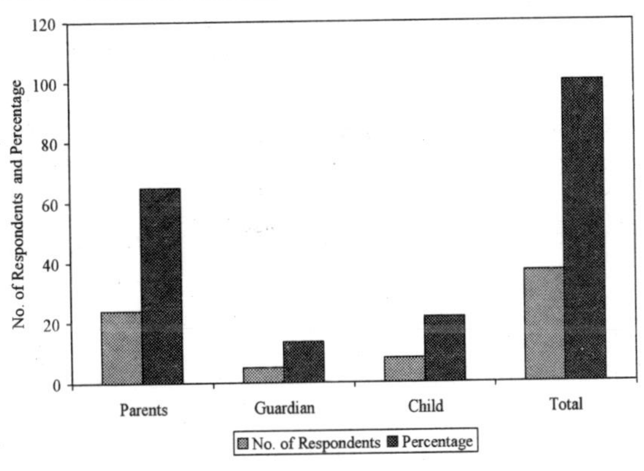

Wages of 64.9% Respondwnts received by their parents, wages of 13.5% respondents received by their guardian and wages of 21.6% respondents received by child himself. The analysis shows that, in majority of cases wages earned by child labourer are received either by parents or guardian directly and children do not get their own earning. The data clearly reveals that the children are reduced the status of slaves.

TABLE 21

Weekly/Monthly Holidays given to the Child Labourer

Weekly /Monthly holidays	*No. of Respondents*	*Percentage*
Given	2	5.7
Not given	33	94.3
Total	35	100.0

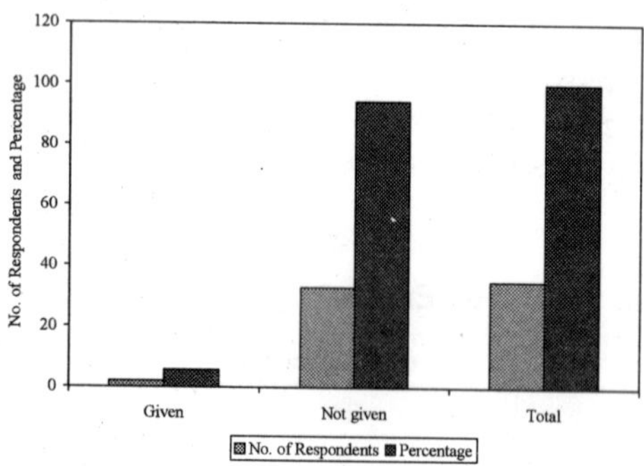

Only 5.7% Respondwnts are given weekly/monthly holidays but 94.3% respondents were not given the weekly/monthly holidays. The analysis clearly shows that, children are forced to work continuously without holidays. This is a clear exploitation of child labourers.

TABLE 22

Wages Paid to the Child Labourers during Holidays

Wages paid during holidays	*No. of Respondents*	*Percentage*
Yes	2	5.6
No	34	94.4
Total	36	100.0

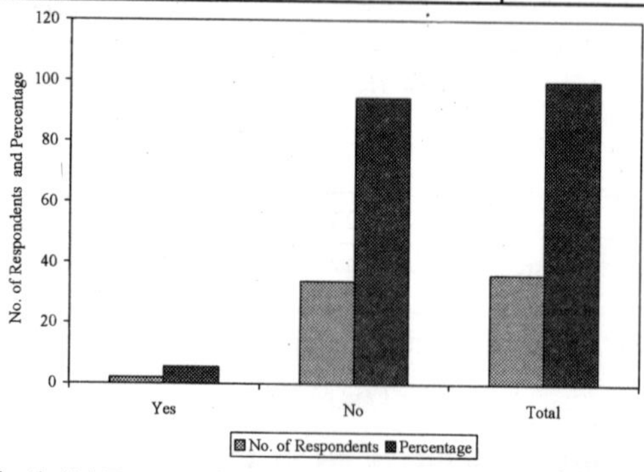

Only 5.6% Respondwnts get the wages when they worked during holidays and rest of the respondents, i.e., 94.4% respondents do not get any wages, although they worked during holidays. The analysis shows that, children are exploited, first, they are not given holiday and secondly, they are forced to work during holidays. Lastly, children are not given any wages when they worked during holidays. This indicates exploitation and abuse of children.

TABLE 23

Wage Rate for Boys (Child Labour)

Wage Rate for Boys	*No. of Respondents*	*Percentage*
Less than Rs. 25	8	22.9
Rs. 25 to Rs. 45	27	77.1
Total	35	100.0

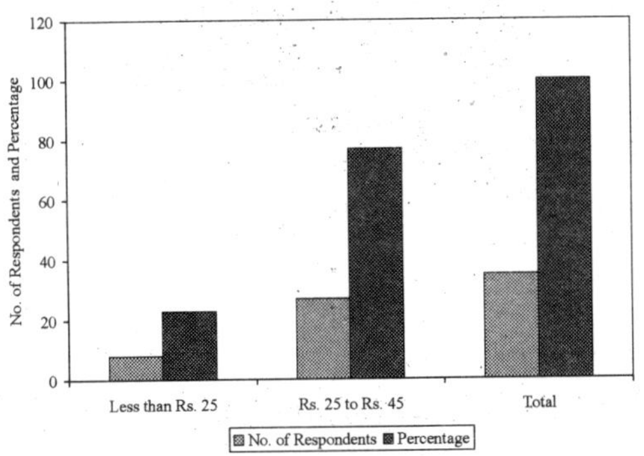

22.9% Respondwnts earn less than Rs. 25 as wages per day and 77.1% respondents earn wages Rs. 25-45 per day.

TABLE 24

Wage Rate for Girls (Child Labour)

Wage Rate for Girls	*No. of Respondents*	*Percentage*
Less than Rs. 20	4	14.8
Rs. 20 to Rs. 40	23	85.2
Total	27	100.0

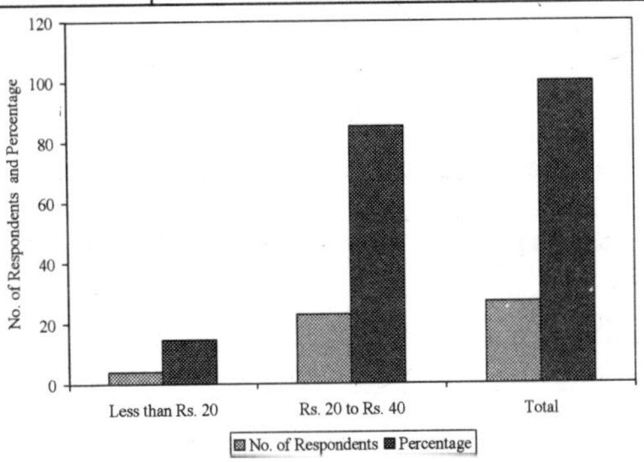

14.8% respondents earn wages less than Rs. 20 per day and 85.2% respondents earn wages from Rs. 20-40 per day. This clearly establishes that the employers practice gender discrimination.

TABLE 25

Wage Rate for Adult Labourers

Wage Rate for Male (Adult)	*No. of Respondents*	*Percentage*
Less than Rs. 100	16	51.6
Rs. 100 to Rs. 150	15	48.4
Total	31	100.0

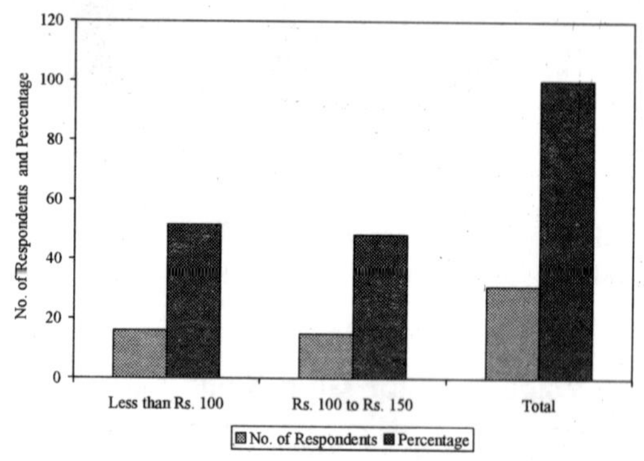

51.6% Respondwnts (male adult labourers) earn wages less than Rs. 100 per day and 48.4% respondents earn wages from Rs. 100-150 per day.

TABLE 26

Wage Rate for Adult Women Workers

Wage Rate for Female (Adult)	*No. of Respondents*	*Percentage*
Less than Rs. 80	12	44.4
Rs. 80 to Rs. 150	15	55.6
Total	27	100.0

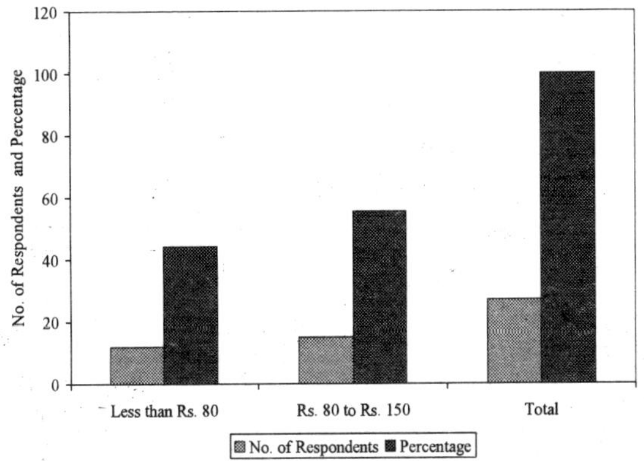

44.4% female adult labourers earn wages less than Rs. 80 per day and 55.6% female adult labourers earn wages from Rs.80 to Rs. 150 per day. Analysis from Tables 23 to 26 reveals that 70.1% of boys child labourer earn wages from Rs. 25 to 45 and 85.2% girl child labourers earn wages from Rs. 20 to 40 per day, while 51.6% male adult labourers earns less than Rs. 100 per day and 44% female adult labourers earn less than Rs. 80 per day. This clearly shows that gender discrimination of boy and girl child labourers and male and female adult labourers.

TABLE 27

Working Conditions of Child Labourers

Employment Working Conditions	*No. of Respondents*	*Percentage*
Comfortable	2	5.6
Non-comfortable	34	94.4
Total	35	100.0

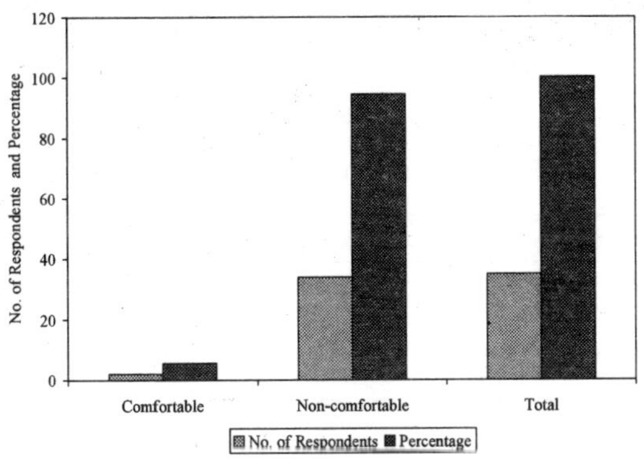

According to 5.6% respondents working conditions are comfortable. But for 94.4% of them feel that their working conditions are bad.

TABLE 28

Behaviour of the Employer

Employer Behaviour	*No. of Respondents*	*Percentage*
Good	7	21.2
Ill-treatment	15	45.5
In different	9	27.3
Punitive action	2	6.1
Total	33	100.0

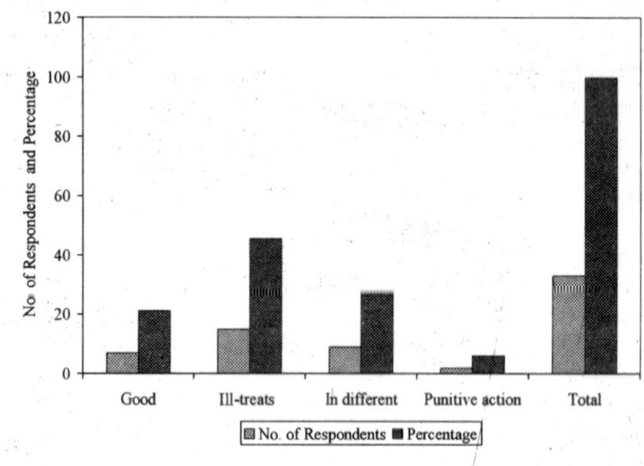

21.2% Respondwnts opined that employer behaviour is good 45.5% respondents opined that employer does not treat them properly, 27.3% respondents opined that employer behaviour is indifferent and 6.1% respondents said employer take punitive action. This clearly established that the child labourers are not properly treated by their employers.

TABLE 29

Punishment by the Employer

Form of Punishment	*No. of Respondents*	*Percentage*
Scolding	20	57.1
Beating	2	5.7
Expelling	13	37.1
Total	35	100.0

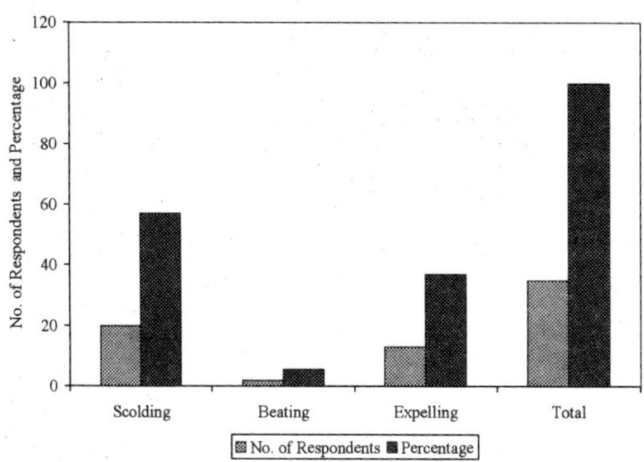

57.1% Respondwnts opined that their employer punished by scolding when they fail to work satisfactorily, 5.7% respondents opined that their employer punished them by beating, and 37.1% respondents opined that their employer punished by expelling them from work.

TABLE 30

Various Kinds of Benefits Availed by the Children

Kinds of Benefits	*No. of Respondents*	*Percentage*
Incentives	6	54.5
Clothes	2	18.2
Tips	3	27.3
Total	11	100.0

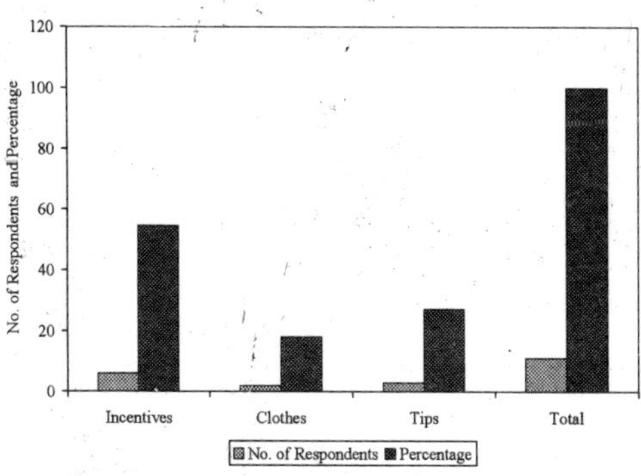

54.5% Respondwnts are given benefits other than wages in the form of incentives, 18.2% respondents receive the benefits in the form of cloths, and 27.3% respondents receive the benefits as tips.

TABLE 31

Health Problem of Child Labourers in the Occupation

Health Problem	*No. of Respondents*	*Percentage*
Yes	27	67.5
No	13	32.5
Total	40	100.0

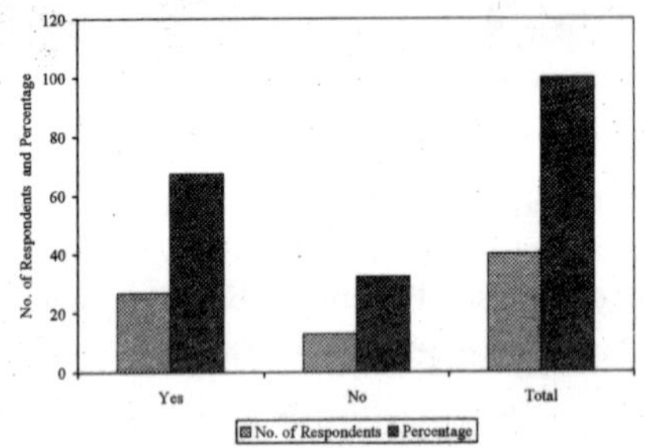

67.5% Respondents opined that they have problem of health in their occupation where they are working and 32.5% respondents of the view that they don't have any health problem. The analysis shows that majority of children are suffering with health problem which affect their physical growth and development.

TABLE 32

Availability of First Aid at the Workplace in Case of Emergency

First Aid Facility	*No. of Respondents*	*Percentage*
Yes	1	2.6
No	37	97.4
Total	38	100.0

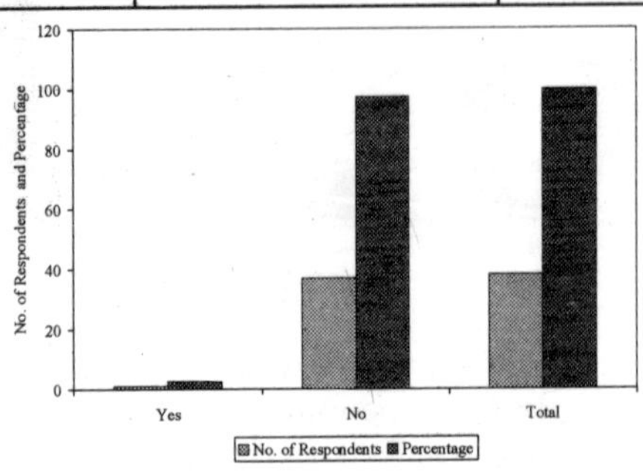

2.6% Respondents opined that they had First Aid facilities in the work place and whereas 97.4% respondents opined that they did not have any First Aid facilities in the work place. This shows the indifference of the employers towards child labour.

TABLE 33

Working during Night Time

Night Work	*No. of Respondents*	*Percentage*
Yes	30	78.9
No	8	21.1
Total	38	100.0

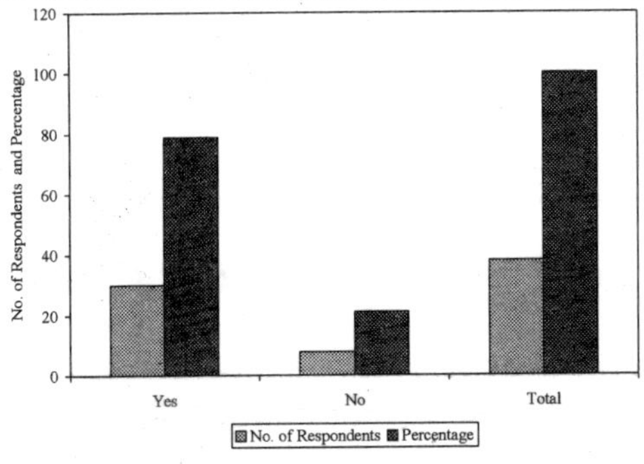

78.9% Respondents opined that they work at night also whenever required by employer and 21.1% respondents said they do not work at night. The Table shows that, more than 78% of children are forced that to work at night, which deprive their right to rest/leisure and affect to their health.

TABLE 34

Habits of Child Labourer

Habits	*No. of Respondents*	*Percentage*
Smoking	11	30.6
Gutka	10	27.8
Narcotic	1	2.8
Gambling	14	38.9
Total	36	100.0

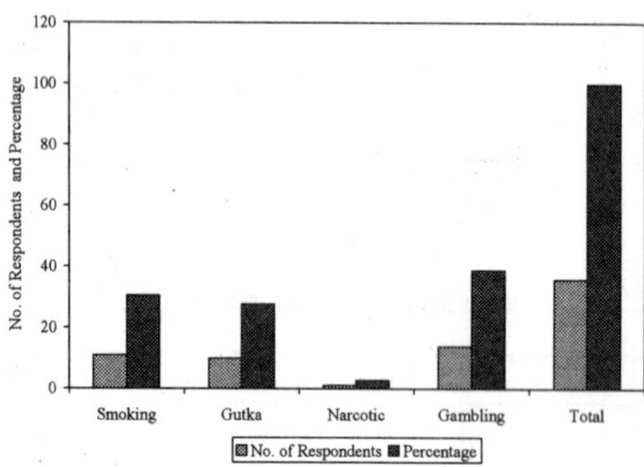

30.6% Respondents had the habit of smoking, 27.8% respondents had the habit of chewing gutka, 2.8% respondents had the habit to take narcotics, and 38.9% respondents had the habit of indulge in gambling. The analysis shows that child labourers have fallen prey to bad habits. These habits affect the health and development of children which are socially disapproved. Further, number of children are engaged in gambling which is rally a serious matter of concern.

II. ANALYSIS OF DATA FROM EMPLOYERS

Table 35

Nature of Employment

Nature of Employment	*No. of Respondents*	*Percentage*
Hazardous	33	94.3
Non-Hazardous	2	5.7
Total	35	100.0

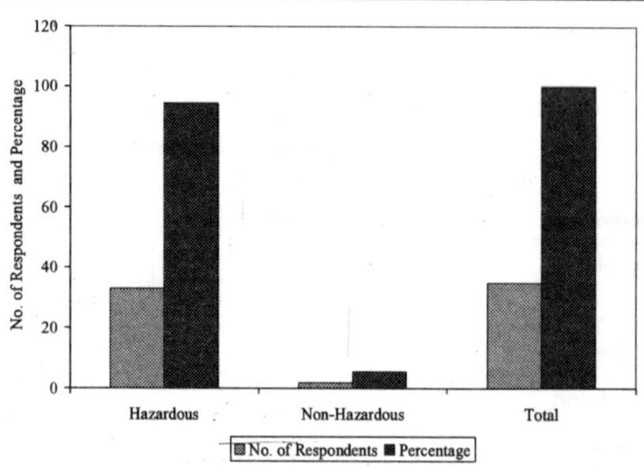

From the Table it is found that 94.3% of employers of child labourers carried hazardous activities and 5.7% carried non-hazardous.

TABLE 36

Nature of Employment

Weekly Holiday	*No. of Respondents*	*Percentage*
Given	3	8.6
Not given	32	91.4
Total	35	100.0

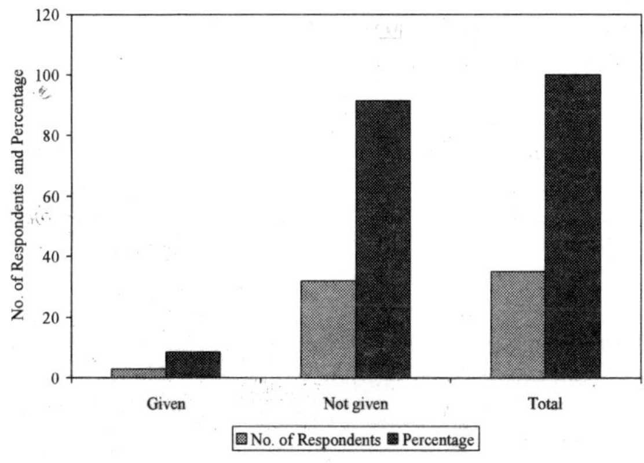

8.6% Respondents give weekly holidays to the child labourers and whereas 91.4% respondents do not give weekly holidays to the child labourers. The analysis clearly shows that employers force the children to work continuously without holidays, denying their right to enjoyment and recreation facilities. This is a clear exploitation of children.

TABLE 37

Reason for Employment of Child Labour

Reasons	*No. of Respondents*	*Percentage*
Cheapness (cheap labour)	8	20.5
Parental Pressure	8	20.5
Poor Economic condition	23	59.0
Total	39	100.0

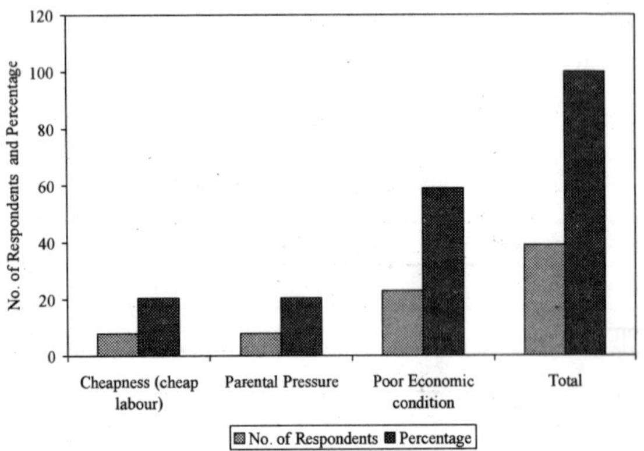

20.5% Respondents employ child labour because they are cheap, 20.5% respondents employ children due to parental pressure and 59% respondents employ children as child labour due to children's poor economic condition. From the analysis it is evident that, majority of employers employ children due to poor economic condition and poverty of parents.

Table 38

Payment of Wages to Child Labourers

Time of Payment	*No. of Respondents*	*Percentage*
Daily	7	18.9
Weekly	17	45.9
Monthly	13	35.1
Total	37	100.0

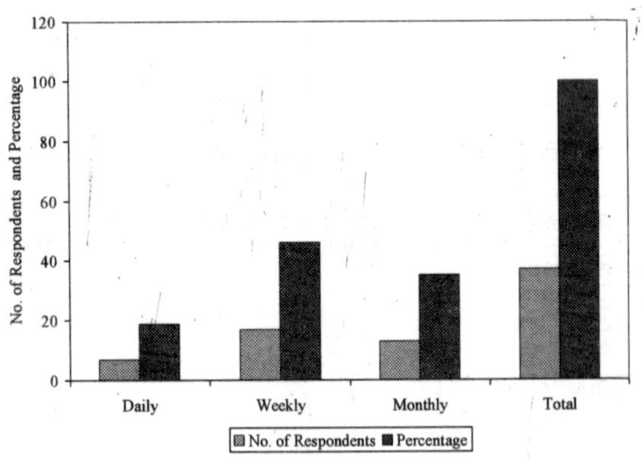

18.9% Respondents make payment of wages to the children on daily basis, 45.9% respondents make payment of wages on weekly basis and 35.1% respondents pay wages on monthly basis. The analysis clearly shows that majority of employers make payment of wages on weekly basis, i.e., at the week end preferably on Saturday (Hafta day)

TABLE 39

Mode of Payment of Wages

Mode of Wages	*No. of Respondents*	*Percentage*
Cash	17	45.9
Cash and Kind	20	54.1
Total	37	100.0

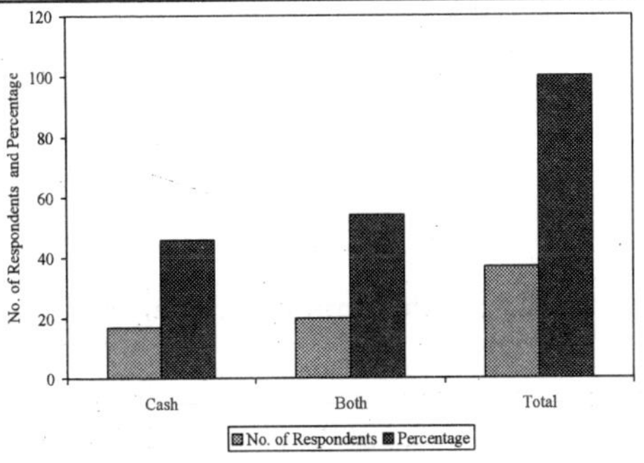

45.9% Respondents pay wages to children in the form of cash and 54.1% respondents pay wages to the children in both forms, i.e., Cash and Kind. The Table shows that majority of employers followed age old crude practice of payment of wages in the form of cash and kind which is illegal. This is a clear violation of rights of children and denial to get wages in the form of current currency/coins.

TABLE 40

Rate of Wages Per Day

Rate	*No. of Respondents*	*Percentage*
Rs. 40	22	61.1
Rs. 60	10	27.8
Rs. 80	3	8.3
Rs. 100	1	2.8
Total	36	100.0

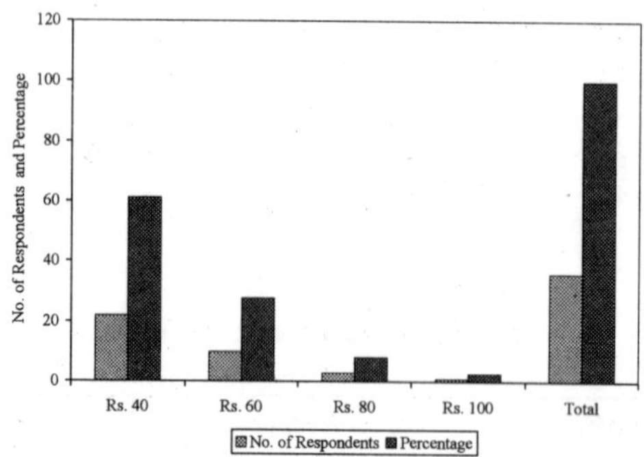

61.1% Respondents pay wages to the child labourer @ Rs. 40 per day, 27.8% respondents pay wages to the child labourer @ Rs. 60 per day, 8.3% respondents pay wages @ Rs. 80 per day and 2.8% respondents pay wages @ Rs. 100 per day. The analysis clearly shows that maximum number of child labourers are paid very meager rate of wages, i.e., Rs. 40 per day which is contravention of the rule equal pay for equal work. Further, there is discrepancy between the statement of employers and child labourers regarding the rate of wages paid.

TABLE 41

Deduction made in Wages

Dedication	*No. of Respondents*	*Percentage*
Yes	35	97.2
No	1	2.8
Total	36	100.0

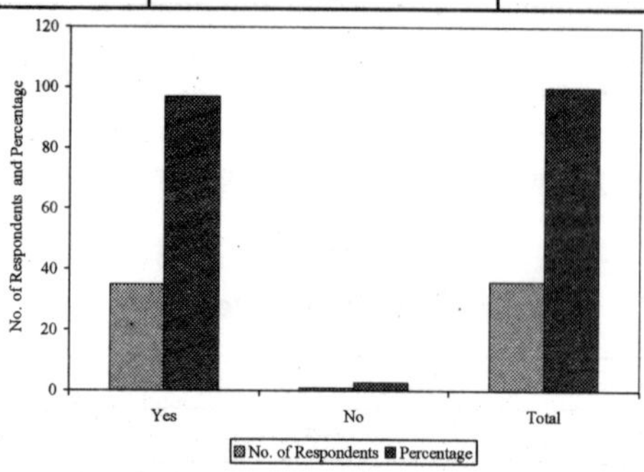

97.2% Respondents make deduction in wages and 2.8% respondents do not made deduction in wages. The Table indicates that more than 90% employer makes unlawful deduction of the wages earned by the children and they are economically exploited.

TABLE 42

Person who Receive the Wages

Receiver	*No. of Respondents*	*Percentage*
Child	3	8.3
Parents	29	80.6
Guardian	4	11.1
Total	36	100.0

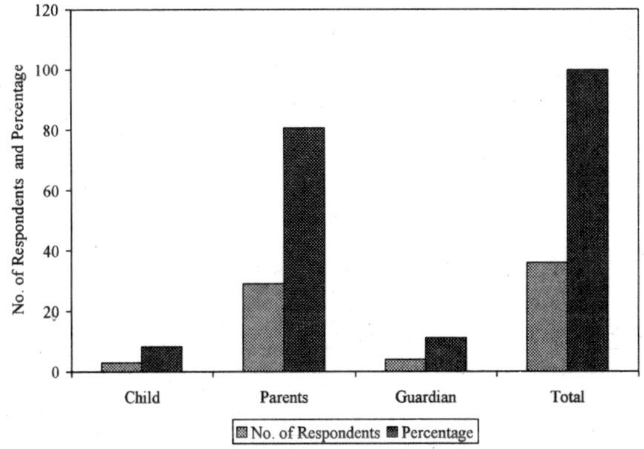

8.3% Respondents say that the child receives the wages, 80.6% respondents says parent receive the wages and 11.1% respondents says guardian receive the wages. The Table shows that more than 80% employers pay the wages to the parents of child labourers and thereby children's right to receive wages are denied by both employers and parents.

TABLE 43

Advance given to Parents

Loan	*No. of Respondents*	*Percentage*
Yes	6	18.2
No	27	81.8
Total	33	100.0

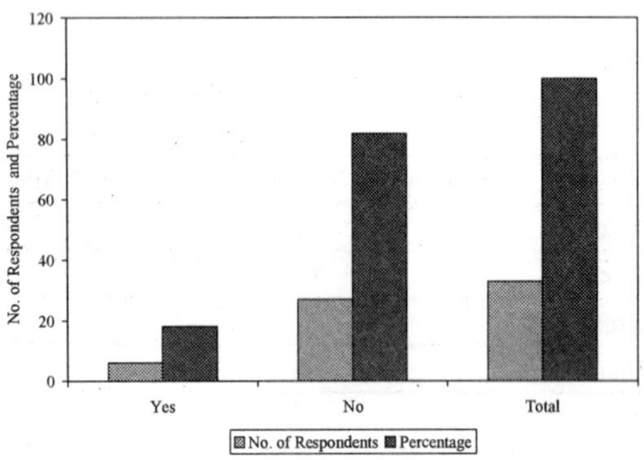

18.2% Respondwnts said parents of the child labour took advance as loan and 81.8% respondents said parents of the child labour did not take wages in advance.

TABLE 44

Rate of Interest Charged for Loan

Rate of interest	*No. of Respondents*	*Percentage*
2.5	8	44.4
3	10	55.6
Total	18	100.0

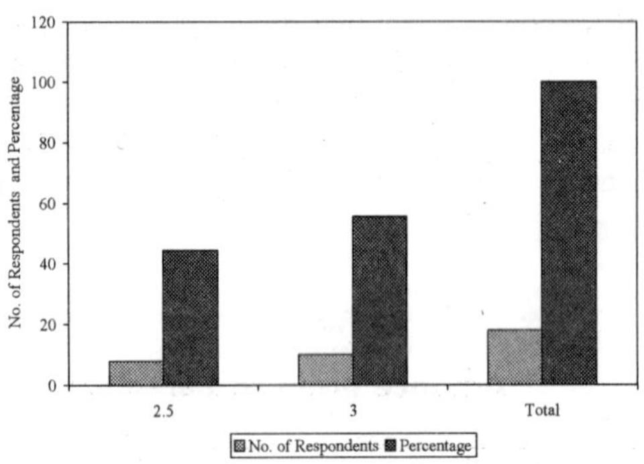

44.4% Respondwnts charge interest @ Rs.2.5% per month for loan amount and 55.6 respondents charges interest @ Rs.3% per month for loan amount. Levying of rate of interest on the money taken in advance is a worst form of exploitation of economic helpless section of the society.

TABLE 45

Interest Deducted from Wages with Regard to Loan amount Payable by the Child Labourer

Interest Deducted	*No. of Respondents*	*Percentage*
Yes	2	5.6
No	34	94.4
Total	36	100.0

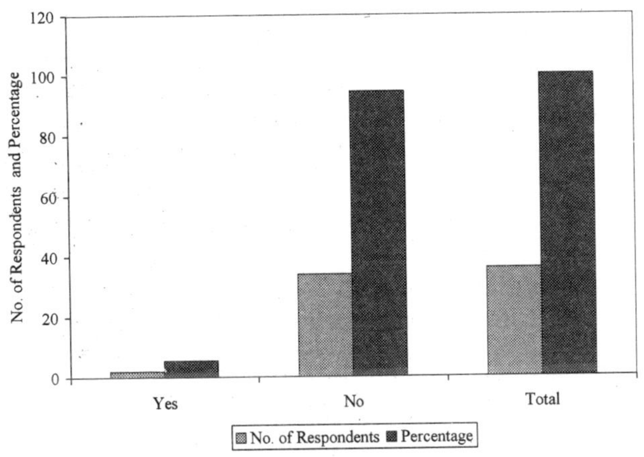

5.6% Respondwnts deduct interest from wages with regard to loan amount payable by child labourer/parent and 94.4% respondents do not deduct interest from wages.

TABLE 46

Knowledge of Law on Employment of Child Labour

Idea	*No. of Respondents*	*Percentage*
Yes	3	8.3
No	33	91.7
Total	36	100.0

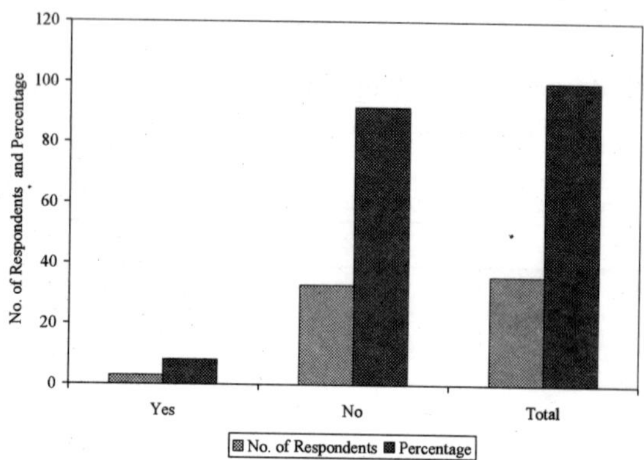

8.3% Respondents have the idea about law on employment of child labour and 91.7% of Respondents do not have the idea about law on employment of child labour. The analysis clearly shows that, more than 91% employers are ignorant about child labour legislation which equally contributes for the cause of perpetuation of child labour.

TABLE 47

Age of Child Labour during Joining to the Work

Joining to the work	*No. of Respondents*	*Percentage*
8-10 years	17	41.5
11-12 years	12	29.3
13-14 years	12	29.3
Total	41	100.0

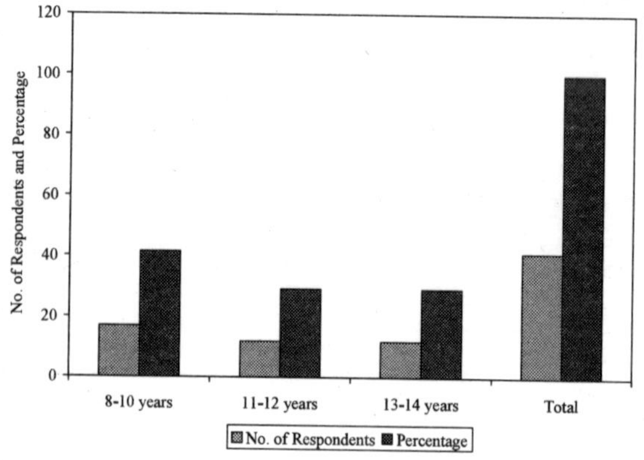

41.5% Respondents said children join to the work in the age group of 8-10 years, 29.3% Respondents said children join to the work in the age group of 11-12 years and 29.3% Respondents said children join to the work in the age group of 13-14 years. The Table clearly shows that majority of employers were of the view that, children join to the work in the age group of 8-10 years which is clear case of violation of the basic rights of children to enjoy childhood.

TABLE 48

Prosecution of Employer

(A) Prosecution

Prosecution	*No. of Respondents*	*Percentage*
Yes	-	-
No	34	100.0
Total	34	100.0

(B) Punishment

Punishment	*No. of Respondents*	*Percentage*
Yes	-	-
No	24	100.0
Total	24	100.0

(C) Nature of Punishment

Nature of Punishment	*No. of Respondents*	*Percentage*
Yes	-	-
No	1	100.0
Total	1	100.0

(A) 100% Respondents are not Prosecuted,
(B) 100% Respondents are not punished, and
(C) 100% Respondents have not suffered any nature of punishment.

The Table shows that, no employer was prosecuted nor punished which indicates a poor enforcement of child labour law and failure on the part of enforcement machinery.

III. DATA OF NON-GOVERNMENTAL ORGANISATIONS (NGOs)

TABLE 49

Registration of NGOs

Registration	*No. of Respondents*	*Percentage*
Yes	6	100.0
No	-	-
Total	6	100.0

The Table shows that 100% Respondents (NGOs) are registered.

TABLE 50

Nature and Object of NGOs

Rehabilitation of Child labour	*No. of Respondents*	*Percentage*
Yes	6	100.0
No	-	-
Total	6	100.0

The Table shows that 100% Respondents (NGOs) nature and object is for rehabilitation of child labour.

TABLE 51

Periodical Receipt of Funds from Government

Mode	*No. of Respondents*	*Percentage*
Quarterly	3	60.0
Half yearly	2	40.0
Total	5	100.0

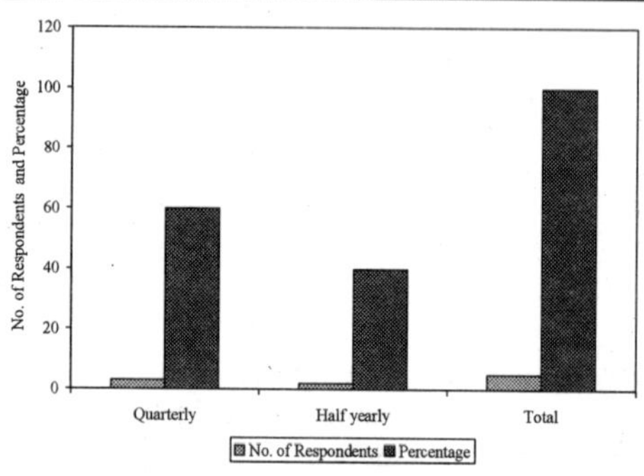

60% Respondents receive funds from Government on quarterly basis, and 40% respondents receive funds from the Government on half yearly basis. Analysis shows that the Government is generous in releasing funds to some NGOs and is indifferent with regard to other NGOs in releasing funds.

TABLE 52

Children Rehabilitated by NGOs during 2007-08

No. of Children	*No. of Respondents*	*Percentage*
20-40	2	40.0
41-60	1	20.0
61-80	-	-
81-100	1	20.0
100 and above	1	20.0
Total	5	100.0

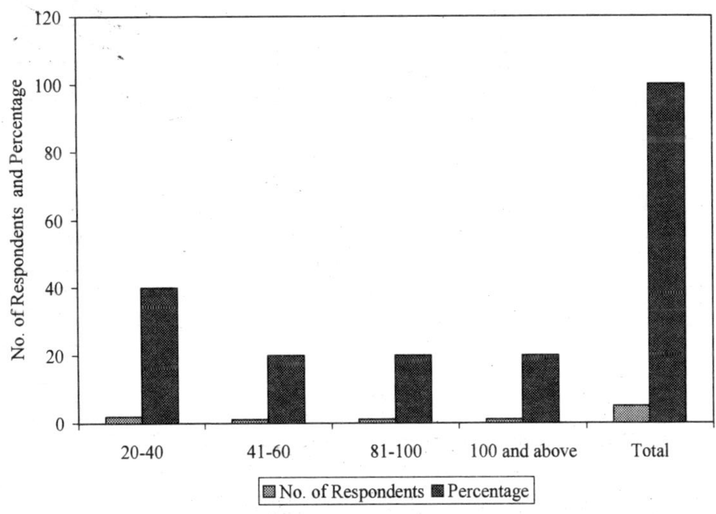

40% Respondents rehabilitated 20-40 number of Children, 20% Respondents rehabilitated 41-60 number of children, 20% Respondents rehabilitated 81-100 number of children, 20% Respondents rehabilitated 100 and above number of children. Table shows that during 2007-08, 40% NGOs rehabilitated the children from 20-40, and rest of NGOs 20% each rehabilitated children from 41-60, 81-100 and 100 and above respectively.

TABLE 53

Children Rehabilitated by NGOs during 2007-08

No. of Children	*No. of Respondents*	*Percentage*
20-40	2	40.00
41-60	1	20.00
61-80	-	-
81-100	2	40.00
100 and above	-	-
Total	5	100.0

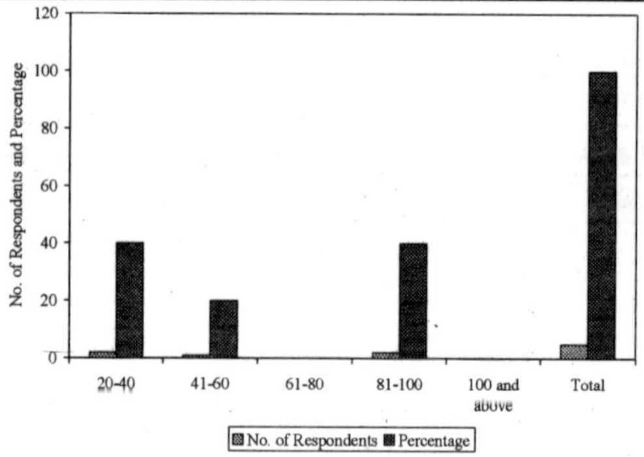

40% Respondents rehabilitated 20-40 number of children, 20% Respondents rehabilitated 41-60 number of children, and 40% Respondents rehabilitated 81-100 number of children. Table shows that 40% NGOs rehabilitated children from 20-40, and 20% NGOs rehabilitated children from 41-60 and 40% NGOs rehabilitated from 81-100.

TABLE 54

Children Rehabilitated by NGOs during 2007-08

No. of Children	*No. of Respondents*	*Percentage*
20-40	2	40.0
41-60	1	20.0
61-80	1	20.0
81-100	1	20.0
100 and above	-	-
Total	5	100.0

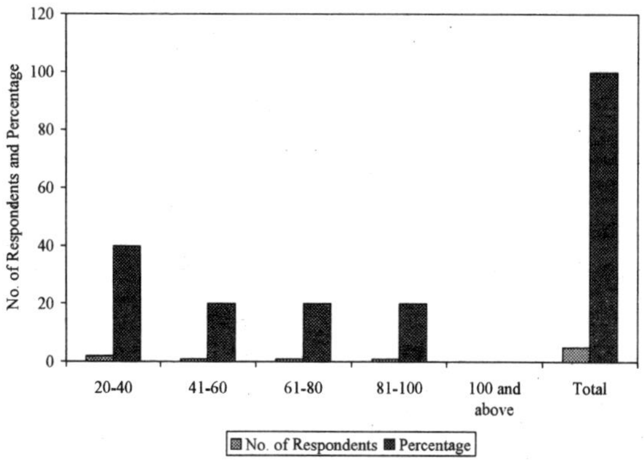

40% Respondents rehabilitated 20-40 number of children, 20% Respondents rehabilitated 41-60 number of children, 20% Respondents rehabilitated 81-100 number of children, 20% Respondents rehabilitated 100 and above number of children.

TABLE 55

Children Rehabilitated by NGOs during 2010-11

No. of Children	*No. of Respondents*	*Percentage*
20-40	-	-
41-60	1	50.0
61-80	-	-
81-100	1	50.0
100 and above	-	-
Total	2	100.0

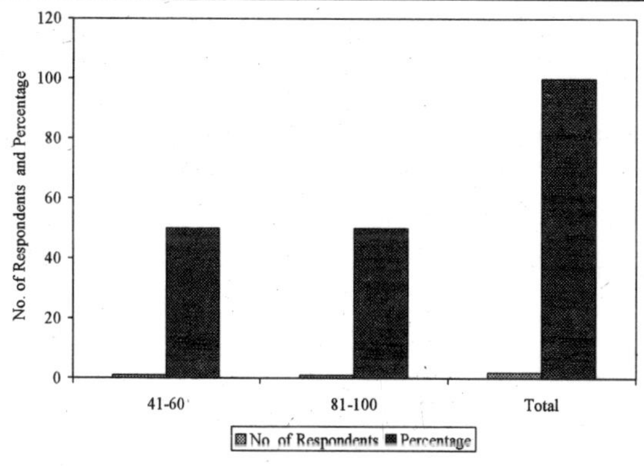

50% Respondents rehabilitated children from 41-60 during 2010-11 and 50% Respondents rehabilitated children from 81-100 during 2010-11.

TABLE 56

Admission of Child in NGO

Admission of child	*No. of Respondents*	*Percentage*
Parent	2	33.3
Public	3	50.0
Others	1	16.7
Total	6	100.0

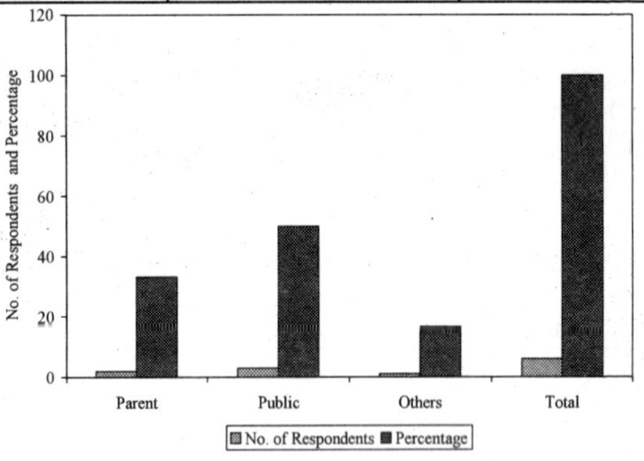

33.3% Respondents said parent will admit the child in NGO, 50% Respondents said public will admit the child in NGO, and 16.7% Respondents said others will admit the child in NGO. The Table shows public response is very good in admitting children in NGOs than the parent and others.

TABLE 57

Co-operation/Support for Rehabilitation of Child Labour by other Departments

No. of Children	*No. of Respondents*	*Percentage*
Labour Department	2	40.0
Employer	2	40.0
Parents	1	20.0
Total	5	100.0

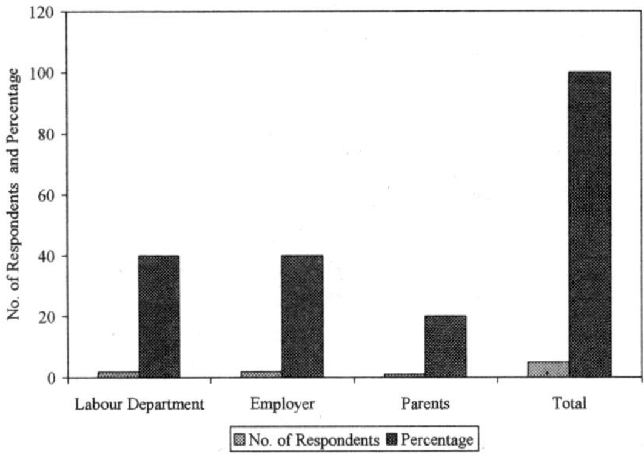

40% Respondents get the co-operation/support for rehabilitation of child labour from Labour Department, another 40% Respondents get the support from the employer and 20% Respondents get the support from the parents. The Table indicates Labour Department and employer are more supportive for rehabilitation of children than the parents.

3. CONCLUSION

From the above analysis it is evident that, most of the child labourers belong to underprivileged, backward communities of the society. Most of the child labourers are school dropouts and they are forced to child labour by their parents. Most of the employers do not treat the child labourers properly and it has also been found that, the enforcement agencies are not discharging their duties properly and NGOs in the field are doing a commendable work in rescuing and rehabilitation of child labourers.

11

Conclusion and Suggestions

> *"I am the child. All the world waits for my coming. All the earth watches with interest to see what I shall become. Civilization hangs in the balance. For what I am, the world of tomorrow will be. I am the child. You hold in your hand my destiny. You determine, largely, whether I shall succeed or fail. Give me, I beg you, that I may be a blessing to the world".*
>
> —***Mamie Gene Cole***

I. CONCLUSION

Children constitute the nation's valuable human resources. The future well-being of the nation depends on how its children grow and develop. The great poet Milton said "Child shows the man as morning shows the day". So it is the duty of the society to look after every child with a view to assuring full development of its personality. Children are the future custodians and torch bearers of the Society: they are the messengers of our knowledge, cultural heritage, ideologies and philosophies. Children are really future components in the form of great teachers, scientists, judges, rulers, doctors, planners, engineers, politicians on whom the entire society is founded. Unfortunately, millions of children are deprived of their childhood and right to education and thereby they are subjected to exploitation and abuse.[1]

The age of the child has been defined differently in different laws. There is no definite criteria or scientific parameters in defining the age of the child. The Constitution of India under Art. 24 defines 'Child' as any one below the age of 14 years and who shall not be employed to work in any factory or mine or engaged in any other hazardous employment. Under Child Labour (Prohibition and Regulation) Act, 1986 'Child' means a person who has not completed his 14 years of age. Article 21-A of the Constitution states that the state shall provide free and compulsory education to all children of the age of six to fourteen years in such manner as the State may by law determine. Now, amended Article 45 of the Constitution states that, the state shall endeavor to provide early childhood care and education for all children until they complete the age of six years. But according to Art. 1 of the United Nations Convention on the Rights of the Child, 1989, a child means every human being below the age of 18 years unless, under the law applicable to the child, majority is attained earlier.[2] Under Juvenile Justice (Care and Protection of Children) Act, 2000 the age is fixed at 18 years. Thus, there is no uniform fixation of the age of a child.

Unfortunately, the children in India are subjected to various forms of abuse. National Study on Child Abuse recorded its findings very exhaustively on various forms of abuse of children. They are child labour, physical abuse, emotional abuse, substantial abuse, Girl child neglect, sexual abuse, etc.[3]

Socio-economic conditions prevailing in the society are strongly responsible for the abuse of child in different forms. High literacy and low literacy rate, equally contribute to the problem of child abuse. Among the various forms of abuse of children it would be more pertinent and relevant to focus on child labour. Child labour is a abuse and exploitation of children and children pre-maturely leading an adult like life. They receive low wages and work for long hours under conditions that are likely to damage their health as well as physical and mental development. According to a National Study on Abuse of Children, out of 12,447 children covered under the study 19.70% are found to be at work. Only 17% of working children are paid for their work.[4] Thus, the study has revealed that the child labour is being largely underpaid, overworked and exploited.

"Child Labour" is not a phenomenon or feature peculiar to India. This has been there all over the world. The pathetic conditions of a child forced to labour for his employer described by Charles Dickens in his well known novel '*Nicholas Nickleby*'.[5] The concept of child labour is complex in its nature. It is very difficult to define and give a valid definition of child labour. But International bodies, like UNICEF, ILO, Research Groups, had made their best endeavour to define the concept of child labour in a more logical manner based on time and space factors.

Taking consequences of child labour into account, the ILO has provided a comprehensive definition: "Child Labour includes Children prematurely leading adult lives working long hours for low wages under conditions damaging to their health and their physical and mental development, some times separate from their families, frequently deprived of meaningful educational and training opportunities that could open up for them a better future".[6]

In this context, child work and child labour often used synonymously, but have different connotations and understanding. All work is not bad for children because, some light work properly structured and phased is not child labour.[7] This implies that work which does not detract from other essential activities for children such as leisure, play and education are not child labour. 'Child labour', therefore, is the work which involves some degree of exploitation, namely, physical, mental, economic and social and therefore, impairs the health and development of children. Thus, child labour is a subset of child work which implies that "all child labour can be termed as child work but all child work cannot be child labour". Thus, there is a gap between two concepts, although, both appears to be one and the same, when it is investigated forensically difference can be made out.

Children work in different sectors, namely in the agrarian sector, industrial sector and service sector. There are various factors responsible for the prevalence of child labour.

Child labour is a complex economic problem. In a country where millions of children go to bed hungry, without having a single full meal a day, total elimination of child labour by mere legal recourse can never be said to be a practical proposal. It may suppress the malaise but cannot cure it. Samuel Johnson opined that, "Poverty is a great enemy to human happiness; it certainly destroys liberty, and it makes some virtues impracticable and others extremely difficult". The poor children thus become instrument to augment family income and are seen as a means to alleviate poverty. Thus, there is vital link between poverty and child labour. Weak and tardy enforcement of the child labour legislations and defective legislation and policies also contribute more for the incidence of child labour.

Thus, the phenomenon of child labour is multi-dimensional complex problem and deep-rooted in the socio-economic fabric of society. So it may not be wise to rely on one single approach to deal with it. So a comprehensive integrated approach is required to tackle and combat the problem of child labour.

The international community has shown its concerns about the problem of human rights in general and child labour in particular by adopting a number of instruments. There were two Pre-United Nations Instruments, namely, the Geneva Declaration of 1924 which provides that, the child must be protected against every form of exploitation and the U.N. Charter 1945 and Human Rights focussued on the dignity and worth of the human being which includes children. In the United

Nations Instruments, the United Declaration of Human Rights, 1948 under its Article 25(2) says that "Motherhood and Childhood" are entitled to special care and assistance. All children whether born in, or out of wedlock shall enjoy the same social protection. The United Nations Declaration of the Rights of the Child, 1959 was indeed a very important event as regards the international recognition of right of the child. International Covenant on Economic, Social and Cultural Rights, 1966 provides that children and young persons should be protected from economic and social exploitation. The International Covenants on Civil and Political Rights, 1966 [8] under its Article 24 stated that, every possible social and economic measures should be undertaken to prevent forced labour and prostitution.

The United Nations Convention on the Rights of the Child, 1989 is a most important human rights document focusing and concentrating on children . The Convention contains 54 Articles and it provides Civil, Political, Social, Economic and Cultural Rights to every child, and out of 54 Articles 41 related to the rights of children. These rights are the Right to Protection, the Right to Development, the Right to Participation and the Right to Survival. Article 32 prohibits practice of child labour and recognizes the rights of the child to (i) be protected from economic exploitation and performing any work, i.e. likely to be hazardous; or (ii) interfere with his education; or (iii) be harmful to the child's health or physical, mental, spiritual, moral or social development.[9]

World Conference on Human Rights: The Vienna Declaration and Programme of Action, 1993 reiterates the principle of "First Call for Children" and addressed to combat exploitation and abuse of children and their root causes.

There are specialized agencies of United Nations for the protection of the child. It is the policy and objective of International Labour Organisation to abolish child labour. It's objective based on the Convention states that "Childhood should be consecrated not to work but to education and development, that child labour often jeopardizes children's possibilities of becoming productive adults and that child labour is not inevitable, its elimination is possible when the political will exists".

International Labour Organization is committed to the abolition of the worst forms of child labour and gradually other forms also. This is the first child labour convention, which prohibited, the work of children under the age of fourteen in industrial establishments. The protection of child against exploitation in employment is one of the major concerns of this Convention. It has moved totally 19 Conventions. International Labour Organisation's Worst Forms of Child Labour Convention, 1999 (No. 182), Minimum Age Convention, 1973 (No. 138),

Minimum Age Recommendation, 1973 (No. 146) and International Programme for the Elimination of the Child Labour (IPEC).

Thus, among the Specialized Agencies of the United Nations, International Labour Organization plays a vital role and directly committed for elimination of child labour. Apart from ILO, there are other specialized agencies like United Nations Educational, Scientific and Cultural Organization, United Nations Children's Emergency Fund (UNICEF), South Asian Association of Regional Countries (SAARC) and World Health Organization (WHO), etc.

International Instruments provide for codification of children rights into one international document and recognises aspirations which mankind has for its children. It can be said that, Conventions and Declarations make provisions and set high aspirations. But the state parties face practical difficulties in implementation due to socio-economic and cultural and political systems. There are no implementing provisions either in the conventions or in declarations. There is no responsibility and accountability upon the state parties for their acts and omissions.[10]

A comparative analysis of the problem of child labour which exists in different countries has been made. In United States of America there are various Acts, like Fair Labour on Standard Act, 1938 (FLASA) and which was amended in 1966, still the children work in dangerous industries in United States.

The problem of child labour also exists in Russia. The state has shown its concern by curbing female child labour working for more than 8-10 hours. Soviet State had taken various steps to protect its women and children by legislations. The problem of child labour exists in China in different forms and age groups. The history of child labour in this country parallels the development of public education system. China has evolved the education policy in order to combat child labour. It had made sincere efforts to reduce the incidence of child labour and formulated elimination strategies. In South Africa child labour was prevailing in the form of socialization, acculturation. In this country child labour distinguished between economic and non-economic activities. In South Africa Schools were not fully supported by Government funds. Families must pay a fee for their children to attend school and Government of this country has recognized a need for comprehensive approach to combat child labour.[11] By and large child labour problem was prevailing in various countries of South Asia, namely, Bangladesh, Thailand, Philippines, Nepal, Pakistan, Srilanka and Afghanistan. Thus, it is observed that the problem of child labour is a global phenomenon which is found in both developed and developing nations.

The practice of child labour in India or in any country of the world is an age old phenomenon. Since ancient time child labour existed in the Indian society in one form or the other. During ancient time the child labourer were regarded as 'child slaves'[12]. Tender aged children who were under eighteen were treated as chattels. Kautilya was not in favour of employment of children. But children were engaged in different occupations and even in agricultural sector and were exploited by landlords.

During the medieval period child labour was prevailing in India. Landless labourers used their children to help in their economic activities and children were required to help them in rendering their traditional crafts or family occupations at the young age. Children were frequently mortgaged and sold like movable properties.[13] The rulers made no effort to abolish this practice.

In the modern era, during British rule significant changes were brought by the then Government. The first protective Child Labour Act was enacted in 1881, this was known as Indian Factories Act, 1881. During the Modern era, before independence efforts had been made by bringing various legislations for elimination of child labour.

The history of child labour law found little improvement under the Indian Factories (Amendment) Act, 1922 which was enacted to give effect to the ILO Convention on the minimum age for admission for children into employment, hours of work and night work of young persons and women.

At present there are 14 legislations to control and regulate child labour in India. Children (Pledging of Labour) Act, 1933 was the first statutory enactment dealing with child labour. Then, the Employment of Children Act, 1938 was enacted which had been in force till repealed and replaced by Child Labour (Prohibition and Regulation) Act, 1986. The main object of the Act was to prevent the employment of children under the age of 14 years to work in occupations and curbed the exploitation of the Child Labour. One of the drawbacks of the Act was it had not provided for any provision with regard to the health, safety, medical examination and welfare of children. This Act was amended as many as five times during the year 1939, 1948, 1949, 1951 and 1978 only to ameliorate working conditions of children.

The Factories Act, 1948 raised minimum age of employment of children in factories to fourteen years and section 67 of the Act enacts an absolute prohibition of employment of child in any factory. The Minimum Wages Act, 1948 defines a child as a person below 15 years and it provides for minimum wages for children and apprentices. The Plantation of Labour Act, 1951 prohibited the employment of children under 12 years in plantations and now by amendments under the provisions of Child Labour (Prohibition and Regulation) Act, 1986, age of the child has been increased to 14 years. The Merchant Shipping Act, 1958 prohibits children under 15 to be engaged to work in any capacity in any ship, except in certain specified cases. Again the Motor Transport Workers' Act, 1961 prohibits the employment of children who are less than 15 years in any motor transport undertaking. In the same year the Apprentices Act, 1961 was enacted which prohibits the apprenticeship/ training of a person of less than 14 years. The Beedi and Cigar Workers (Conditions of Employment) Act, 1966 prohibits (a) the employment of children under fourteen year in any industrial premises manufacturing beedies or cigars, and (b) persons between fourteen and eighteen years from working at night between 7 pm and 6 am.

Constitution contains several provisions under Article 15(3), Article 21, Article 24, Article 39(e) and (f) and Article 45 for preventing exploitation and protecting children. Article 24 of Constitution prohibits employment of children below 14 years in factories, mines and in any other hazardous employment. In order to fulfil the constitutional mandate after 36 years of independence and to respond to the National Policy for Children, 1974, Government has enacted Child Labour (Prohibition and Regulation) Act, 1986 which prohibits the employment of children below 14 years and imposes stringent punishment in cases of violation of the Act. The Act suffers from some serious shortcomings. They are, the Act is contradicting in its goals, as it provides for both prohibition and regulation of Child Labour. There is controversy relating to the age of the child, misuse of proviso annexed to section 3 of the Act, absence of any measures for rehabilitation of the child, absence of addressing children who are working in large scale in agricultural sector (farm-lands), and policy perspectives relating to children and childhood are confused. Therefore, there is an immediate need for amendment of the Act, so as to bring it on par with the international standards laid down in the U.N. Convention on the Rights of the Child.

The debate about whether child labour should be banned or regulated is not new. It surfaced in 1985 when the Govt. of India claimed that "Child labour was a harsh reality"[14] and found it more prudent to regulate rather than ban it. The Child Labour Act, 1986 is an Act without teeth and innumerable loop holes. It does not cover children working in agriculture. Today the largest employers of children are farmers growing B.T. Cotton in State like Andhra Pradesh, Gujarat and Karnataka where according to D. Venkateshwaralu's recent study more than 2 lakhs children below 14 work from day break to dusk in cross-pollination work. The Child Labour Act, cannot effectively control child labour because (i) The Act is silent about welfare of child labour, (ii) and does not abolish child labour in all employments below certain age.

In all the Five Year Plans progressive steps were taken by the Government of India for the elimination of child labour. National Policy of Children, 1974 was introduced and it recognized that, "The Nation's children are supremely important asset" and declared that "the nation is responsible for their nurture and solicitude". In February 1979 Government constituted 16 member committee on child labour under the chairmanship of Shri M.S. Gurupadaswamy to look into the cause leading to and the problems arising out of the employment of children in organized and unorganized sectors. After a detailed study, Committee found that "Child Labour involves the use of labour at its point of lowest productivity, hence it's an inefficient utilization of labour power. Child labour represents pre-mature expenditure rather than saving". Committee remarked that, child labour is economically unsound, psychologically disastrous and physically as well as morally dangerous and harmful. National Child Labour Policy 1987 was introduced and implemented National Child Labour Projects in 1988 for the rehabilitation of child labour. In the dawn of the new millennium, Government of India brought various legislations and made amendments to the existing laws. The Second National Commission on Labour, 2002 which has recommended the repealing of the existing Child Labour (Prohibition and Regulation) Act, 1986 and suggested a new model Act as child labour (Prohibition and Rehabilitation) Act, "To prohibit employment of children in all employments and to regulate employment of children where permitted".

Thus, right from the ancient period to present day, the problem of child labour has been in existence and perpetuated in one or the other form, due to several socio-economic and political factors. In the post Independence era, due to the human rights orientation the child labour was considered abominable and various legal provisions have been made to abolish/regulate child labour. New polices and new laws have been adopted to deal with child labour.[15]

The judiciary has played an important role in the protection of fundamental rights of citizens in general and children in particular. Judicial interpretation and activism had created new hope and aspiration among the citizens because of tremendous growth of statutory intervention in the present era due to emergence of liberalization, privatization and globalization and movement of protection of human rights of children. Time and again judiciary has pronounced judgments for eliminating the problems of child labour in India. With regard to this, Justice K. Subba Rao, a former Chief Justice of India observed : "Social Justice must begin with children. Unless a tender plant is properly tended and nourished, it has little chance of growing into a strong and useful tree. So, the first priority in the scale of social justice shall be given to the welfare of children".

In *Rajangam* v. *State of Tamil Nadu*[16] employment of children in beedi manufacture was considered as violating the Beedi and Cigar Workers (Conditions of Employment) Act, 1966 and the Child Labour (Regulation and Prohibition) Act, 1986. The Court observed, "Tobacco manufacturing has indeed health hazards. Child labour in this trade should therefore, be prohibited as far as possible and employment of child labour should be stopped either immediately or in a phased manner".

The Supreme Court has directed the state government in *M.C. Mehta* v. *State of Tamil Nadu*[17] to enforce the statutory requirements of the Factories Act for providing recreational facilities and Medical aid to the workers of Match Factory at Sivakasi.[18] It has also been suggested that every employee working in this factory should be brought under a group of insurance scheme.[19]

There is a plethora of cases,[20] wherein judiciary has made significant contribution to the cause of child workers. The Court has given new dimension to several areas, such as *locus standi*, minimum wages, and employment of children and gave decisions which deal with the payment of minimum wages to the children and protection of their fundamental rights and sexual exploitation of children in hazardous occupations which reflect the judicial creativity in the field of the welfare of the children including the child workers.

The Judicial mandate clearly demonstrate that Right to Education is necessary for the proper flowering of the children and their personality. The Supreme Court of India in *J.P. Unnikrishanan* v. *State of Andhra Pradesh*[21] declared that, upto secondary education every child has fundamental right to education. Similarly in a number of cases the Supreme Court emphasized the importance of education for the children.[22]

The verdict of the Supreme Court and pressure built by child rights organization culminated in the amendment of the Constitution in 2003. In pursuance of this the Right to Education Act was passed in 2009. The Right to Education Act is the first legislation in the world that puts the responsibility of ensuring enrolment, attendance and completion on the Government. The Government of India is committed to ensuring that all children irrespective of gender and social category have access to education. The 86th Amendment to the Constitution and the Right to Education Act act as a tool to provide quality education to all our children. This Act serves as building block to ensure that every child has his or her right (as an entitlement) to get a quality elementary education, and that the state, with the help of families and communities, fulfils this obligation.

Non-Governmental Organizations also play a very vital and

significant role in the task of elimination of child labour. NGOs work at grass root level, they will have an intimate knowledge and experience about the day-to-day problems of child labourers. It is the NGOs which can identify child labourers working in their area and understand the causes and factors which force the children to become child labourers. The working children may be successfully rehabilitated in NGOs run child labour schools and mainstreamed. Today, several NGOs, across the nation and within Karnataka, are working relentlessly for the prevention and elimination of child labour. Global March Against Child Labour at Delhi, Butterflies at Delhi, M.V. Foundation at Andhra Pradesh, and Concerned for Working Children (CWC) in Karnataka, Child India Foundation (CIF) Childline are working as NGOs for the cause of elimination of child labour and rendering valuable services to the community.

Lastly, it may be concluded that, in India large number of children are working as child labourers due to various socio-economic factors. Poverty, illiteracy, ignorance of people are the root cause for the prevalence of child labour. Though there is a plethora of laws dealing with problem of child labour due to their faulty implementation by the law enforcement agencies, child labour practice is far from eradication.

In order to tackle the problem of child labour, the following suggestions have been made.

2. SUGGESTIONS

1.Constitutional Amendment: Art. 24 of the Constitution should be amended as below:

1. "No child below the age of fourteen years shall be employed to work in any factory or mine or engaged in any other employment".
2. The present title of Child Labour (Prohibition and Regulation) Act, 1986 should be amended as Child Labour (Prohibition and Rehabilitation) Act, so that more focus should be given to rehabilitation rather than regulation.
3. Proviso annexed to section 3 of Child Labour (Prohibition and Regulation) Act, 1986 should be amended to prevent the misuse of this provision by employers under the heading of family occupations and no exceptions should be provided. Section 3 of the Act should be amended as, "it shall be presumed that occupier is also the employer for the purpose of the Act and the onus to prove that the child is a member of his or her family would rest on the occupier".

4. Distinction made between Part-A and B Schedules annexed to section 3 of the Child Labour (Prohibition and Regulation) Act, 1986 shall be removed, as both Schedules namely, occupations and processes, are equally hazardous to the health of children. Therefore, prohibition to employ a child should exist in both.
5. Under section 9 of the Child Labour (Prohibition and Regulation) Act, 1986, it should be made mandatory that every occupier after establishment should send a notice to the Inspector containing the information regarding the employment of a child, either in the affirmative or in the negative, annually.
6. The age of the child provided under Child Labour (Prohibition and Regulation) Act, 1986, i.e., 14 years should be enhanced to 18 years so as to bring it on par with United Nations Convention on the Rights of the Child, 1989.
7. The advisory function of the Technical Advisory Committee under section 5(1) of the Child Labour (Prohibition and Regulation) Act, 1986 should be expanded so that it shall receive petitions from individuals, etc. for addition of occupations and processes to the Schedule.
8. The punishment for violation under section 14(3) of Child Labour (Prohibition and Regulation) Act, 1986 shall be enhanced to three months simple imprisonment or fine which may extend to fifty thousand rupees or with both.
9. In Section 16 of Child Labour (Prohibition and Regulation) Act, 1986 a time limit from Six months to One year should be fixed for the disposal of the case so that, the aggrieved party may get relief on time.
10. Government of India should ratify the Convention No. 182 and Recommendation No. 190 which deal with the "Prohibition and Immediate Action for the Elimination of the Worst Form of Child Labour". The Convention was adopted in 1999 but the Government has not yet ratified it.
11. The Employment of children in any other employment including Agricultural/Farm Sector should be made a cognizable offence, non-bailable and non-compoundable.
12. A separate and independent body should be constituted under Labour Ministry at Centre, State and District level for monitoring the affairs of child labourers after 14 years who were rehabilitated and mainstreamed.
13. Every State Government shall frame Rules under the Right to Education Act, 2009 immediately for the proper implementation of the provisions of the Act.

14. Laws on child labour and Education should be implemented in a mutually supportive way.
15. The Judiciary should be more sensitive in dealing with child labour cases. The general rule of 'benefit of doubt' cannot be given to the offending employers. When guilt is proved, offending employer should be punished with imprisonment and not with fine. In punishment policy, sentence of imprisonment should be made a general rule and imposing fine should be an exception. This deters the employers. Further there is a need to increase the conviction rate.
16. Government should encourage the NGOs for elimination of child labour by granting proper budget periodically and accountability should be fixed on NGOs to ensure that the funds are utilized for the purpose for which it is given.
17. To deal with apathy and indifference on the part of the law enforcing agencies in the discharge of their duties, there is need to conduct periodical orientation and training programmes to sensitize them adequately.
18. It is suggested to give more focus on implementation and enforcement of child labour laws and other laws meant for the protection of the children.

It is humbly submitted that, if all the above suggestions are implemented, the menace of child labour can be effectively tackled and eventually it can be eradicated.

Notes and References

1. *Supra*, Chapter-II.
2. *Ibid.*
3. *Supra*, Chapter-III.
4. *Ibid.*
5. *A. Sriram Babu* v. *The Chief Secretary of the Government of Karnataka and Others* cited in the Child Labour (Prohibition and Regulation) Act, 1986, 4th edn., Bangalore: *Karnataka Law Journal Publication*, 2010, p. 89.
6. *Supra*, Chapter-IV.
7. *Ibid.*
8. *Supra*, Chapter-VI
9. *Ibid.*
10. *Ibid.*
11. *Supra*, Chapter-VII.
12. *Supra*, Chapter-V.
13. *Ibid.*
14. *Supra*, Chapter-VIII.

15. *Ibid.*
16. (1992) 1 SCC 221; 1992 SCC (L & S) 105.
17. AIR 1991 SC 417.
18. See *M.C. Mehta* v. *State of Tamil Nadu*, AIR 1996 (JT, 1996 (II) SC 685).
19. A sum of Rs. 50,000 per children.
20. *M.C. Mehta* v. *Union of India, Salal Hydro Project* v. *Jammu & Kashmir, Laxmikanth* v. *Union of India, Bandhua Mukti Morcha* v. *Union of India* and *M.C. Mehta* v. *State of Tamil Nadu, Asiad Workers case.*
21. AIR 1993, SC 2178.
22. *Supra,* Chapter-VIII.

Bibliography

Books

Bajpai, Asha, *Child Rights in India*, 2nd edn., Delhi: Oxford University Press, 2006.

Bakshi, P.M., *The Constitution of India*, 9th ed., Delhi: Universal Law Publication, 2809.

Basu, Durga Das, *Human Rights in Constitutional Law*, 2nd edn., Agra: Wadhawa and Company Law Publishers, 2005.

Bhat, Ishwar P., *Law and Social Transformation*, 1st edn., Luknow: Eastern Book Company, 2009.

Burra, Neera, *Born to Work Child Labour in India*, New Delhi: Oxford University Press, 1995.

Campaign Against Child Labour—ILO-IPEC Karnataka Child Labour Project (Supported by the Govt. of Italy).

Cathryne, L. Schmitz, Elizabeth Kimjin Praver and Desi Larson, *Child Labour: A Global View.*

Chandra, U., *Human Rights*, 6th edn., Allahabad: Law Agency Publications, 2006.

Chaudhary, Radhakrishna, *Economic History of Ancient India*, 1982.

Desta, Sunil, Desta, Kiran, *Law and Menace of Child Labour*, 1st edn., New Delhi: Anmol Publications Pvt. Ltd., 2000.

Dhani, S.N., *Jurisprudence : A Study of Indian Legal Theory*, 1985.

Dr. Bhakhry, Savita, *Children in India and their Rights*, New Delhi: National Human Rights Commission, 2006.

Govt. of Karnataka Budget—2010-11, Bangalore: Sun Publications, 2010.

Gulbarga District at a Glance—2009-10, Publishers, District Statistical Officer, Gulbarga.

Halambi, H. Kamalakar, Sanjay Kumar, *Hand Book for the Employer's Organization Member and Office Bearers and Elimination of Child Labour*, New Delhi, ILO-IPEC Karnataka Child Labour Project (Funded by Govt. of Italy), 2008.

Iyer Krishna, V.R., *Jurisprudence of Juvenile Justice: A Preambular Perspective.*

Jois Rama, M., *Legal and Constitutional History of India,* Bombay: N.M. Tripati, Pvt. Ltd. 1990.

Kautilya, *Artha Shastra*, Part-3, Chapter 13, Prakaran 65.

Kothari, G.M., *A Study of Industrial Law*, 3rd edn., Bombay: N.M Tripathi Pvt. Ltd, 1978.

Krishna Iyer, V.R., *Legally Speaking*, Delhi: Universal Law Publishing Company Pvt. Ltd., 2003.

Kulshresta, J.C., *Child Labour in India*, New Delhi, 1978.

Malik and Raval, *Law and Social Transformation in India*, 2nd edn., Faridabad: Allahabad Law Agency, 2009.

Mehta, P.L., S.S. Jaswal, *Child and the Law*, New Delhi, Deep and Deep Publications, 1996.

Mishra, Laxmindhar., *Child Labour in India,* New Delhi: Oxford University Press, 2000.

My Name is Today—Children in News, New Delhi, *Butterflies'* Programme with Street Children, Vol. XVI, 2009.

Naikar Lohit, D., *The Law Relating to Human Rights*, Bangalore: Puliani and Puliani, 2004.

Nanjunda, D.C., *Child Labour and Human Rights—A Perspective,* Delhi: Kalpaz Publications, 2008.

Panth, Dr., *Economic History of India under the Moghals*, 1990.

Patil, G.B., *Child Labour: A Stigma on Humanity*, 1st edn., Bangalore, KILPAR Law Studies, 2009.

Rahman, M.H., Rahman Kanta, S. Meharaj Begum, *Child Labour and Child Rights—A Compendium*, New Delhi: Manak Publications, 2002.

Rajashekhar, C., *Social Revolution and the Indian Constitution—Interrelationship between Fundamental Rights and Directive Principles*, New Delhi: Deep and Deep Publications, 1993.

Rao, Mamata, *Law Relating to Women and Children*, 2nd edn., Laknow: Eastern Book Company, 2008.

Sekhar, R. Helen., *Child Labour Legislation in India—A Study in Retrospect and Prospect*, Noida: V.V. Giri National Institute of Labour, 1997.

Sekhar, R. Helen., *Child Labour Situation and Strategies for Elimination*, Noida, V.V. Giri National Labour Institute, 2007.

Sekhar, R. Helen., *Towards Combating Child Labour*, 2nd edn., Noida: V.V. Giri National Labour Institute, 2005.

Shandilya, Tapan Kumar and Shakeel Ahmed Khan, *Child Labour: A Global Challenge,* New Delhi, Deep and Deep Publication Pvt. Ltd., 2006.

Shrivatsva, M.P., *Child Labour Laws in India*, Allahabad, Law Publishing House, 2006.

Shukla, C.K, S. Ali, *Social Economic Dimensions*, New Delhi: Swaroop and Sons, 2006.

Singh, Bharat, *Crime Against Child Labour.*

Staljar, S.J., *Children, Parents and Guardians,* 4, INT, L. Ency. of Company Law.

Subba Rao, K., *Social Justice and Law*, Delhi: Publication House, 1974.

Venkateshwar Rao, D., *Child Rights—A Perspective on International and National Law,* New Delhi: Manak Publications, 2004..

Verghese, Jose, *Law on Employment of Children*, New Delhi: Capital Foundation Society.

Articles

Anand, A.S. J., Article on "Neglect of Economic and Social and Cultural Rights—A Threat to Human Rights", Vol. 5, (2006), New Delhi, *Journal of the National Human Rights Commission.*

Bangalore Law Journal, Bangalore,Vol. 2, No. 1 (2007).

Corlett, C., "Impact of the 2000 Child Labour Treaty on United States Child Labourers" (2002), *1919 Arizona Journal of International and Comparative Law.*

Dhaka Rajiv, S. and Narwal, Jagbir, "Child Labour in the City of Rothak : A Study", Vol. XXXVII (2005), 1 January-March, *Nagarlok.*

Elis-Mendelievitt, "Child Labour", Vol. 18, No. 5 (1979), *International Labour Review.*

Gupta, Meera, 'Special Problems of Enforcement of Child Labour and Regulations", Vol. XX, Nos. 7-12, *Awards Digest Journal of Labour Legislation,*

Hegde, B.N., "Hungry Mouth's Day", Vol. 55, No. 12 (2009), Mumbai: *Bhavan's Journal Bharatiya Vidya Bhavan.*

Jayanti, P.P., "Child Labour a Socio-Legal Study", Vol. 1 (1998), Tiruvantapuram: *Kerala University Journal of Legal Studies,* Department of Law, University of Kerala.

Jha, Praveen, Pooja Parvati, "Right to Education Act, 2009: Critical Gaps and Challenges" Vol. XLV, No. 13, (2010), Mumbai: *Economic and Political Weekly.*

Khanam, Rasheda and Mohamad Rehman, "Child Labour in Developing Countries: The Role of Education, Poverty and Birth Order"., Vol. 10, No. 2 (2008), New Delhi: *Journal of Social and Economic Development.*

Mehandale, Archana, "Realities of Child Labour and Contextualising the

Legal Strategy—A case study of India" cited in Small Hands in South Asia, Child Labour Perspective (2004), New Delhi: IDPAD-Manohar.

"My Name is Today: Children in News", New Delhi, *Butterflies.*

Nambir Bindu, M., "Children and Human Rights", Vol. 5-149 (2007), Kottayam, *Journal of Indian Legal Thought.*

Padhi, P.K., "Child Labour: Yesterday, Today and Tomorrow" (2004), Journal Section, Lab LC.

Pandiaraj, P., "Elimination of Child Labour in India : Towards a glorious illusion ?", Vol. 46 (2006), *Indian Journal of International Law.*

Patel, Vibhuti, "Law Concerning Protection and Empowerment of Girls in India", Vol. 23, No. 8 (2009), *Legal News and Views*, New Delhi: A Social Action Publication.

Paul, Thomos, "Child Labour Prohibition *v.* Abolition; Untangling the Constitutional Tangle", Vol. 50, No. 2 (2008), New Delhi: *Journal of Indian Law Institute.*

Pillai, Sheeba, "Right to Education and the Fishing Community in Kerala", Vol. I (2008), *Mysore University Law Journal.*

Polly, Vizard, Review by Prof. B.B. Pande, "Poverty and Human Rights – Sen's Capability Perspective", Vol. 5 (2006), New Delhi: *Journal of Human Rights Commission.*

Sahu, Umesh C., "Child Labour in Surat Industry Social Change", Vol. 20, No. 3, September.

Sharma, Ravi, "Frontline" (2006), Nov. 17, Bangalore: *Magazine.*

Sharma, Subhash, "Trends, Causes and Consequences of Child Labour in India", Vol. LV, No. 2 (2009), *The Indian Journal of Public Administration.*

Sharma, Sudesh Kumar, "Child Labour: Problems and Prospects" (2009), Cochin *University Law Review.*

Singh, A.N., "The Child Rag Pickers" (1996), *Socio-Economic Perspective and Interaction Strategies.*

Smolin, David M., "Strategic Choices in the International Campaign against Child Labour", Vol. 22 (2000), *Human Rights Quarterly.*

Spirit of Human Rights—A Manual of Gulbarga University, (2005), Gulbarga: Law Department.

Umar, Harish, "Human Rights to Children: Agenda for implementation" (2000), *Cochin University Law Review.*

Reports

'Child Labour', "Challenge and Response"—A Status Report on Indian Initiatives towards the elimination of child labour, V.V. Giri National Labour Institute, Noida, 1996.

"National Study on Child Abuse", Conducted by Prayas in collaboration with the Ministry of Women and Child Labour, Govt. of India, Supported by UNICEF and Save the Children Fund, UK-Executive Summery Report, 2005.

Archana Mehandale, "Elimination of Child Labour –A study of the Role of Law and Non-Governmental Organizations from a perspective of the Rights of the Child", National Law School of India University, Bangalore, 1997.

Association for Development (AFD), News Letter Issue XXIX, Oct-Dec 2007.

Children and Work—Annual Report, 2004-05 (Department of Women and Child Development, Govt. of India).

Committee on Child Labour, 1979

Gurupadaswamy Committee, Govt. of India Report, 1981.

Convention and Rights of the Child, Country Report, India February 1997, Department of Women and Child Development, Ministry of Human Resource Development, Govt. of India, New Delhi, 1997.

Critic of ILO Global Report, "The End to Child Labour—Within Reach", The Concerned for Working Children (CWC).

Draft Declaration and Agenda for Action of the National Consultation and Child Labour, Delhi, 4-5 August, 1997.

Fact Finding Report of Second World Children Congress, Delhi, 2005.

Gazette of India 1938, Part-V.

Govt. of India Census, 2001.

India-Vision 2020, Published by Planning Commission of India.

India Alliance for Child Rights, 2003, Citizens Alternative Review and Report on India's Progress Towards CRC, Realisation, 2003, New Delhi.

Jain, Mahaveer, "Child Labour in India"—A Select Bibliography, National Labour Institute, Noida, 1995.

Jeen, Fares and Dushyanth Raju (2007), "Child Labour Across the Developing world Patterns and Co-relation", The World Bank Report, Policy Research Working Papers-4119.

Law Commission Report, Chapters 3 and 4, 205th Report.

National Crime Record Bureau, Ministry of Home Affairs, Govt. of India, 2005, Crimes in India, New Delhi.

Press Information Bureau, Govt. of India, MLD L-53 (cpi-iw) 1-8-2006.

Sanat Mehta Committee Report, 1984.

The National Plan of Action for Children, 2005, Working group on development of children for the Eleventh Five Year Plan (2007-2012)—A Report.

The Report of Second National Commission on Labour (2002).

The State of the World Children, 2005, Childhood Under Threat, UNICEF.

Towards Faster and More Inclusive Growth, An Approach to the Eleventh Five Year Plan, Planning Commission, Govt. of India, New Delhi, 2006.

UNICEF, State of World's Children Report, 2009.

Workshop on Model Development for the Juvenile Justice Board Members under Juvenile Justice Act, 2000, Sponsored by UNICEF held at Administrative Training Institute, Mysore from 2nd to 4th February, 2009.

Newspapers

The Times of India, 10th June, 2003.

The Hindustan Times, New Delhi, 25th Mar, 2005.

The Hindu, "India Dangerous for Children", 22nd July 2006.

The Hindu, "Ban on Domestic Child Labour comes into effect", Oct. 11, 2006.

Deccan Herald, 15th October, 2006.

The Indian Express, New Delhi, 18th Dec., 2007.

The Asian Age, New Delhi, 2nd May, 2008.

The Kashmiris Times, Jammu, 6th June 2008.

DNA, Mumbai, 25th July, 2008.

The Hindu, Chennai, 20th Aug., 2008.

The Tribune, New Delhi, 11th October, 2008.

The Hindustan Times, New Delhi, 23rd October, 2008.

The Hindu, 11th June, 2009.

Deccan Herald, 14th August, 2009.

Website

http://www.chldlabour.in

http://www.wcd.nic.in

http://www.kar.women & child development.com

http://www.bba.org.in

http://www.socialjustice.nic.in.

http://www.Education.nic.in

http://www.rural.nic.in

http://www.all4children, org

http://www.echoindia. Org/htm

http://www.manak publication.com

http://www.nhrc.in
http://www.global march.org
http://www.crin.org.
http://www.labour.nic.in
http://www.unicef.org
http://www.wcd.nic.in
http://www.pratidhi.org
http://www.children compaign.org
http://www.ncrb.nic.in
http://www.cuts.international.org

Index